H Jo...

John Wilsey was born in 1939 and was educated at Sherborne School in Dorset. He was commissioned from Sandhurst in 1959 into The Devonshire and Dorset Regiment. As a young officer with H Jones, he served in Cyprus, Libya, Malta, British Guiana and Germany, as well as in Northern Ireland, where some 20 years later he became GOC and Director of Operations. In 1996 General Wilsey, then C-in-C Land Command and Joint Commander of all British Forces in the former republic of Yugoslavia, retired from the Army.

He is now Chairman of Western Provident Association, Vice Chairman of the Commonwealth War Graves Commission and Chairman of Salisbury Cathedral Council. He is a patron of Hope and Homes for Children and is involved with several other charities.

John Wilsey is married with two children. He breeds alpacas and enjoys skiing and sailing. This is his first book.

Reviews

'This is the story of an unconventional man from an unusual family which clearly illuminates the personal qualities and professional abilities of Jones; it also sheds light on the structure, ethos and activities of the British Army during the post-war years' *Times Literary Supplement*

'An excellent contribution to the recent military history of Britain' *Osprey Military Journal*

'A gripping and thorough biography' *Warship IFR*

'This is the author's first book and one would hope for more; it places in perspective Colonel Jones's leadership qualities, especially during the battle for Goose Green, and corrects the misrepresentation by the media, in print and on television' *Despatches*

'A carefully researched biography of an extraordinary man' *Soldier*

H JONES VC

The Life and Death of an Unusual Hero

JOHN WILSEY

ARROW

Published by Arrow Books in 2003

1 3 5 7 9 10 8 6 4 2

Copyright © Kingsbroke Settlement, 2002

Foreword © John Keegan 2002

The right of John Wilsey to be identified as the author of this work has been asserted
by him in accordance with the Copyright, Designs and Patents Act 1988

First published in the by Hutchinson in 2002

Arrow Books
The Random House Group Limited
20 Vauxhall Bridge Road, London SW1V 2SA

Random House Australia (Pty) Limited
20 Alfred Street, Milsons Point, Sydney
New South Wales 2061, Australia

Random House New Zealand Limited
18 Poland Road, Glenfield
Auckland 10, New Zealand

Random House (Pty) Limited
Endulini, 5a Jubilee Road
Parktown 2193, South Africa

The Random House Group Limited Reg. No. 954009

www.randomhouse.co.uk

A CIP catalogue record for this book is available from the British Library

Papers used by Random House are natural,
recyclable products made from wood grown in sustainable forests.
The manufacturing processes conform to the environmental
regulations of the country of origin.

Typeset by MATS, Southend-on-Sea, Essex
Printed and bound in the United Kingdom by
Cox & Wyman Ltd, Reading, Berkshire

ISBN 0 09 943669 8

To James –
about the godfather you never knew

Contents

Illustrations

Second Section
H as Adjutant of the Devon and Dorsets in Germany
H receives the Queen's Jubilee Medal from Sir Norman Strong
H briefs Roy Mason
Captain Robert Nairac
H on Remembrance Day in Belize
2 Para practising landing drills at Ascension (*photo: H Jones*)
H's cabin on Canberra (*photo: H Jones*)
GPMG team on Canberra (*photo: H Jones*)
San Carlos Bay on land and at sea (*photo: H Jones*)
2 Para prepare defences on Mount Sussex (*photo: H Jones*)
Mount Sussex: H's sangar, another position on the mountain and a
    photo of 2 Para moving off (*photos: H Jones*)
Reconstruction of H's assault and death
Commander Tim Jones RN visits H's grave
H's grave at San Carlos Military Cemetery
Sara, Rupert and David Jones at the VC Investiture at
    Buckingham Palace

*The above photos come from the private collections of Sara Jones
and members of H's family.*

Maps

Foreword
John Keegan

H Jones was about to leave Sandhurst when I joined the academic staff in February 1960 and I never knew him as a cadet. John Wilsey, the author of his biography, I knew well as a captain instructor later in the 1960s and we have remained friends ever since his Sandhurst days. It is a great pleasure to contribute a foreword to what I think is a remarkable book.

John Wilsey has written an inherently convincing portrait of a brother officer. Though I did not know H, I perceive his character clearly in the picture John gives of him. Although out of the ordinary as a soldier, perhaps because his ample private means gave him the self-confidence to defy convention, he was not so much out of the ordinary in his time and place. The Army, when I first knew it forty years ago, was full of young officers who behaved with a disregard for the rules that I, who had never been a soldier and had come straight to Sandhurst from an Oxford college whose undergraduates were much in awe of the dons, thought breathtakingly wilful. Juniors from regiments which counted as grand in the Army's complex pecking order blatantly condescended to seniors from regiments less grand or corps not reckoned grand at all. Captains who felt a glittering career in front of them were little more than formally respectful to majors whose careers were dwindling to a close. It was an archaic world, in many ways not much changed since the days of purchase, when officers with money could buy promotion by the purchase of commissions. Yet it had this virtue: it kept young officers constantly on their mettle. Those with the bravado to cut a dash but avoid rebuke by keeping just within the limits of what was permissible arrogance developed very forceful personalities. That stood them in the best of stead in command of soldiers and in the face of the enemy.

H Jones, in John Wilsey's depiction, may be thought to have followed such a path of career development. After a diffident beginning he became very strong-willed and given frequently to argument, often with seniors, particularly if they were not from his own Regiment. Like all really ambitious young officers, however, he was careful not to alienate the seniors who wrote his annual confidential reports or to have blood-quarrels within his own Regiment.

Readers may well think that John Wilsey's real achievement is to have written an account of life inside a British regiment more authentic than any generally available. Regiments like the Devon and Dorsets are institutions perhaps unique to Britain. In one aspect they are ancient monuments: the Devons were raised in the seventeenth century and fought at the Battle of the Boyne in 1690; the Dorsets have as their motto 'First in India' (*Primus in Indis*), which they were in the mid-eighteenth century. In another aspect they are vital social organisations of the here and now, rooted in the localities where they recruit and officered and manned by local people. H was a Devonian and so were many of his soldiers, unless they came from Dorset. Cousinage abounds in county regiments, so does inter-marriage. A county soldier's good name has therefore to be preserved at all costs, for reports of cowardice or disloyalty soon reach relations as well as regimental headquarters.

Because of the peculiar intimacy of county regimental life, careers have to be constructed with great care. Men soldier together usually for a whole military lifetime. The ordinary upsets of family life – differences of opinion, disappointments, temporary jealousies – erode with time but there are certain sorts of misbehaviour that are remembered and never forgiven. Currying favour with authority, particularly by deceit or tale-telling, wins an inexpungeable bad name. Success earned on merit, by contrast, is not resented, not at any rate in the long run. As in any family, and county regiments are very family-like, a sort of communal agreement operates about who deserves what, up to and including regimental command. A curious consensus comes into play, often working from the bottom upwards. Those at the top learn, by tacit indication, whom it is that regimental opinion regards as eligible for elevation. Unhappy the officer, or senior sergeant, who wins promotion to the highest rank without regimental endorsement.

John Wilsey's portrayal of H's transit of the regimental circuit, from platoon commander to lieutenant-colonel, is absolutely authentic, in part because he has made it himself. It gains immeasurably, however, from his skills as a writer, of which I had no inkling when he first told me that he proposed writing H's life. At that early stage he asked me, as an experienced author, if I would be prepared to help. 'Let's see if you can write, first,' I said. The draft of his first chapter persuaded me that he could. John, indeed, is a natural writer and what he has produced is a worthy tribute both to the man he calls 'an unusual hero' and to the ethos of British army in which he lived and died.

John Wilsey has also made an important contribution to the chronicling of Britain's war in the Falklands, the last conflict this country fought single-handed and perhaps ever will. He conveys, as a writer who is himself an experienced soldier and commander only can, the tensions and uncertainties that surrounded the decision to send the Task Force, its voyage south and its landing on a hostile shore. Having interviewed many of those who took part, he also succeeds in describing with uncanny realism the harshness of the environment in which they fought and the strains of action. As he himself acknowledges in the preliminaries to the text, over twenty books, to say nothing of official reports, have already been published about the Falklands. John Wilsey's life of H, his brother officer, is nevertheless an important addition to the history of a conflict from which Britain's late twentieth-century renaissance as an international power may be dated.

Acknowledgements

Since the end of the Falklands War in June 1982, more than twenty books and hundreds of articles and reports, official and unofficial, have been published about the battle for Darwin and Goose Green. There have also been various television programmes on the subject.

Darwin and Goose Green – one overall battle but two distinct engagements at twin settlements three kilometres apart – was the first land battle of the campaign. Uniquely, 2nd Battalion, The Parachute Regiment (2 Para) was involved in another major battle, a fortnight later. This was on Wireless Ridge, one of the concluding battles outside the capital, Stanley, which preceded the surrender of the Argentinians.

Since I was not professionally involved in the Falklands, except as an informed bystander, I began my research by reading Major-General John Frost's *2 Para Falklands*. It was Frost, commanding 2 Para's predecessors at Arnhem in 1944, who was responsible for the heroic, but eventually unsuccessful, defence of the bridge there. As one of the Regiment's heroes – indeed, a founding father – he had unrestricted archival access to the Battalion after the Falklands War. However, there was surprisingly little there to guide him.

The records were minimal, even for a unit engaged so fully in action – or perhaps because of that. For example, 2 Para's battle 'log' no longer existed, so Frost apparently drew heavily on an informal internal report prepared on the voyage home by Captain (now Colonel) David Benest. Subsequently Benest, who had been

H JONES VC

Lieutenant Colonel H Jones's Regimental Signals Officer in the early stages of Darwin and Goose Green, commented that for a variety of reasons some significant errors were evident when *2 Para Falklands* was published in 1983. However, as this was one of the first accounts – enhanced by the authority of the admired Frost* – it carried credibility and has often been quoted since.

The next three books I read were most instructive, and I am grateful to the authors for allowing me to quote from them. The well-known journalist and writer, Robert Fox, published a contemporary account of the battle soon after the campaign. He had come to know H well, and had formed a high opinion of him. Fox did not witness the Commanding Officer's action at Darwin, but his *Eyewitness Falklands* contains many anecdotes about H, and his descriptions of some of the events and the atmosphere leading up to the battle are illuminating.

Brigadier Julian Thompson's book *No Picnic* carries considerable authority by dint of his appointment, and his integrity. As Commander 3 Commando Brigade, he was H's immediate superior and understood precisely the mission on which he sent 2 Para, even though he had severe reservations about its relevance and wisdom at the time.

The Battle for the Falklands by Max Hastings and Simon Jenkins is considered one of the most comprehensive and authoritative accounts of all aspects of the campaign – political, diplomatic and military. Hastings also regarded H highly, although he was nowhere near Darwin when H was killed.

Initially, therefore, I concentrated my search for details of Lieutenant Colonel Jones's last hours on the published material relating specifically to the twin battles for Darwin – where his renowned action took place – and for Goose Green. This came from three authors: first, two books by the historian Martin Middlebrook – *Operation Corporate* and *The Fight for the 'Malvinas'*, published in

*He died in 1993.

1985 and 1989 respectively – which looked at the campaign from the protagonists' different viewpoints. Second was Mark Adkin's *Goose Green – A Battle Fought to be Won*, published in 1992; and third was Spencer Fitz-Gibbon's distinctive *Not Mentioned in Despatches*, first published in 1996. I found all four books invaluable as they covered the conflict from very different angles, including, in Middlebrook's case, an insight into Argentinian attitudes and thinking. I am indebted to each of these authors for allowing me to quote from his work.

For insight into the activities and contribution of the Royal Navy, I drew on *Amphibious Landings Falklands*, co-authored by Commodore Michael Clapp and Major Ewen Southby-Tailyour, from which they kindly gave me permission to quote.

My thanks go to Andrew Orgill, the librarian at RMA Sandhurst, and his staff for their help, as well as to the MOD Library, and the Department's Historical Records branch for their assistance.

One of the delights of writing H Jones's biography has been meeting, renewing contact and discussing my subject with so many of his friends and acquaintances. I have interviewed nearly 150 people – only one refused me – and my thanks go to all for giving so generously of their time, and patiently sharing their recollections.

Three merit specific mention in view of the quality and quantity of their contributions. First Lieutenant Colonel Chris Keeble, on whom command of 2 Para suddenly devolved when H was killed. As Jones's key confidant – by virtue of appointment as well as personality – Keeble was very much in H's mind in the last five months of his life. His contribution has been uniquely helpful in interpreting some of the personal interactions that occurred during Jones's tenure of command, and on the final battlefield.

The second significant contribution was almost accidental. While routinely researching H's motor-racing days, I made contact with Bill Sanders-Crook, a club car racing enthusiast, former Parachute Regiment officer and now in public relations. As an author, and so familiar with the world of publishing, Bill helped me avoid some of the pitfalls that can attend the novice biographer, particularly one whose subject touches upon deep sensitivities. I am extremely grateful for his conscientious assistance, and for enhancing my enjoyment of the whole project.

The third crucial contribution came from Donald Mildenhall, formerly editor of the *Western Gazette* and of *Pulman's Weekly News,* two leading West Country newspapers. In that capacity Donald followed, for some forty years, the fortunes of The Devonshire and Dorset Regiment, H Jones's Regiment for the first twenty years of his service. Donald painstakingly edited and transcribed H's many letters to Sara which provide such an invaluable insight into their relationship, and to contemporary events.

Throughout my research I taped, with permission, all important conversations for the record and I returned the transcripts and draft texts, as appropriate, for checking. I hope in this way to have minimised error and misattribution. Some matters were discussed in confidence, trusting that I would not publish them. Appreciating regimental and wider military sensitivities, I was content to give such undertakings. The biography did not need extra spice, and those confidences did not alter the thrust of my work in any significant respect. All the material I have gathered will be placed in an archive for another generation to explore, if so inclined.

There are others too whose contributions have been so substantial, prolonged and generous that I wish to mention them. John Keegan first, because without his wisdom and consistent encouragement I doubt I would have started, let alone completed, this biography. It was John who put me in touch with Hutchinson and Tony Whittome, who became respectively my supportive publisher and most patient and delightful editor.

Having written nothing of this nature before, I knew little initially of their work and skill. Both corporately and personally, Hutchinson and Tony Whittome, with his persuasively gentle touch, have proved to be formidably impressive and agreeable in every respect. I count myself lucky to be in such experienced hands. I am grateful also to Roger Field, who advised on aspects of the text, James Nightingale, Hutchinson's helpful assistant editor, and Barry

Featherstone, the ever-supportive production director. To Jo Cumberlege, my proof-reader, I am indebted.

I have many friends to thank who have been particularly patient and helpful throughout the entire project. First and foremost has been Sara Jones herself. It cannot have been easy to have someone exploring H's and her own private and public life for well over a year, and she has been most tolerant of the inevitable intrusions. Unconditionally she made available all H's letters, and many of her own from key moments of their life together – including even some of hers returned unopened from the Falklands after he had been killed. These had been unread for twenty years. It struck me that only someone completely at peace with herself, and secure in her memories, would be prepared to countenance such a thing.

Sara gave me, as did her sons, David and Rupert, a completely free hand, at no stage trying to influence me or guide my pen. I am indebted to her, and them, and profoundly admire her resolve and courage to see the biography through.

I have had the run of the family photograph albums, newspaper cuttings and historical papers. H's brothers Tim and Bill helped me and my occasional researcher, Bryanne Deal, with their American ancestry and other aspects of H's early life. I am most grateful to them.

My thanks go to those friends who read draft chapters or passages and helped with my research; and to others who generously provided peaceful bolt-holes in lovely surroundings, often abroad, in which I could think and write.

Lastly, I owe an enormous debt of gratitude to my own family: to my sister, an author and journalist in Rome, to whom I sent my draft offerings and who has been so astute in her advice; to my own children for their good-humoured tolerance of my preoccupation; and above all to my wife Lizzie, who, in addition to enduring the disruption of the whole undertaking, has typed the manuscript and patiently guided and sustained me throughout.

For her it must have been as if H had come to stay for a couple of years. Fortunately, like me, she thoroughly approved of him.

Preface

H Jones was godfather to my son James, who was only three when H was killed. I wanted James to learn something of the godfather he never knew – a man who, despite everything he had on his mind, remembered to send James a birthday card as he sailed to war in the Falklands, from where he never came back.

I intended to jot down a simple pen-picture of this interesting and most unusual friend. But the story became increasingly intriguing as I delved into H's American ancestry, his youth in wartime Britain and his post-war education, of which I had known almost nothing.

Background research can become intrusive, so I sought his family's permission to delve deeper. One of my godsons is Rupert Jones, H's youngest son, who was only twelve when the Falklands War began. His interest in learning more about his father matched my growing enthusiasm for the project, and so what began as a short pen-picture became, with Sara Jones's consent and his sons' support, H's biography.

I was a twenty-one-year-old subaltern when I first met H in Libya, where my Regiment was exercising in 1960. It was obvious from the start that an engaging character had joined us. Over the ensuing years, H and I became close friends, and so we remained until his death in 1982.

For much of our service we were together more or less daily – on and off duty – although in the last year of his life I saw him only once. That was because, by then, we were commanding officers of units in different commands: I was based in Germany, then in Colchester, with a tour of Northern Ireland thrown in, while H was commanding a parachute battalion in Aldershot, and later in the Falklands.

His death occasioned deep sorrow among his friends, but little real surprise once the initial shock had passed. Those who knew him best understood that H had prepared his life for a supreme challenge somewhere along its course. We had sensed that when he found it, his intense commitment, harnessed to a profound sense of duty, honour and vocation, was likely to demand, and secure, the ultimate sacrifice.

Over the ensuing years, I have at times found it hard to explain this convincingly to those who did not know H, especially if they were unfamiliar with the British military ethos. Too often I have noticed comprehension leave the eyes of those to whom I was explaining what motivated my friend, and why he reacted as he did.

I became aware, too, how the uninitiated could mistake valour in a soldier for folly, see swift decisiveness as impetuous haste, and interpret zest for action – and its thrill – as immature excitability. Moreover, while wishing to understand and identify with our military heroes, we perversely place them on pedestals, hoping perhaps to discover Greek gods. That is no more realistic on the battlefield than it is in the boardroom, in a pulpit, or around a Cabinet table. Furthermore, we should guard against judging historical characters – as H, a generation on, now is – by the behavioural benchmarks of our own times. We stray into moral confusion if valour is viewed as near lunacy or if we perceive our heroes to be just celebrities.

H Jones was no god. He had many of the imperfections that burden us all. He could be awkward, opinionated and stubborn; and he was unusually impatient. But the virtues he did possess were noble and strong: courage, honour, loyalty and devotion to true friend and cause alike. Old-fashioned these may seem – although he certainly was not that himself – but they were genuine and pre-eminent. Moreover, he was passionate and intuitive, and in no sense a military metronome.

My hope is that those who read, to the end, this account of H's life and death will arrive at an understanding of how his gallantry, recognised by the world's most renowned decoration, derived from the natural consequences of his background, personality, character and life.

When the ultimate professional challenge confronted him, by any yardstick H triumphed. Yet his actions have been scrutinised often, and sometimes interpreted unfavourably. Battlefields are brutal, violent places, where the participants are invariably confused, frightened and exhausted. Wet and cold, or hot and thirsty, and hungry too when the fight is hard and long, soldiers are literally fighting for their survival and are divorced from normality.

In these circumstances, one man's recollection of an event may vary distinctly from another's, even though both might have been present together. Experience shows also that some acquit themselves well in action, others less so, and a few not well at all. Revision – collective and personal – afterwards is not unknown. An undefined brotherhood exists of comrades who have fought together. This distances and distinguishes them from those who were not there and hence were not privy to their shared experience, which they jealously guard.

For all these valid reasons, it has been hard to establish exactly what happened on H's battlefield, though I always sensed his reputation did not deserve the wilder myths and misconstructions relating to his final hours. There has never been any suggestion that what he did was anything other than conspicuously brave. Yet hints here that it was not really necessary, and a whisper there that it achieved nothing, have generated doubt and myth.

Myths attend all leaders, especially military ones, where the influence of one man – for good or ill – can be profound; and where personality cults and a sense of theatre find fertile breeding ground. H never deliberately courted such artifices, but myth, theatre and criticism did attach themselves unavoidably to a man with his strength of personality and uncompromising views.

Not that H would have minded. One of his attractions was the ability to laugh at his own misfortunes, and he was familiar with criticism. He had received it often enough at school, at Sandhurst and as a young officer. Moreover, as he climbed the professional ladder, he was free with it himself.

One of H's many contradictions – and part of his interest – was that this energetic and seemingly assertive man was essentially shy and private. He was surprisingly vulnerable and needed more gentle reassurance and discreet approval than most. Never gregarious, he chose friends carefully. Few got really close to him, but those who did found friendship warmly reciprocated and upheld.

To record H's life and death and attempt to capture some of the character, colour and style of this unusual hero has been my privilege.

Introduction

Easter fell early in 1982. The prospect of a fortnight's skiing over the school holidays appealed to H Jones and so, on 26 March, he bundled his family into the car and headed for Meribel in the French Alps. He drove fast because he always did, and his wife, Sara, who used to support his motor racing in his youth, was resigned to it by now.

Herbert Jones was known to virtually everyone as H. He hated being called Herbert which, he said, was permitted only to his mother. His sons, David, aged fifteen, and Rupert, twelve, also called their father H. To those who thought this unusual, he would explain that they were more than sons: they were his friends, too, and friends called him H.

The holiday began in earnest as they crossed the Channel, and it picked up momentum with every passing mile. H could look back on the last twelve months with satisfaction. He had just completed a most successful first year in command of the 2nd Battalion, The Parachute Regiment (2 Para), no mean feat for an officer transferred in to command from outside the Regiment. His Brigade Commander had said as much in H's confidential annual report.

H had taken his Battalion on exercise to Kenya where, away from the restrictions and distractions of barrack life in Aldershot, they had trained hard up-country. Commanding officers (COs) relish getting their officers and men away on their own, and H had used those seven weeks to stamp his authority on his command, to inject fresh ideas and to bond his team together.

The family had recently attended an investiture at Buckingham Palace for H to be appointed by the Queen an Officer of the Most Honourable Order of the British Empire (OBE). This unusual honour, given sparingly, was in recognition of his outstanding staff work in planning the deployment of the British Monitoring Force in what was then Rhodesia.*

Things were also going well domestically. David had settled in happily at Sherborne, his public school in Dorset, and Rupert, who was due to take his Common Entrance in May, was predicted to pass easily and would then join his elder brother in the same House. Sara and H were in the eighteenth year of a close and happy marriage, given the various usual arguments and rows that punctuate most unions between strong personalities.

Meribel, in the Haute Savoie region of France, is some 120 kilometres south-east of Geneva, at the centre of the famous Trois Vallées, where there has always been a strong British influence. The development of this beautiful spot began when the mostly English pioneers of skiing deserted the slopes of Austria after the Anschluss of 1938. Among them was a Major Peter Lindsay who, that year, founded a company to build a ski resort in Les Allues Vallée. A wartime Special Operations Executive (SOE) officer, Lindsay was well respected and influential locally, and he ensured that the village was developed sympathetically.

It was here that H Jones and his family came year after year. They took an apartment near the centre of the village with good access to the slopes and settled in comfortably. The pound sterling that week was worth a healthy 10.71 francs, and it had recently snowed. An excellent holiday was in prospect. H was a competent but not a graceful skier; the boys were fast but inclined to be reckless, as boys on skis at that age are; and Sara, although technically the most proficient and stylish, had some difficulty keeping up. Such is the lot of the wives and mothers of keen husbands and high-octane-burning sons in every mountain resort.

*Now Zimbabwe

On the other side of the world, in Buenos Aires, on Friday 26 March, unbeknown to many in London and certainly to any skier in Meribel, the military Junta in Argentina was taking the first formal steps towards ordering an invasion of the Falkland Islands. That weekend naval leave was cancelled, and stores and equipment were rushed to the major naval base of Puerto Belgrano and to Commodore Rivadavia, the nearest air base to the Falklands.

Previously there had been reports of an illegal landing of an Argentine scrap-metal merchant, Constantino Davidoff, and forty salvage men on South Georgia with the declared intent of removing material from the abandoned whaling station at Leith. In fact, they had a proper contract: the removal of an eyesore of sheds, old barges and rusting iron. But instead of clearing their arrival with the British Antarctic Survey base twenty kilometres down the coast at Grytviken – as their permit required – they landed at Leith on 19 March, hoisted the Argentine flag and set to work. Whether this omission was by design, or by accident, as Davidoff vigorously maintained, has never been properly established.

Either way, alarm bells began to ring in London. The press picked up the scent and wrote initially about a gang of 'comic-opera' scrap-metal merchants causing an international incident. It is unlikely that H Jones read these reports in Meribel, where British newspapers arrive, if at all, the day after publication. He certainly did not know that on Monday 29 March an order from 10 Downing Street to dispatch three nuclear submarines to the South Atlantic reached the Ministry of Defence across the road in Whitehall.

All submarine deployments are kept secret for obvious reasons, but the indication that something was seriously afoot was there for alert observers. HMS *Spartan* was recalled from the NATO exercise 'Spring Train' off Gibraltar, and her practice torpedoes were exchanged for live ones in the dockyard there. She sailed for the South Atlantic within forty-eight hours, to be followed from Faslane by HMS *Splendid* on 1 April and by HMS *Conqueror* three days later.

That day – Sunday 4 April – was the end of the Joneses' holiday. They had booked a passage on a cross-Channel ferry that evening, and so it is not true – as is claimed in most accounts – that H cut short his leave to hurry home lest he miss some of the impending action. Myth also has it that he heard the news of the deteriorating situation in his chalet on the BBC World Service and that he abandoned his holiday at once. The truth is more prosaic, as it is about much of the ensuing story.

The Joneses packed their Renault estate after breakfast and set off down the winding mountain road towards Moutiers. As they left the mountains, and reception improved, H switched on the car radio. The news was riveting. The Falkland Islands had been invaded at dawn on Friday 2 April and were now in the hands of Argentinian armed forces. A Royal Navy task force was being made ready and would sail the next morning.

Most unusually, the House of Commons had been in session on Saturday, debating the crisis, during which the Prime Minister, Margaret Thatcher, announced her intention '. . . to see the islands returned to British administration'. Lastly, they heard that the United Nations in New York had passed Resolution 502 demanding an Argentine withdrawal.

The effect of this news on H was electric and his passengers remember it well. 'The whole mood in the car changed and every-one went silent,' recalls Rupert, the younger son. David remembers H driving even faster in an atmosphere of deep concentration. Sara's principal recollection is of H stopping en route at various telephone kiosks to ring his old Headquarters at Wilton, near Salisbury, from where any Army response to the crisis would be mounted. She realised, too, that she had 'lost' her husband. Not lost in any final sense, for she had no reason to imagine that H could possibly become involved in the Falklands – 2 Para was about to deploy to Belize. But lost in the sense that their happy holiday had ended, and her husband's attention was now focused on more immediate professional matters.

Although none of them knew it as they reached their Army quarter in Aldershot in the early hours of Monday 5 April and went wearily to bed, H's life had just fifty-three days to run.

CHAPTER ONE

American Influences

H Jones's ancestry is an interesting mix of rich American and impecunious Welsh, set against the backdrop of American and European history over the last four centuries. The American strands can be traced back to 1650 and the first white settlers, and the Welsh, on his maternal side, to the middle of Queen Victoria's reign. H's father, also Herbert, was an American millionaire whose wealth derived from a major zinc-mining operation in Wisconsin. His mother, Olwen, was the ninth and youngest child of an impoverished, fiery Welsh family from Anglesey.

H's father was born on 16 May 1888 in Chicago, Illinois, and his mother in Liverpool on 6 January 1902. They were married at a civil ceremony in New York in May 1938, shortly after the 'Reno divorce' of Herbert from his first wife, Loe Kann, a rich, drug-addicted patient of Sigmund Freud. Six years later, after Loe had died, Herbert and Olwen solemnised their marriage in a religious ceremony at Totnes, in Devon. These arrangements must have raised eyebrows in contemporary circles but there is no doubting H's legitimacy. Among other things, it was unusual at the time for such a relatively elderly couple to produce children successfully – Herbert was fifty-two years old and his wife thirty-eight when H was born in 1940; and two further brothers, Tim and Bill, arrived in 1942 and 1945 respectively. By then Herbert was almost sixty, and Olwen over forty.

Whereas Herbert's second marriage was mature and founded on

mutual respect and affection, his first was far more unconventional. In 1907, at the age of nineteen, he had gone up to Princeton to study geology, having completed his secondary education in Chicago. He graduated three years later with a Bachelor of Arts degree cum laude. He had developed a love and aptitude for poetry and painting at university, where he won the Baird Prize in Poetry in 1910. On graduating, therefore, it was not surprising that this rich and talented young American should head for Europe to explore and develop his appreciation of the arts.

So began Herbert's travels, which took him to England, across Europe and to the Middle East. He developed a profound admiration for the richness and variety of European history and culture, and soon became a devout europhile. Just before the First World War, a friend encouraged Herbert to explore the world of art and the *demi-monde* in Vienna. It was here that he met and fell in love with Louisa Dorothea Kann, known as Loe (pronounced Lou), a beautiful and wealthy Dutch Jewess. At the time Loe was married* to another Jones, Doctor Alfred Ernest, who was a psychiatrist disciple of the father of modern psychology, Sigmund Freud. Jones would become Freud's biographer.[1]

In the summer of 1912, whilst attending with Freud the Weimar Psychoanalytic Conference, Ernest Jones discussed with Freud Loe's ill-health – her abdominal pains, her kidney stones and her morphine addiction. According to Freud, '[Jones] offered me her treatment',[2] whereupon he embarked on the 'cure through love' of Loe Kann Jones. As he recorded: 'She is a highly intelligent, deeply neurotic, Jewess, whose disease history is easy to read. I will be pleased to be able to expend much Libido on her.'[3]

Freud found Loe truly to be 'a treasure of a woman', and from 1912 onwards she occupied a place at the centre of his circle in Vienna. It was there that she met Herbert 'Davy'† Jones, when he

---

*Possibly she was just Ernest Jones's mistress. However, Freud referred to her as Ernest Jones's wife.

†Freud's set referred to him as 'Davy', or Jones ii, to differentiate from Ernest Jones.

embarked on his first European tour. The account of their initial meeting is contained in one of Herbert's many sonnets, entitled 'O Mistress Mine!'.[4] He had been encouraged by a friend against his better judgement to go to Vienna, rather than Paris, to meet a girl he did not know:

> We sat and waited. Being somewhat bored,
> I entertained the gravest doubts about
> The wisdom I had shown in my accord
> With him about Vienna: had we gone
> Straightway to Paris we could there have found
> Better to do than waiting on and on
> For hope's sake – when the hope might not be sound.
> But this bad-tempered meditation died
> Suddenly, after living scarce a minute. –
> A sound of rapid steps: the door flew wide:
> And all the room was light when she was in it.
> – A beauty? Never. Something far more rare:
> A spirit bright and flame-like, straight and clear,
> That shone from laughing eyes and filled the air
> Around her: knowing neither doubt nor fear; –
> A little out of breath, with glowing cheeks,
> As if the sun and tingling frost were brought
> Into the room with her; – and when she speaks,
> Her quaint and happy phrases come unsought.

This was not just poetic licence. Herbert was at once deeply smitten by Loe and determined to marry her, which he did in Budapest on 1 June 1914. Sigmund Freud attended the wedding,* having facilitated the match by persuading Ernest Jones that his patient's best interests would be served if Jones and Loe parted amicably, which they did.

---

*Freud attended only three weddings, including his own, in his lifetime.

By now war seemed increasingly likely and, recognising the unpleasant undercurrents of anti-Semitism in parts of Europe, Herbert took Loe to safety in England. His relatives in America must have watched these developments with some alarm. They were from successful and respectable American and Welsh families, and would have harboured severe misgivings at Herbert's involvement in such an avant-garde – even loose – circle. Many in America and Europe were suspicious of psychoanalysis, and especially of Freud's modern theories on sexual behaviour and attitudes. As Freud's biographer records: 'He and his followers were regarded not only as sexual perverts but as either sexual or paranoiac psychopaths as well, and the combination was felt to be a real danger to the community.'[5] So Herbert's marriage to someone they almost certainly saw as the disreputable mistress of the man who had founded it all must have greatly alarmed his relatives.

Herbert's immediate family in America consisted of his parents, a younger brother, Owen, and three younger sisters. His father was David Benton Jones, who had married Nora Lois Bayley in Platteville, Wisconsin, in 1879. The Bayley connection is historically interesting on two counts. First, Nora Bayley was one of that select band: a direct descendant of the First Families of America.

The earliest Bayley ancestor in America was John Bayley (1590–1651), who had emigrated from Chippenham, in Wiltshire, on the *Angel Gabriel*, believed to have been the first such ship wrecked off the New England coast. He survived, and was later joined by the great-grandson of another Bayley, Henry Bright, who set sail in the *Winthrop Fleet* (named after John Winthrop, the first Governor of Massachusetts) in 1630. Together, these immigrants formed the nucleus of the original Massachusetts colony, and so established the First Families of America.

The second interesting historical connection concerns the Reverend James Bayley (1650–1707), one of Nora's ancestors, who was the first preacher in Salem, Massachusetts, notorious later for its witch trials. The story of the Salem Witches began in the bitter winter of 1691–2, when several young girls gathered regularly at the

Parish House to witness the palmistry and black magic of a Negro servant woman named Tituba. These sessions fired the girls' imagination, and several of them began to believe themselves possessed of evil spirits. One participant was twelve-year-old Ann Putnam whose aunt, Mary Carr, was James Bayley's wife. It was on the evidence of Ann Putnam and others that some of the alleged witches were hanged and, by the time the hysteria had subsided, twenty people had been executed for witchcraft. Minister Bayley stayed several years in Salem and then departed, under duress, for Connecticut. There he almost certainly assisted, as was the wont of dissident preachers from Massachusetts, in the foundation of the University of Yale.

Two hundred years later, the Bayley connection had a much more practical and beneficial impact on all subsequent generations of the Bayley and Jones families. On Christmas Day 1878, Nora Bayley's father, Elija (1811–78), was gored to death by a young bull. This was just before Nora's wedding to David Benton Jones, and the fortune left to Nora enabled her to lend her husband the money to buy the Mineral Point Zinc Company, of which he became president and which was to form the cornerstone of the family history.

Lead – or 'mineral' – was discovered in the 1820s by prospectors swarming over the hills of south-west Wisconsin. A 'lead rush' began, and the mining camp which developed round the diggings was eventually named Mineral Point. There were other camps in the area but Mineral Point quickly became pre-eminent, ultimately to become the county seat of Iowa County, Wisconsin.

In the 1830s Mineral Point was a bustling, expanding city that attracted many politically significant and influential people. John P. Jones (1819–92) was one of them. He was David Benton Jones's father, and therefore H Jones's great-grandfather. In early 1851 he and his wife, Phoebe Davies, who was seven years older than him, had left their village of Soar, or Star, in the parish of Clydey* in Pembrokeshire to begin a new life in America, joining her parents,

---

*Also spelt Clydau in Welsh.

who had emigrated to Wisconsin five years earlier. Of their four sons, three – William, John and David Benton – had been born in Wales. A fourth son, Thomas, was born in America in 1851, his mother having carried him through the arduous weeks under sail across the Atlantic.

Strongly Welsh, Phoebe refused to speak English, which she considered to be the 'devil's language', although she could read and understand it perfectly well. She passed on her dislike of the English – on what particular grounds is unclear – to her four sons, who went on to express their Celtic sentiments and anti-English feelings at every opportunity. The family contemplated slate mining in Pennsylvania, but because Phoebe's parents were already in Wisconsin, where there was a thriving Welsh community, John Jones and his family moved on and settled in the same corner of Wisconsin, at Pecatonica on the Pecatonica River, near Platteville.

That was where David Benton and his younger brother Thomas grew up and attended a local school. Later, they were sent east together for a year's cramming and were accepted into the illustrious Princeton University, a remarkable achievement at that time for boys from rural Wisconsin. Both David and Thomas were bright, apparently led their class all through college, and were specially commended by the president of the university when they graduated in 1876.

After a year studying in Germany, the brothers went to Chicago to read and practise law and set up their own law firm, Jones and Jones. Their elder brother William, meanwhile, had become a teacher in Mineral Point and was duly appointed Superintendent of Schools for Iowa County. By 1884 he had become a leading citizen, and was one of the founders of the First National Bank of Mineral Point. Further honours befell William when, thirteen years later, President McKinley appointed him 'US Commissioner of Indian Affairs'.

The Jones family's involvement in politics was to continue. In the first decade of the 1900s, David and Thomas (H's grandfather and great-uncle respectively) threw their considerable talent and resources behind the major educational and social reforms of the then president of Princeton University, Woodrow Wilson, whose wider political ambitions beyond academia were already developing. By 1910, H's grandfather had become such an important benefactor and confidant that Wilson sought his advice at a crucial turning point in his life, writing in July of that year:

> Would you mind telling me with perfect frankness what you and your brother think my present duty in regard to politics.
>
> It is immediately, as you know, the question of my nomination for Governorship of New Jersey; but that is the mere preliminary of a plan to nominate me in 1912 for the Presidency.
>
> In order to go into this properly, I feel I must get the free consent of yourself and your brother ... who have guaranteed money to the University and who ought not now to be embarrassed by any action of mine.[6]

In a long reasoned reply by return of post, David concluded:

> I think it [politics] offers a more important field of service than even the reform of our educational institutions ... you [are] under no obligations to anyone interested in Princeton. You have immeasurably contributed more to that institution than anyone else ...[7]

Two years later, with Woodrow Wilson duly installed in the White House, the President sought David's views on policy measures relating to new trust fund legislation which Wilson was keen to enact, and on various appointments to office. In June 1914, H's great-uncle Thomas was nominated to the newly created Federal Reserve Board, but his nomination was vetoed by two Senators, invoking the apparent fury of the President, who wrote privately to David from the White House:

> ... I cannot tell you how often I think of you and your brother

or how deeply I nurse the grudge I have against certain gentlemen in high station for blocking his appointment to the Reserve Board. I am small enough to be waiting for a day of reckoning when I can get their scalps.[8]

David's own non-interventionist and somewhat jaundiced attitude to international affairs at the start of the First World War had been revealed earlier in a letter to the President:

Even at this distance it does not require imagination to realize your burdens. With a half strangled nation at our very door [referring to Mexico], and Europe inclined to sneer and to snarl because we do not send in an army to shoot and to be shot at, chiefly to save a few individuals from material loss, it is difficult enough to keep one's mind on internal problems.[9]

It is interesting to reflect that when David wrote this, his son Herbert was himself travelling in the geographical heart of Europe and would be married to Loe within weeks.

President Wilson kept enticing Thomas to hold office. Eventually, after turning down several minor posts, he was appointed during the President's second administration to the War Trade Board, and then, on 28 December 1919, was offered Secretary of the Interior in most unusual circumstances. With the President unwell, his wife, Edith Bolling Wilson,* wrote in her own hand:

This afternoon the President asked me to write for him and dictated the following – 'Will you permit me to nominate you Secretary of the Interior and complete my official family and fulfil my dearest birthday wish' . . .

The letter continued with Edith urging Thomas to accept:

---

*Also known as Edith Gault.

Just now he needs this assurance for he has so many things that necessarily must come directly to him – that he longs to have you . . . to depend on while he is convalescing.

Thomas, however, seems to have declined. According to his descendants, an ambassadorship to a major European capital was mooted, but nothing came of that either. Nevertheless, the financial support for the Wilsons provided by Thomas Jones and others (David died in 1923) remained rock solid. Just before Woodrow Wilson died,* he wrote in a shaky hand:

I owe a debt of inexpressible gratitude for having lifted Mrs Wilson and me out of the mists of pecuniary anxiety and placed us on firm ground of ease and confidence.[10]

The origin of the Joneses' money is an important part of the family history. In 1882, two years before William had founded his bank, a local consortium set up the Mineral Point Zinc Company with $3,500 capital. They built a zinc oxide plant to convert the raw material into white zinc oxide, the basic ingredient of good paint. However, at some point the lawyers Jones and Jones received an urgent message from William. His bank had over-loaned money to Mineral Point Zinc, which was threatened with foreclosure through inadequate security. Not only would this have bankrupted the zinc company, it would have endangered the bank, tarnished the growing reputation of William and the Joneses, and lost them money and influence all round. So David Benton and Thomas dropped their Chicago practice and hurried to Mineral Point, where they both worked exhaustively to improve the management and production of the company. Soon the mine and works were back in business, and within a year the existing shareholders had been bought out and the company's capital increased by $400,000 – mostly through Nora

---

*In Washington DC on 3 February 1924.

Bayley's inheritance. By 1891, Mineral Point was the largest zinc oxide operation in America, and probably in the world.

Capitalising on their success, the Jones brothers diversified. Between 1899 and 1905 they constructed a railway both to service the mines and to expand the community. Then came the war. Largely as a result of munitions production, the zinc industry peaked in 1917, but with the ending of the conflict in Europe it rapidly declined. With spectacular good timing and shrewd business acumen, the brothers sold out before that happened, and ahead of the Great Depression. Mineral Point is now owned by New Jersey Zinc, which in turn has Mobil/Exxon as its residual owner.

H's grandfather David had shrewdly decreed: 'Never hold on to stock for sentimental reasons.' This was particularly wise advice, for by now his health was deteriorating and in 1923, whilst on the West Coast, he was diagnosed with cancer. His brothers hired a private train to take him home to Chicago, where he died later that year. By then, he and his brothers had prudently set up family trusts to take care of the needs of his thirty-five-year-old son, Herbert, and the other members of the family. These trusts still exist and provide for their descendants today.

David's wife Nora had predeceased him by twenty-four years, dying of a sudden heart attack in 1899 at their grand home, Pembroke Lodge, when Herbert was only eleven. One of H's American cousins[11] tells a bizarre tale: 'On the day of her death a dinner party had been arranged and apparently the children were sent out as each guest arrived to explain that their mother had died, and the dinner was cancelled.'

The loss of maternal influence at such a vulnerable age must have had some effect on Herbert, and may explain his subsequent independence. A nanny had already been engaged but, in view of his age, she would not have exercised much influence for long. Soon a talent for poetry was evident, and Herbert began to develop into a sensitive and gentle young man. His love of home emerges in one of his early works, entitled 'Pembroke', to be found among five books of poetry, including sixty-two sonnets, published in the early

1920s.[12] Herbert was to pass on this love of poetry to his son.

Whether Herbert would have virtually abandoned America and his family for Europe on completion of his education had his mother survived is not clear. Similarly, what she would have made of Loe Kann and her bohemian circle can only be imagined. What is known is that Herbert and Loe established themselves in England after their marriage in 1914, buying a flat in St John's Wood near Lord's cricket ground, and a house in Dorking. Although Herbert did not need to earn a living, he kept himself busy with his painting, of such quality that he exhibited at the Royal Academy. He continued to write fine poetry, he sailed and he rode.

He was also an active philanthropist and, during the First World War, as an American and a non-combatant, he volunteered for Red Cross duty. He bought a Rolls-Royce, which he had converted into an ambulance to drive the wounded, who were returning in great numbers to Channel ports from the Western Front, to London reception centres and hospitals.

Meanwhile, Loe remained a morphine addict. She stocked up on the drug at the onset of the war claiming that it was for the wounded soldiers being recovered by her husband. It is unlikely that she bore Herbert any children, probably because she had miscarried earlier with Dr Ernest Jones's child. However, the possibility of issue exists in view of a sonnet Herbert wrote to her:

> You are my night and morning, all my life,
> You are my soul, my courage and my pride:
> The one to whom in trouble I have cried,
> Whose arms have sheltered me when storms were rife;
> Whose hand slips into mine amid the strife,
> Whose clear warm spirit I have found beside
> Me everywhere, however wild and wide
> The seas between us – mother, mistress, wife![13]

Although the last line could be taken to indicate that Loe had borne Herbert a child, equally it could mean simply that she provided the maternal love and support he had been without since the age of eleven.

Bill Jones, H's youngest brother, who has researched the matter carefully, is adamant that there were no offspring from that marriage. Practical evidence supports him. First, Loe was probably incapable of childbearing. Second, no provision was made in Herbert's will for any children other than H and his two brothers. Herbert, a genuinely sensitive and kind man, would not have overlooked or ignored such a responsibility. Thirdly, Loe made no such provision in her own will, which appears well drawn up. In it she bequeathed her two properties in Ewhurst, in Surrey,[14] to Anna Freud, with whom she maintained an intense and passionate friendship all her life. It is unlikely she would have ignored the prior claim of a child if one had existed. Fourthly, no record or mention of such a possibility has ever surfaced in the extended Jones family in the eighty years since the poem was written.

After the war, although not in robust health according to some of Freud's friends, Herbert remained busy. He researched the letters of Stendhal, the French author of *Le Rouge et le Noir*, but did not publish them because a rival writer did so first. He wrote and presented a West End play, and crafted a wide range of sculptures, mostly in bronze. He funded the British School of Archaeology in Athens and attended various archaeological digs in the Middle East.

Herbert – tall and distinguished-looking, with a hawk-like nose – emerges in his mid-life period between the wars as a gentle and generous man, at peace with himself and his life in Europe despite the fact that Loe, with her addiction and constant pain, could not have been an easy companion.

As he began to break his ties with America during the 1930s, the focus of his life moved towards Europe, and to England in particular. He asked that his name be dropped from a 1932 Princeton alumni survey, but not before recording that he was a Democrat, that his favourite study was French and his occupations were 'writing and painting'. Much later, with the ties almost severed, he drew up a will specifying that his children should not be

'. . . brought up in the United States of America or in the Roman Catholic Church'.[15]

As the clouds over Europe darkened and another war began to look inevitable, Loe's condition deteriorated. Her behaviour became increasingly erratic and life with her, even for the tolerant Herbert, must have been difficult. As a distraction he focused his energy on his leisure pursuits, becoming a keen horseman and an accomplished yachtsman.

He sailed a fifty-foot ketch, *Sea Bear*, with a professional crew, on long passages around Britain and became involved with the yachting fraternity. In the thirties there was fierce competition between the United States and Great Britain in many of the one-design yacht classes. In the six-metre class,* the boats raced for the Seawanhaka Cup. Great Britain had never won this trophy, and although Herbert, as an American, was not eligible to race for Britain – or indeed to be actively involved – it seems that he discreetly backed the building of a challenger, *Circe*. This beautiful yacht enabled Britain not only to compete on equal terms but to win the cup in 1938 and to defend it successfully the following year.†

Around this time, Loe underwent a series of kidney operations performed by another friend of Sigmund Freud, the famous surgeon Sir Wilfred Trotter. (It was Trotter who helped secure political asylum for Freud in Britain after the Nazi occupation of Austria in 1938.) Sir Wilfred had arranged a team of private nurses to assist Loe's recuperation and, when Loe felt better, she gave a small party for those attending her. One of the nurses, Mary Pritchard-Jones, asked if she might bring along her younger sister, also a nurse. Thus Herbert met Olwen, and they promptly fell in love.

Loe had another six years to live. Drugs and illness had taken so much out of her that any normal existence became impossible

---

*38.5 feet long with a 6.1-foot beam and a sail area of 452.5 square feet.
†The best six-metre helmsman of the day, John H. Thom, was declared as *Circe*'s owner. However, later he is shown as J. Herbert Thom, an apparent acknowledgement in yachting circles of Herbert's contribution to their success.

and she and Herbert agreed that their marriage should end. Nevertheless, a remarkably strong bond of loyalty and affection remained – with Loe inviting Herbert to look after her financial affairs, which he did with care and discretion until she died in 1944. Loe must have been a tolerant and unselfish woman to free Herbert at a time when probably she needed him most. Perhaps she accepted that Herbert, by now nearly fifty, had a dynastic need to father children.

Whatever the reasons, events moved quickly. According to Herbert's youngest son, Bill, Herbert and Loe were divorced in Reno, Nevada, in January 1938. 'I went through my father's diaries diligently,' says Bill, 'and all I discovered was that in January 1938 he was in Reno. He does not say why but there is one intriguing entry: "Went dancing with Olie [Olwen]. She dances divinely, so do I!" '[16]

There must have been more to it than that. Olwen was fourteen years younger than Herbert but she was not a young beauty, neither was she notably vivacious or intellectually stimulating. She was not well connected or rich – not that the latter would have worried Herbert – and her rather severe personality and Welsh upbringing were hardly compatible with Herbert's artistic and liberal lifestyle. Perhaps her appeal lay in her very contrast with Loe: her dependability, doggedness and unemotional stability. On 20 May 1938, Herbert Jones and Olwen Pritchard-Jones were married at the City Bank, Brooklyn, in New York. They returned to an England on the brink of war and bought a spacious flat in Whitehall Court,* with fine views over the Thames.

The Pritchard-Joneses were a professional family from North Wales. Olwen was the youngest child of eight daughters and one son, Hugh. Their parents, Robert Jones and Ellen Pritchard (hence Pritchard-Jones), had married sometime between 1875 and 1880 and survived into their eighties. But unlike H's paternal relations, they were not a prepossessing couple. Robert was said to be an alcoholic,

---

*Flat 81, 3 Whitehall Court, lies between the Thames and the Old War Office, now part of the Ministry of Defence.

although his age – eighty-four when he died – suggests otherwise. Ellen allegedly went into decline after her husband's death in 1940 and was bedridden for the last ten years of her life.

Of the nine children (some with odd family nicknames like 'Fire' and 'Foot') only two, Hugh and Olwen, are recalled with affection. Hugh served with the Royal Welch Fusiliers and lost a leg on the first day of the Third Battle of Ypres. Money had run out for the private education of the two youngest Pritchard-Joneses and Olwen had little or no secondary education, so Hugh generously paid for her training as a nurse at Charing Cross Hospital. Here she told of considerable poverty – of walking home to Marble Arch barefoot because her feet had swollen on the hospital rounds and she could not afford larger shoes.

However, Olwen's fortune was about to change at the bedside of her sister's patient. The resulting union of Herbert, the rich, gentle, artistic American, and Olwen, the determined, impoverished Welsh woman, would shortly produce a warrior son whose deeds would one day earn him his country's highest recognition for valour.

CHAPTER TWO

Early Life

H's birth was announced in *The Times* on 16 May 1940:

> JONES – on May 14, 1940. In London to OLWEN
> wife of HERBERT JONES, 81 Whitehall Court – a son.

The joy of the occasion was tinged with sadness because Olwen's father had died the day before. That news was kept temporarily from her lest the shock should cause undue distress and complications at a critical time.

Olwen's confinement was in the private nursing home of Dr Grosvenor Millis at 7 Gwendolen Avenue, Putney, in south-west London. Millis was a long-standing friend of Herbert's from the Great War, when they had sheltered together from the Zeppelin raids over London. He was later to be appointed a trustee of Herbert's estate and a nominated guardian should Herbert and Olwen die whilst any of their children were minors. H's birth, at eight in the morning, under the sign of Taurus – many of whose mythical characteristics he was to possess – was free of complications, except that Olwen, whilst bathing in Anglesey late in her pregnancy, had been stung by a jellyfish and it was thought that this accounted for an inherited allergy which made H prone to rashes.

National events at the time were momentous. On Monday 13 May, the day before H was born, Winston Churchill, who had been appointed Prime Minister of the National Government three days earlier, made his famous speech in the House of Commons: 'I would say to the House, as I said to those who have joined this Government, I have nothing to offer but blood, toil, tears and sweat.' Churchill was in the process of forming his War Cabinet, and on the following day Lord Beaverbrook was appointed Minister for Aircraft Production and Ernest Bevin took up his post of Minister of Labour.

In Europe, on 14 May, the Dutch forces were ordered to stop fighting and the next day the Nazis occupied The Hague. Mussolini was about to join the Axis and declare war, and the preparations for gathering together a flotilla of small ships to evacuate British soldiers from the Dunkirk beaches were underway.

Whether Herbert Jones took a conscious decision to move out of London with his wife and infant son because of the deteriorating war situation, or for other reasons, is not clear. What is known is that a fortnight after H's birth, Herbert acquired and moved into The Grange, a substantial estate in Kingswear, Devon. On the face of it, this move in something of a hurry was uncharacteristic – Herbert and Loe had stayed in London throughout the First World War and contributed to the war effort from the capital. They were familiar with wartime London, though perhaps that might have hastened their evacuation.

On the other hand, as a cosmopolitan and well-connected American millionaire, Herbert enjoyed the city. His political credentials, plus his involvement in high-profile international yachting, brought him at least into social contact with the US Ambassador, Joe Kennedy, a fellow Democrat, and gave him some prominence in, and access to, those circles.

It has been suggested that Herbert was involved in intelligence work for America or her allies, but extensive research has virtually eliminated that possibility. So, as often occurs in recounting Herbert's life, the trail goes cold at a critical moment. Why they decamped from London to remotest Devon quite so suddenly remains a mystery.

What does ring true is how the family came to acquire The Grange. Herbert's enthusiasm for sailing and racing in the late thirties used to take him along the Devon coast, and the story goes that one day he sailed round Start Point and across the bay to the mouth of the River Dart. Taking in the glorious headlands and magnificent views, he fell in love with the area. He spotted from the sea a fine-looking house that stood at the head of a valley bounded by woods, and within a fortnight of H's birth had acquired it.[1]

The property is a mile to the east of Kingswear, overlooking Start Bay. Kingswear lies opposite its more famous neighbour, Dartmouth, which is on the west bank of the river. Old ferries ply across the Dart connecting the two communities, which are steeped in nautical tradition; the whole area was, and still is, one of the prettiest places in the West Country. The presence of the imposing Britannia Royal Naval College perched on the side of a hill overlooking the town and river gives Dartmouth something of an aura and international renown, and was later to be the scene of some of H's wilder exploits.

It was here at The Grange, a white, gabled late-Victorian house, that H and his two younger brothers grew up; Tim and Bill were respectively two and five years younger than H.* H's closest friend then and throughout much of his life was Tobin Duke, a boy nine months older than himself, whose parents – a serving Army officer and his wife – had been befriended by Herbert and now rented a cottage on the estate. The Jones family and the Dukes struck up a close relationship which endured at The Grange throughout the war and continued long afterwards. It is from Tobin Duke that most of the recollections of H's early life come.

H's childhood was happy and carefree despite the austerities of wartime Britain. These were ameliorated somewhat by the fact that throughout the war Herbert regularly received food parcels from Marshal Field, Chicago's largest store. Tobin was conscious of the family's wealth – H had plenty of toys, many imported from

---

*Tim was born on 11 February 1942; Bill on 16 February 1945.

America, and his father was generous and carefree with his possessions.

The Joneses had another asset. Herbert, who was too old for active service with the US Forces and not eligible for call-up in Britain, volunteered to join the local Home Guard unit. He found himself in charge and offered to provide the unit transport – his grey Austin 8 saloon. This became known as the 'Home Guard Car', and with it came an entitlement to petrol coupons that helped the family in those days of strict rationing.

Six miles from The Grange, across Start Bay, lies Slapton Sands which was the scene of one of the most tragic and mysterious events in the preparations for D-Day in 1944. That part of the coast closely resembles Normandy and the proposed invasion beaches; accordingly, it was requisitioned for rehearsals by US and Allied amphibious forces. By late 1943 Slapton had been evacuated, which involved the removal by edict of a hundred villagers, and the declaration of a 'cordon sanitaire' for miles around.

In the early hours of 28 April 1944, a flotilla of landing craft ploughed steadily in a calm sea across Lyme Bay towards Slapton Sands. German radio intercept on the Cherbourg peninsula picked up heavy radio traffic and sent some Fast Patrol Boats to investigate. They were amazed to find this apparently unprotected flotilla of ships and attacked immediately. Torpedoes hit three of the landing craft, two of which sank in minutes, trapping below decks hundreds of soldiers and sailors. Others, already on deck, leapt into the sea, soon to drown weighed down by their waterlogged clothing and equipment. Chaos ensued, not helped by some panic among those running the exercise, who could not initially determine what was happening. When dawn broke, the toll of dead and missing stood at 198 sailors and 551 soldiers, a total of 749 Americans lost. A possibility then emerged that the Germans had taken prisoners. As ill-luck would have it, ten officers aboard the doomed landing craft had been closely involved in D-Day planning and knew the exact location of the landing beaches in France. There was deep consternation for several days that the secrets of the forthcoming invasion would be extracted from them. In fact, all ten had drowned and their secret remained safe.

Slapton Sands was a serious setback. Not only was it a demoralising blow to the whole Allied Command effort at a crucial time, but there were severe recriminations over the failures that were revealed. An order was issued imposing the strictest secrecy on all those who knew, or might learn, of the tragedy, including the doctors and nurses who treated the survivors. It was vital that the enemy should not realise what they had accomplished, or be given any clue that might link Slapton Sands to the planned US main effort on Utah Beach. However, the suppression of bad news on that scale, even in wartime, can be self-defeating because exaggerated rumour then takes flight. In this case, stories of a massive cover-up still persist. Half a century later, the belief endures locally that the full extent of the tragedy has always been suppressed and that, notwithstanding a granite Memorial on the beach,* total casualty figures have never been officially declared. No coherent explanation of what happened, and why, has been given and there is still some reluctance around Slapton to talk about the tragedy.

It seems difficult to believe that Herbert Jones, who must have been the only prominent American citizen living within sight of Slapton Sands, should not have been involved in some way, particularly in his Home Guard capacity. In daylight he could not have failed to see the ships and landing craft in the bay, or missed the increase in activity and traffic in the aftermath. But no one ever heard Herbert, or anyone at The Grange, mention the subject then, or at any time thereafter.

Other things, however, were well remembered. Tobin Duke clearly recollects the character and nature of each member of the Jones family from the time that he was four. He recalls H's father as:

> . . . a tallish, very thin man with grey hair and a large beaky nose. He was rather loose-jointed and his clothes always looked too

---

*The Memorial carries the figures mentioned in this chapter.

baggy and too short in the arm or leg. A very gentle person, he made even a small boy feel as though he was glad to see him. He talked to us about all sorts of subjects, some of which were a bit beyond us at the time but he patiently explained things, and he never talked down to us.[2]

Although to Tobin Herbert seemed quite old, with his greying hair and gaunt appearance, this never prevented him doing things with the boys right up to the time that he was taken ill. This, Tobin reported, was in marked contrast to his own far younger father, who always claimed he was too old to play at whatever it was the boys wanted.

The fact that Herbert Jones was at home, and therefore an influence on the family, throughout the war was unusual. The heads of most local families in and around Kingswear were away for long periods on active, or equivalent, service. So The Grange was a stable and secure home and the Joneses did not suffer the wartime anxieties and separations of most families. Herbert was nominally the disciplinarian as head of the family; however, he was a liberal one and generally adopted a benign role in the upbringing of his sons. Untypical of fathers in those days, he did not inflict corporal punishment on his children – at least not smacking them; rather, he used to flick the children hard on the side of their heads with his fingers as one would flick a fly off food. Duke recalls that H was generally argumentative. He was also fussy over his food, and was frequently 'flicked'.

H's mother, Olwen, who was called Dia* by her sons, although H sometimes called her Gus, was stricter than their father and set the domestic rules, such as meal times. Tobin remembers Dia favourably: 'She was strongly Welsh and could be fierce, emotional, tough and argumentative. But she was a jolly good mother and ferociously protective of her chicks.' She had a stormy but loving relationship with H, who was equally argumentative – even at that

*Pronounced 'dear'.

age. Dia appeared kind and gentle, but Tobin recounts that behind that façade 'was a very determined lady who knew what she wanted and was conscious of her husband's wealth and the value of money'.[3]

Jim Maker, the son of the tenant farmer at The Grange, and a contemporary of H's youngest brother, Bill, remembers Mrs Jones more with respect than affection: '. . . rather daunting – a bit of a schoolmistress and not someone who enjoyed small talk'.[4]

The Joneses employed a couple, Colin and Julie Armstrong, to help at The Grange. Colin, a true and shrewd Devonian, long since retired, recalls H's parents as 'local gentry – highly respected and well liked. They weren't toffee-nosed in any way. Mr Jones was gentle, kind and generous – a fine gentleman, in fact.'[5]

On the subject of H's mother he was more circumspect: 'She was more reserved and slightly formal; she gave you the feeling that you had to be on your best behaviour. Don't forget she had been a nurse for over twelve years and it showed.' Although only five foot two inches tall, Olwen had presence and an air of authority, but in the early days at The Grange she found it difficult to handle men, give instructions or get things done in a straightforward, easy manner. On the other hand, she was a generous benefactor locally of good causes.

Herbert and Olwen's relationship with each other and their sons was warm and loving, and the boys reciprocated. Olwen once told Bill that she only ever had one argument with his father in eighteen years – over him. However, as older parents, they exercised only loose control and discipline over their children, who were left with the two Duke boys largely to their own devices around the soft green acres of The Grange.

An additional attraction was another of Herbert's boats, a thirty-two-foot motor ketch called *Duckling* (*Sea Bear* had been sold), in which the children learnt to sail under Colin Armstrong's supervision. A more perfect childhood in wartime could not be imagined. Unsurprisingly, H became accustomed to an unusual degree of latitude and independence and, as the eldest son, he was undoubtedly spoilt.

Tobin Duke and his younger brother Jonathan were accepted as honorary members of the family, at least in part because they came from well-established, respectable British stock of some standing. This was important to Herbert, who had a strong sense of dynasty, and being an anglophile, encouraged what he saw as these favourable influences upon his sons. He very much wanted them to develop into proper English gentlemen, and as part of this process, with the family roots now deeply established in England, he applied for and was granted British nationality.*

H's early characteristics were soon evident. These were conflicting and unusual – an assessment which would recur throughout his life. On the one hand he could be awkward and solitary, retiring to immerse himself in a book in his bedroom if someone came to the house. On the other he could be boisterous and irresponsible. Tobin and H embarked on frequent daring and imaginative escapades. One day H led Duke through the quarter-mile-long Greenway railway tunnel between Paignton and Kingswear, with no apparent concern for what would happen if a train came along.

Relationships are often difficult between any three young siblings – one often gets excluded – and the two Duke boys enlarged the group further. Tobin was physically bigger and stronger than H, and the pair of them dominated the others. Although theirs was the attraction of like-minded boys, by nature Tobin was more prosaic and he provided a restraining influence on his younger friend. From an early age H was obsessed by the concept of family and its cohesion, and was intensely loyal both to it and to his friends. As the eldest, he was fiercely protective of his two younger brothers, and according to Duke 'would go to war for them'. This was repaid in full by Tim and Bill and exists even today in their diligent protection of H's memory and record. However, it did not at the time preclude fierce arguments and fights among the boys during which H, when

---

*Granted by Home Office Certificate AZ 25035 dated 22 June, 1947. He gave his occupation as a 'painter'.

not initiating them himself, tended to take up cudgels on behalf of whomever he perceived to be the underdog.

One of Duke's recurring memories was that H always had to win any argument. Tim was less aggressive and more responsible, and a far better sailor; while Bill, physically less well developed and co-ordinated than his brothers, was mostly excluded from their games and activities. Bill had had whooping cough when he was very young and his brothers rather unkindly nicknamed him 'Belsen Bill'. He was not excluded on that count, but because he was the one who always got caught if they were mischief-making, or out of bounds. Nevertheless, if Bill himself ever got into trouble or was attacked by one of the others, H was the first to jump to his defence. It was H's idea to build an assault course at The Grange designed to develop and toughen Bill up. With stopwatch in hand, he would record his young brother around the circuit, shouting appropriate encouragement.

Until the summer of 1948, H attended, along with his brothers and the Dukes, the local private day school, Tower House, high on Townstal Road in Dartmouth, where Miss Gates was headmistress. This involved a daily drive, or a thirty-minute bicycle ride, which included crossing the Dart by ferry. Tower House was a small and undemanding establishment, one that Tim remembers as a happy experience. Few records of H's attendance or academic performance exist; however, the easy and agreeable tempo of life at home was barely disturbed.

When he turned eight, it was time to move on. In her last report Miss Gates concluded kindly: 'Herbert's work is coming along very well. He is gaining confidence in himself. We shall miss him.' More to the point, he was going to miss them. Things were about to change.

In September 1948, H was packed off to St Peter's preparatory school, 250 miles away, in Seaford, East Sussex, where his brothers were to follow in due course. In those days, St Peter's was the archetypal prep school. The imposing, red-brick Edwardian establishment, set in acres of mown grass, had a far from cosy aura. Seaford was the mecca of south coast prep schools, and it was a fine sight to see the boys and girls of over a dozen such private schools walking in a crocodile to church on Sundays. Herbert chose St Peter's because of its good reputation, particularly as a traditional feeder school for Eton, which was where he had already determined to send his sons next. Eton was then Britain's most expensive school, and Herbert, knowing little of English education, had been advised that it was also the best, which settled the matter. Nevertheless, that was not to stop H and Bill pronouncing later that they loathed the place.

The shock of boarding must have hit H hard, not that the regime at St Peter's was especially tough under the kindly Mr Knox-Shaw and Mr Talbot, the joint headmasters. However, after the war, the ethos and conditions in all preparatory schools were universally spartan and strict, no matter how benign and civilised a headmaster might be. Parents primarily sent their sons away to be well taught and prepared for successful admission to the public school of their choice five years or so later. This involved a certain amount of mental and physical rigour, conformity and personal development which was accepted as a necessary prelude to public school, and coping subsequently with life in the outside world.

St Peter's was a far cry from present-day preparatory schools with their carpeted small dormitories or cubicles, and teddies nestling on pillows to add homeliness and warmth. When H's generation went off to their various boarding schools, rationing was still in force – today's choice of menu would have been unthinkable – and the unheated dormitories were large and forbidding. Christian names were never used; cold baths were compulsory and the administration of discipline was swift and harsh by today's standards. Boys were beaten with various wooden implements, often on their bare bottoms, for relatively minor misdemeanours or indifferent work – punishment that few juniors seemed to avoid in the course of a term, and some endured several times. H would have derived little comfort from hearing that this was good preparation for public school.

Prowess on the games field was important and often of more

significance than performance in the classroom; and boxing was compulsory. There were no half-terms or exeats, and parents visited, if at all – many fathers were still serving overseas after the war – on one Sunday a term; or perhaps they came to watch a match and take their sons out to tea afterwards.

H started well academically and collected three alpha pluses in his first term, but it did not last. The following term one report read: 'Not a good start. Scrappy and rather idle. I have spoken my mind so something may start to happen.' It did. Michael Farebrother, who would shortly become one of the joint headmasters, took H under his wing when he joined his class in the autumn of 1950. Records show that H moved up to the top of his Latin set. Nevertheless, years later, Farebrother was to recall* that overall H's academic progress was inconsistent and remained a cause for concern:

By now the need to qualify academically for entry to Eton was well over the horizon and H was being urged on by both school and home to work harder. He was never one to ask for help, make a fuss or draw attention to himself, but he must have taken what was said to him to heart because we find among the form prize winners for the autumn of 1952: H Jones. He was also appointed Captain of a small dormitory, his first command!

Among fellow pupils, the few who remember him at all recall a gentle, sensitive boy. H's father made more impression on them, arriving in the family Rolls-Royce and taking H and his friends off for picnics. They would park up under some trees in the country and Herbert would dispense luxuries from a wicker basket. One school friend who still remembers these outings recalls that 'there were many things in that basket, such as quails' eggs, that I had not seen let alone tasted before in times of rationing. And I hardly came from a world that could be described as deprived.'

Another recollection gives an early insight into H's thoughtful

---

*In an article written after H's death.

and compassionate nature. Robin Ashburner, who was the same age
as H, had to move schools and was distraught at leaving St Peter's
where he had been happy.

> I well remember the day I was told the earth-shattering news that
> I was not to return to St Peter's. It was the very last day of term
> and every boy except Jones and me had left. We were there
> because we were not travelling on the school train but were being
> picked up by our respective parents. Jones was a real brick. To this
> day I remember his concern and sympathy as I finally emptied my
> locker never to return. He was loyal, always with thought for his
> friends, especially if they needed sympathy.

At one stage H got caught up in an unusual and unpleasant
incident. There had been a theft from one of the boys and all those
who could have been involved were lined up and questioned about
it. When asked, H said something like: 'I don't think I took it, but
I might have done in my sleep.' This was quickly accepted as an
admission of guilt. However, it transpired later that he had taken the
rap on behalf of the others because they had all been threatened with
collective punishment. This was typical. Throughout his life, H
possessed an unusually strong sense of justice and fair play and even
as a young boy would have sensed the inherent injustice of a
collective punishment.

H's letters home were characteristic of that generation of prep
school boys – mostly factual, and devoid of any intimacy or clues to
their feelings. The results of school matches were listed, as was his
form order, and he made various demands, such as to keep a guinea
pig in the holidays. But mainly he wanted more and more books. In
one Sunday letter he first thanked his parents for sending *Riders of
the Range* and *Yankee RN*. Then he asked for the *Roy Rogers Annual*,
and went on to enquire persistently about another five books he had
ordered but which had not arrived: 'Has the rest of the series come
in yet because it's about time they did! Isn't it?'

H's last report from St Peter's came shortly before he took his

Common Entrance. It noted many distinctions – first place in Latin and maths; second in French, English and history – and concluded that: 'He has left us in no doubt about his intentions this term and has acquitted himself right nobly . . . I do congratulate him. Now for the next big step.'

St Peter's had been a success. Mr Farebrother noted H leaving 'with quiet courtesy and sincere gratitude to those who helped him but with very little demonstration'. Certainly Herbert Jones must have been well satisfied with the progress and development of his eldest son – and later his younger ones – because generously he donated a swimming pool to St Peter's* in appreciation of the start they had given his children.

---

*The school closed in 1982 because of falling numbers.

CHAPTER THREE

'Floreat Etona'

Eton College, over five hundred years old, is the most famous public school in Britain, and indeed the world. Early in the summer term of 1953 H, just thirteen, sat his entrance examination and passed it at the first attempt. This was no great intellectual achievement because in those days Eton was relatively undemanding academically, except for King's Scholars, whose abilities obviated their parents paying their fees. It was, nevertheless, the first formal academic hurdle that H had ever faced and so there was cause for celebration when he jumped it.

Sadly, however, he was about to begin five far from happy years, during which he barely left his mark on the school. Indeed, so little impact did H make that when he was killed twenty-five years later, some of his contemporaries proclaimed, with the certainty bred of some Old Etonians, that he could not possibly have been at school with them because, if he had, they would surely have known any future VC.

In many ways H should have thrived at Eton. The school has a tradition of nurturing unusual individuals and coping with late developers in ways that many other public schools with more conformist attitudes do not. We know that H's father wanted the very best for his sons, and we can assume that St Peter's would have advised Herbert had they felt H could not swim in such a large pond; but they did not. Furthermore, as H's two younger brothers followed him to Eton, it may be deduced that there was parental satisfaction with the school. But the fact is that H did not fit in, and perhaps did not want to fit in, at Eton. Certainly he made little attempt to adapt to or go with the flow of contemporary life there.

Eton accommodated around 1,250 boys, with the seventy scholars set apart, living and working in their own College within the school. The rest, known as Oppidans,* were dispersed into twenty-five boarding houses each of about fifty boys. Living conditions at such a supposedly well-endowed school might be assumed to be comfortable; on the contrary, many of the boarding houses were run down and shabby.

Eton in the fifties, under Dr Robert Birley, was going through one of its happier and more successful phases, according to John Wilkinson,† a contemporary of H with a foot in both camps – his father was a Housemaster and Wilkinson himself was a King's Scholar. Birley towered over Eton like some great lighthouse, illuminating everything within range. A large, shambling man with immense presence, he was kind and civilised, if sometimes unworldly. A brilliant, stimulating teacher, he inspired lifelong devotion in his pupils and was considered one of the greatest Head Masters of Eton. There were some, however, who thought him too scholarly and austere. Furthermore, his administration was inconsistent, particularly in replying to letters. One Housemaster recalls writing two letters to Birley. The first was an imaginative proposal for Eton boys to teach English to immigrant children in Slough; the second was a routine note asking permission for a boy to miss the last Chapel of term in order to attend a wedding in Ireland. The second letter brought a two-page reply that had obviously entailed much research into bus, train and ferry timetables, and proved that the unfortunate boy could attend both

---

*Originally meaning boys from the town and denoting non-scholars.
*Now Conservative MP for Ruislip Northwood, former member of the Parliamentary Defence Committee and a Commissioner of the Commonwealth War Graves Commission. He was commissioned into the RAF via Cranwell, but did not know H at Eton.

the wedding and Chapel. The first, on just such a subject as could be expected to touch Birley's heart, remained unanswered.

Assuming the Head Mastership in 1949, Birley quickly established his influence throughout the school. Unusually in such a big place, he came to know many of the boys personally through his insistence on teaching history himself, which he did with great enthusiasm, often writing red-ink notes on boys' essays lengthier than some of their own unworthy offerings.

A boy's House was all-important, not because of the condition of its fabric, which anyway varied, but because traditionally Eton operated a strong House and tutorial system. Each Housemaster exercised considerable autonomy and tutors had an important academic influence. Hence the quality and character of both were crucial, and could make or mar a boy's career, as indeed could his contemporaries in his House.

One supportive Old Etonian father, with three generations of Etonians in the family, was well aware of this. Lieutenant Colonel Desmond ffrench-Blake was killed in action early in the war, but not before writing to his wife from the Western Desert on the subject of the future education of their newly born son. ffrench-Blake wanted him to go to Eton because he believed it to be 'quite the best school', but warned: 'Robert must not go there unless he has the strength of character and the temperament to handle it.' There were too many temptations, he felt, with too much wealth and too much glamour – boys who were well connected and good at games, good-looking and self-confident, wielded too much power and influence.

Reinforcing this, sixty per cent of H's intake in the fifties were sons of Old Etonians, forty-nine boys in H's year were the sons of peers and four were members of the British or foreign royal families.[1] Snobbishness was a problem and homosexuality, certainly in its milder form of the physical attraction of some adolescent boys to others, was endemic. Bullying was commonplace and the administration of discipline was tough and largely in the hands of senior boys.

Eton, perhaps more than most schools, tended to allow the

H JONES VC

'Library' (House prefects in other public schools) and those elected to 'Pop'* full licence, on the basis that they should develop their authority and exercise powers of discipline in preparation for adulthood. There were two by-products of this laudable aim: the first was fagging – that is, junior boys running errands and undertaking chores for senior boys; and the other a tradition of corporal punishment, often savage and ritualistic. The Library would summarily cane boys, often for trivial offences, and so very occasionally would Pop, for severe misdemeanours, in a much more serious and exemplary way. Furthermore, for centuries before and for at least a decade after H left, the Head Master and Lower Master 'flogged' – that is, birched – particularly idle or ill-disciplined boys bent over a wooden block maintained for that very purpose.† All this was generally accepted, often proudly, as part and parcel of Eton's life, with few objections raised. But it did create a robust, rather physical atmosphere in which a sensitive boy could feel vulnerable and alone.

H entered this world in September 1953, arriving at Timbralls, a large, three-storey brick building fronting the main road. This was Tom Brocklebank's House.‡ It was close to the centre of the school and the nearest House to one of the main sports fields, called The Field, just across the road from the famous wall where the Eton Wall Game is played.

In certain respects Brocklebank seemed an ideal Housemaster. He was a keen oarsman who in the Varsity Boat Race had stroked Cambridge to victory on three occasions, and was also an accomplished mountaineer with an attempted Everest expedition behind him. However neither he nor his wife was in robust health,

---

*'Pop', or the Eton Society, was a group of senior boys elected by their peers. This prestigious body was responsible, among other things, for administering school discipline.
†Headmaster Anthony Chevenix-Trench's use of corporal punishment, as recently as 1970, was thought to be so excessive that it provoked a scandal, and flogging was retained as a 'reserve power' and rarely used thereafter.
‡The Houses were referred to by the Housemaster's name.

32

and he lacked charisma – one boy described a meeting with 'Fingers' Brocklebank as a 'monotone experience'. He was moody and could be unkindly sarcastic. Moreover, outsiders viewed Brocklebank's indifferently, claiming the House lacked the qualities to inspire impressionable young men: a style of its own and strong *esprit de corps*. Such intangibles mattered at Eton, as indeed did the type of boy in the House. Those departing from certain conventions could be targets for persecution in some Houses, and the feeling was that Tom Brocklebank did little to curb this unpleasant herd instinct. Nevertheless, at least one of his House Captains insists that quietly he exercised more control than was superficially evident.

Some boys at Eton under the Fleming Scheme,* for instance, were tormented and told to 'go back to the grammar school where you belong'. In Brocklebank's, even Winston Churchill's grandson had a rough time, being considered (as perhaps he might have been) bumptious. In H's case he was half-American, came from a remote part of England and was without any established friends in the school. He was not well connected, and he was awkward and shy. He was hopeless at ball games and lacked any obvious talents or attributes to create a favourable initial impression.

It was hardly surprising, therefore, that he felt insecure, and his isolation was further accentuated by one of Eton's most cherished features. Whereas in most public schools new boys were thrust together in day rooms and dormitories, and so quickly got to know their peers, each boy at Eton was given a room to himself straight-away. This had many advantages: it was easier for a boy to be an individual, and it was possible for him to have privacy if he felt the need. Furthermore, he could talk to his Housemaster privately in his own familiar surroundings, which encouraged a more equal relationship.

Whatever the merits and demerits of these unique traditions, as the terms (or 'halves') went by, a picture of H began to emerge from both staff and contemporaries. Brocklebank remembered him –

---

*Scholarships for boys whose parents needed assistance with the fees.

many years later and only with prompting – as 'smallish in build, wiry and strong, possessed of an engaging shyness which never left him'. His contemporary impressions of H were more scathing, as this letter to Herbert at the end of H's first year shows:

> Some depressing reports here again, I'm afraid. They mostly tell the same story. No-one thinks him wanton in his idleness, but idle he certainly is . . . Too often after tea he is to be found, not working as he should be then, but drifting into a book (not a very good one, either) or into gadgeteering [*sic*] with much mess left on the floor . . . Without more active co-operation on his part, nothing much is likely to emerge from this most likeable boy.

Reflecting years later in H's obituary, Brocklebank explained:

> Those who taught and tutored him were often distressed at not helping him to take fire. He was a classic example of a late developer. Yet there were signs of what was to come, little though we realised it. He began to enjoy reading military history and there was some evidence of character and originality which escaped us all at the time. He was a 'loner' taking his own course – not for him to follow with the herd.[2]

How distant from the herd he stood is well illustrated in a passage from the autobiography of young Winston Churchill, an exact contemporary of H in Brocklebank's. He wrote:

> By my second summer at Eton I had become sufficiently proficient at rowing to abandon my single man 'whiff'* in favour of a 'perfect', crewed by two oarsmen. On 1 March 1955 I reported in a letter to my father: 'Next half I am sharing a "perfect" with a boy called Jones who is quite mad, but very nice. (He thinks of nothing but guns and battleships.)' Apart from this one reference to him in

---

*Small fragile boat.

a letter to my father I, in common with many of his contemporaries at school, have no recollection of him whatever, other than as a quiet reserved boy who would keep very much to himself.[3]

However, Charles Palmer-Tomkinson, another contemporary in the same House, remembers H better because he 'messed' with him at one stage. This was the custom of a few friends in a House eating tea together – a system, incidentally, that broke down the isolation of boys otherwise alone in their rooms. Palmer-Tomkinson remembered H as 'extremely quiet, almost a non-entity really, but an avid reader of war books. He would hardly speak when we messed together, other than to offer me an egg or another piece of toast!'[4] His most distinct memory is of H's mother providing copious quantities of food to supplement their messing. 'Our "sock cupboard"* was always bulging,' he recalls, 'and although wartime rationing had ended, some things were still in short supply.'

Another slightly older boy, Tim Ashburner,† who was in a different House, had a very clear and significant recollection of H's bravery in the boxing ring. H was drawn in the school boxing competition to fight, at featherweight, a very proficient boxer called Michael Hare,‡ who won his weight in all six of his years at Eton. It must have been a daunting prospect for H. Ashburner, along with many other boys, feared for Jones's chances – even for his safety.

The contest began and, as expected, Hare proved to be by far the better boxer and was soon inflicting severe punishment; however, H doggedly fought back and kept upright. Towards the end of the first round the referee and games master, Colonel Ames, stopped the contest and declared Hare to be the winner, announcing loudly from the ring: 'Green [i.e. H in the green corner], you are a very brave boy. You are up against the best featherweight the school has ever had and you have acquitted yourself extremely well.'

---

*Food cupboard.
†Elder brother of Robin Ashburner, H's friend at St Peter's.
‡Later Lord Blakenham, one-time chairman of the Pearson Group.

Further evidence of H's strength of character came at the same time from another boy in the House, with whom he had been friendly. Unpleasant gossip had started to circulate about this contemporary, who remembers vividly H confronting him directly: 'He banged open my door and stood there formally and stiffly blurting out: "You are behaving unacceptably and I shall not speak to you again". And he never did.' It was as if H had reached a decision and felt morally impelled to act on it, irrespective of the circumstances or consequences. Other boys avoided the issue or gossiped behind backs, but this was not H's way. He confronted matters head on, ensuring, honourably, that any wounds he inflicted were open and direct. It now seems that H might have wrongly accused his friend. If so, it reveals another aspect of his emerging character: an impulse to act on principle but without due care for the evidence.

At the age of about fifteen, H started to think seriously about a career. His first inclination was to join the Royal Air Force, reflecting his already keen interest in aeroplanes and flying. This enthusiasm took an unexpected turn in a letter to his father: 'I want to emigrate to Australia and join the RAAF after going to Cranwell, or to its Australian equivalent. Do you think that is a good idea, or not?'

Unfortunately, his poor eyesight – he had been wearing reading spectacles since he was eleven – was becoming more evident. He now had to sit at the front of the cinema to see a film properly, and tests indicated he would not meet the strict RAF eyesight requirements for aircrew selection. He was bitterly disappointed, because he had very much envisaged himself as a pilot, and this perhaps accounts for his scorn later in life for most things involving the RAF.

So he turned his attention to the Navy and became obsessed with ships. This ties in with Churchill's memory of H immersing himself in *Jane's Fighting Ships* and generally enthusing about the Senior Service. With Dartmouth just across the river from The Grange, he also had a local focus. But again, eyesight let him down. The Navy's requirement was hardly less stringent than that of the RAFs, so that avenue was blocked too. However, H's younger brother, Tim, subsequently joined the Royal Navy for a full career.

It might be wondered what encouragement and guidance his parents were giving as H experienced these various disappointments and coped with adolescence. In those days parents tended to leave the development of their offspring to the school; besides, H's father had suffered a mild stroke in 1949 and by now his condition was deteriorating. For the last six years of Herbert's life, which covered almost all of H's time at Eton, he was partially incapacitated and could not talk, while Olwen was preoccupied with running the home and devotedly looking after her husband. For these reasons perhaps things were allowed to drift. However, good news from Eton was imminent.

By the end of 1956, H's work seemed to be showing a marked improvement and, after one notably encouraging report from his tutor,* Herbert felt a corner had been turned. Despite his incapacity, he wrote at once to Brocklebank suggesting his son should try for Trinity or Pembroke, Cambridge. The reply was immediate:

> There is no harm applying but I should warn you straight away that it is extremely difficult for a boy of Herbert's† ability (which is, frankly, very limited academically) to get to the University. And to get to Trinity on a science ticket is about the hardest of all . . .
>
> P.S. What about sending him to Princeton?

But Herbert would not be deflected and persisted with his notion of H trying for Trinity. Meanwhile, Pembroke had shown interest and so Brocklebank tried again:

> I strongly advise you, in the light of the letter you've had from Pembroke, to cancel the entry with Trinity, and tell Pembroke that you have done so and would prefer to aim at Pembroke.

---

*C.H. Taylor wrote: 'Jones has always impressed me by his interest in and command of the English language . . .'

†Brocklebank referred to H as Herbert, or Herbert the Younger, or sometimes as Herbert ii.

Herbert ii wouldn't have a chance at Trinity; of that I'm sure. And you want to be free to try for Pembroke at the *suitable* time, and not after failure for Trinity . . .

One is struck reading the correspondence by the Housemaster's care that Herbert should avoid any misunderstanding – due to his inexperience as an American – of the requirements for Oxbridge. Both men seemed to like and respect each other. Neither was fit, but each was working in what he believed to be H's best interest. Sadly, Herbert would be dead within a year and Tom Brocklebank would soon be convalescing in Australia following a serious illness.

Presumably for these reasons, all initiatives aimed at university petered out, and although H's work continued to progress, his focus turned on the Army, and matters military. The Russian Front in the Second World War captured his imagination. He became absorbed particularly in the details of Operation Barbarossa, Hitler's winter offensive in Russia in 1941, and model tanks replaced the aircraft and ships in his room. On a different plane, he was entranced by Field Marshal Wavell's poetic anthology *Other Men's Flowers*. Academically, he prepared for the Civil Service entrance examination, success in which was necessary for Sandhurst in those days, if a boy was not a graduate.

The outdoor activity H really enjoyed and in which he wanted to make his mark was rowing. Brocklebank's was traditionally a rowing House – their dark blue and yellow blades were prominent on the river, and the House was invariably well placed in races. So H should have had plenty of encouragement; indeed, he may well have done, but he was dogged by misfortune. According to Tobin Duke, who was not at Eton but discussed such things with him in the holidays, H took his rowing seriously. He believed he had the ability to get into the School Eight and he was sufficiently ambitious and determined to train hard. But he was too light, and more seriously, he broke his collarbone falling off his bicycle whilst coaching from the towpath. So he was never awarded his Colours. Nevertheless, he became 'a determined member of a rather good Bumping Four', according to the *Eton Chronicle*. But this was very much second best, and H would have been disappointed.

That did not adversely affect his holidays, however. He sailed with Tobin, and another friend, Bobby Hanscomb, in *Duckling*, living aboard her for days at a time and having a great deal of amusement. Hanscomb was struck by H's boldness and desire for challenge – one holiday he wanted to cross the Channel and explore the French canals. The three of them formed a formidable, assertive trio, not deliberately excluding the younger brothers, but paying them scant attention as they basked in their own self-sufficiency. Tobin was then living in Aldershot, where his father was stationed. Bobby and H often came to stay in the holidays and on exeats, when together they roamed over the local training area, fought mock battles, tackled the assault course and watched the Farnborough Air Show.

Around this time H started to develop an interest in girls, although he was still socially gauche and easily thrown by them. His first declared love was Ellie Kennaway, a girl of his own age whom he described years later as 'startlingly beautiful'. He serenaded her with the song 'My Girl Ellie', played to the tune of a popular regimental march,* but mostly he was hopelessly awkward and shy with her and indeed others. He would often go to a party, find a quiet corner and take out a book to avoid having to make conversation.

Olwen tried hard to get H and his brothers to conform to accepted social conventions, but without much success. She bought the right clothes, arranged dancing lessons, had them Highland reeling and even insisted they learn to carve – a minor social skill at the time. But H in particular resisted all attempts to civilise him and he often behaved stupidly. He could be boorish and rude at parties – often irresponsible, like driving at breakneck speed down the narrow lane to The Grange – and even loutish on occasion. In retrospect, Tobin considered this to be immaturity, lack of

---

*The Royal Tank Regiment's march is 'My Boy Willie'.

self-confidence and absence of parental control. Being part of a gang with Tim, Tobin and Jonathan Duke made matters worse, and in their teens they had a bad reputation locally.

After one incident – one of Dartmouth's fountains was 'found' up at The Grange – Olwen resolved that a more powerful influence should be brought to bear. She enlisted the help of the Dukes, who in turn approached a formidable relation, Geraldine Sangar, the widowed daughter of Field Marshal Sir Cyril Deverill, a former Chief of the Imperial General Staff. In her fifties, Geraldine had been a school matron during the war, had a son of her own – then a Gunner subaltern – and knew about boys. She was part of a respectable and self-assured society in and around Lymington, in Hampshire, and she introduced H and his brothers to a wider and more sophisticated circle of friends than they had in Devon.

Much against H's wishes, he was thrust into the midst of a vibrant social scene – parties, hunt balls and local yacht club functions. At one of these H met Blythe Monro, a delightful girl still at school whose quiet, undemanding and somewhat naïve manner gave him more confidence. She became his next girlfriend, although not in any very passionate way. H was still shy and hesitant, and more often than not he could be found alone, biting his fingernails on the edge of a party.

On 10 September 1957, a few days after the beginning of H's last year at Eton, Herbert died, aged sixty-nine, of hypostatic pneumonia. His ashes were scattered from *Duckling* in a cove off The Grange, in a moving ceremony which H attended wearing his Eton tailcoat. It is not easy to assess Herbert's influence on his eldest son. The family's view is that H was closer to his mother than to his father, whilst the reverse was true of Tim. Unquestionably, Herbert passed on to H his love of poetry and reading, and also the romantic side of his nature.

In view of Herbert's unconventional life, it is remarkable that this gentle, artistic and peaceful man, who had not fired a shot in anger in either world war, should have produced a disciplined warrior son of such ultimate valour and intensity of purpose. Certainly he did nothing to discourage H from a Service career – indeed, he had been the first to suggest the Navy – and so he would undoubtedly have been well pleased with the paths two of his sons were preparing to take.

Back at Eton, H was now at the top of the school, and his contemporaries were being nominated and elected for School and House appointments both lofty and humble. At the apex of the pyramid was the prestigious self-electing oligarchy Pop, which included the Captain of the Oppidans. Then came the Library of each House. The House Captain was appointed by his Housemaster, but thereafter the Library was largely self-electing. Below them, on the bottom rung, came the Debate, enjoying little responsibility or prestige. The Library and Debate selected their new members.*

It was unusual for a senior boy not to be invited to join one or other of the tiers of House governance before he left but H's name was passed over until the last opportunity for such advancement. Midway through his last half, he was summoned by the Library. What happened next is remembered with awe by Mike Wilkin,† a boy two years junior to H:

> We (the boys lower down the House) heard one morning that the previous evening H had been summoned to the Library to be told, reluctantly, that he had been elected to Debate (in other words, made a sort of junior prefect), and that he had had the temerity to decline the honour, and tell the assembled members of the Library why.
>
> In the conditions of the time, this was an event on a par with a Spartacus revolt. It had a dramatic impact on those of us resigned to having been born into some teenage underclass for reasons not explained by our education or upbringing.

---

*Kenneth Rose, the distinguished biographer and columnist, and himself an Eton 'beak', observed drily: 'In the perverse manner of Eton's nomenclature, the Library were not noted for reading and Debate never debated.'

†Wilkin became an American oil executive and wrote to Sara Jones in 1992 with this recollection.

Nor can I forget the attempt by the Library to get their revenge for his spurning Debate by launching a barrage of 78 rpm records and verbal abuse from their windows down on to a friend of H's from Kingswear, in the courtyard below. Eton was a strange place!

H's own account of the incident, in a letter to his mother, was brief and pithy: 'They elected me into Debate last night, but I refused to become a member. I don't think they were very pleased, but there's nothing they can do about it.' H's attitude was that the whole process was bogus at such a late stage of his final term and he would not be party to it.

Before this happened, H was angling to get away from Eton anyway. He prevailed upon his mother to remove him a term early to go to a crammer for the Civil Service Commissioners (or Army) exam. It was generally thought that there was a technique to it, and so H's request was logical. He had by now achieved seven GCE O levels, including the mandatory English and maths, but he did not take any A levels – there was no need, because the Civil Service exam lay parallel to, but outside, the normal O- and A-level syllabus. His mother, now shouldering uneasily all such matters herself, concurred, although without the apparent enthusiasm of H's acting Housemaster.* When informed of Olwyn's decision he wrote simply: 'So be it.' Accordingly, H arrived at Davies, Laing and Dick, the well-established London crammer, in early April 1958 to prepare for his ordeal in late May.

Looking back at his time at school, it was neither a miserable nor a fulfilling period in his life. Tom Brocklebank summed up H's career for the *Eton Chronicle* after his death:

At school he was in no sense a scholar but did his tasks well enough and totally without ostentation . . . he left Eton in March 1958 having made no mark, not complacent about it, but having

---

*The Hon. Giles St Aubyn.

led a rather dull life with undaunted cheerfulness . . . It all reads as a remarkably humdrum career. And he left the Corps as Private H. Jones.

It is difficult to feel that Eton did well for him; in all likelihood, though, he would have fared no better elsewhere at that stage. For he needed longer than most to grow up and find himself, and those who are youthful in this way often turn out to be the most brilliant people. After all, the higher in evolution you go, the longer the childhood of the species . . .[5]

For his part, H looked back on Eton with little affection. But there was no resentment of his time there, or bitterness at his failure to blossom. Occasionally he even wore the distinctive Old Etonian tie, and if he remembered the date, he would draw attention to the Fourth of June;* and he would have a dig at any Old Harrovian if Eton beat Harrow at Lords. He appreciated that Eton was a particular school for a particular type of boy. It had not been right for him, and it should not be the automatic choice for the sons of Old Etonians. When the time came, the Joneses sent their two sons, David and Rupert, to Sherborne.

Perhaps the clearest image of H at Eton comes from Roger Sainsbury,† a contemporary in Brocklebank's who, after H had been killed, summed up the boy and his time at school in a perceptive and moving article published alongside H's official obituary in the *Eton Chronicle*:

When first I heard on the News that the paratroops had captured Goose Green in a fierce battle against enormous odds and that their commanding officer, reportedly revered by his men and known to them as 'H', had been killed in a notable act of bravery and personal leadership I, with most of the rest of the nation, was

---

*Celebration of King George III's birthday.
†Sainsbury became a distinguished engineer, a Director of Mowlem, and President of the Institution of Civil Engineers.

moved by the story. How, I pondered, could a man, who by virtue of his rank had no apparent need to charge a machine gun post, find the courage for such an act? Was he indeed, in an objective sense, right to do it? How, in any case, can one be objective about a supreme personal example which inspires others to complete a glorious victory? What sort of man was this?

Next day, from fragmentary information in a newspaper, it dawned that this was the Jones who had started at Eton on the same day as I; for a long time we had messed together; for much of our five years together at Timbralls he was my closest friend: now he was dead and famous. And I was not surprised.

I had not seen him since schooldays. I was not even consciously aware that he had followed a military career. Why was I not surprised that he had died a national hero? He was after all an outwardly unremarkable boy – search the records and you will be hard put to it to find that he excelled at anything. Not outstandingly bright; competent but far from brilliant on the games field; a leading light in no club or society; a boy whom most would have thought destined for obscurity. And yet there were in him at the age of fifteen all the traits of character which made it seem so natural to me that 'H' the hero was that same Jones.

He loved military books in general and tales of heroism in particular; he was a romantic who even then could be seen measuring himself against Beau Geste and the other literary notables that fired his imagination. He was liable suddenly to embark upon an evening's discussion about the nature of courage. He was to an alarming degree resistant in any boyhood trial in the endurance of pain. Above all he had a highly developed sense of honour; if he somehow formed a conclusion that he ought to act in a certain way nothing, but nothing, would deflect him. Right or wrong, if he thought himself right he did not flinch from being a lone voice, from being the one to stand against the tide. It takes a kind of courage to order other men to their deaths, but it takes another kind to lead them into it oneself. The sense of honour that Jones, as a boy, displayed would inevitably have made him one to lead from the front. Now he has had that one crowded hour of glorious life that is said to be worth an age without a name. But Jones would not have done it for glory; he would have done it in honour. In truth I don't think Eton made him so; this character was formed in him earlier than that. But Eton may perhaps be proud that it did not unform the remarkable character in the apparently unremarkable boy, did not stifle him or mould him into some other person who might have been admirable but would not have been 'H'.

Today a simple round memorial tablet of black slate, in the shape of a parachute seen from above, commissioned by the then Provost, Martin Charteris,* is set in the wall below the steps to the College Hall bearing the inscription:

In memory of Lieutenant Colonel H. Jones VC OBE
killed leading the Second Battalion the Parachute Regiment in the
attack on Darwin and Goose Green, Falkland Islands, 28 May 1982.

It is Eton's formal recognition and mark of respect for H, the school's thirty-seventh holder of the Victoria Cross.

---

*Lord Charteris was Provost of Eton 1978–91, having earlier been Private Secretary to HM The Queen for twenty years.

CHAPTER FOUR

'Serve to Lead'*

At the end of the 1950s, National Service was an established national institution, and the junior ranks of the Armed Forces were largely conscripted. Britain prides herself on not having a large standing army except at times of national crisis, so this was historically unusual. Until 1 April 1958, every young British male of the appropriate age was called up for two years' service, mainly in the Army but also in the Royal Navy or Royal Air Force, unless he was for various reasons deferred or exempt.

When H left Eton, the Army was some 335,000 strong,† deployed worldwide. There was a substantial presence east of Suez, with garrisons and units in the Far East in Hong Kong, Malaya, Singapore, Borneo and Brunei. Another major command was based in the Middle East, with brigades in Aden, Kuwait, Kenya and Oman. HQ Near East Land Forces was in Cyprus, with its subordinate garrisons in Malta and Libya, and in Gibraltar. Of greatest military importance was the large standing British Army of the Rhine (BAOR), which comprised four well-equipped, powerful divisions totalling some 77,000 men on high operational readiness. There was even a military presence in the Caribbean, including significant garrisons in British Guiana and British Honduras, as well

---

*RMA Sandhurst's motto.

†Defence White Paper, April 1958. All subsequent facts and figures in this chapter are from that source.

as a handful of military posts in Jamaica and Barbados. The balance of the Army was held in the United Kingdom, in numerically the largest command.

The Royal Navy and Royal Air Force were similarly deployed, with ships and aircraft with a nuclear capability held at instant readiness against the massive potential Soviet threat. The Berlin airlift of 1949 had shown the lengths to which the West had to go to preserve the integrity of NATO in post-war Europe. Many of the same lessons had applied to the United Nations Force in Korea three years later. The Suez fiasco of 1956 was a recent and painful memory for the Armed Forces, and even more so for the Conservative Party. That same year the Soviet invasion of Hungary emphasised the sense of insecurity in Europe; and worse was to come. In 1961, three years after H joined the Army, the Berlin Wall went up overnight, with no apparent warning, followed by an extension of this artificial barrier along the Inner German Border. The following autumn the Cuban Missile Crisis* broke, drawing the world to the edge of another world war. Against this background, Britain's Armed Forces were busy and in demand.

The alternative to being called up for National Service was voluntary regular service. This was the route H chose. In those days, a young man hoping for a regular commission direct from school needed to jump three hurdles before admission to the Royal Military Academy Sandhurst (RMAS). First was the necessary academic qualification, which by the summer of 1958 H had secured. Second, he had to pass a Medical Board (the source of jokes about Army doctors grabbing the testicles of unsuspecting young candidates and telling them to cough), which rejected more candidates than might be imagined, often with medical conditions of which they were unaware. Here, H very nearly came unstuck, with his earlier broken, perhaps brittle, collarbone and impaired vision. The latter was of more concern to the Board, and H only passed with the lowest possible grading. Weighing ten stone, and only five foot nine inches

*October 1962.

47

tall, he was formally assessed as: 'Fit for RMAS but only as a candidate for the Royal Pioneer Corps.'*

The third hurdle was the Regular Commissions Board (RCB). This involved three days of tests, interviews and assessments in a country house at Westbury in Wiltshire. There, candidates were – and still are – put through a series of aptitude and academic assessments, and dynamic practical tasks – such as getting their teams across a notional crocodile-infested river in a set time, with only a barrel, a length of rope and a couple of wooden planks too short to reach the other side.

Despite sceptics and management consultants, the RCB procedures have stood the test of time remarkably well, and indeed have been widely imitated in industry and commerce. The RCB's aim was – and continues to be – simply to identify a candidate's potential as an Army officer after the necessary training at Sandhurst. The Board was headed by the Commandant – a major-general in H's day – supported by a brigadier and a dozen specially selected officers, who together assessed each candidate over the three days. Independent bodies, including various headmasters, career specialists and industrialists, often observed the proceedings. Some would arrive dubious about the integrity and value of the whole process, but they invariably left satisfied that the RCB was scrupulously fair, professionally conducted and tended to get the right results. The example of Candidate 25 on Board 632 of 27 July 1958 may be considered a case in point. He was one Mr H Jones.

Viewed objectively, H cannot have been deemed a strong candidate. His academic record was unexceptional. His report from Eton may have been loyally supportive, but it must have lacked the lustre of most other Eton candidates, for headmasters cannot avoid differentiating between their pupils. Furthermore, his medical record was only just acceptable and his general demeanour would have been at best shyly enthusiastic, and at worst awkwardly hesitant.

---

*Later to be incorporated into the Royal Logistic Corps.

Luckily a record exists, albeit sketchy, of H's RCB. He attended as Candidate 25 in Yellow Group – candidates were referred to by their number and colour, not name, to ensure all were on an equal footing. His Officer Intelligence Rating was 8, on a scale of 0 to 10. In the words of one of the Staff: 'This was a high score showing a very sound effective (not basic IQ) intellect in the top 20 per cent of the RCB candidate population. It would also be above average in his civilian peer group.'

His Education Standard was rated as 'Adequate (A)'. The Board would then have considered his showing in the various interviews, discussion groups and practical tests, noting how H related to other candidates and vice versa. Finally they would have discussed his potential and commitment. The result was that all members of the Board agreed on a D8 grade. Robin Searby,* a former President of the RCB, explained:

> The vast majority of successful candidates receive a D grade, which is a good solid pass. Very few mortals receive gradings C to A. Overall, H Jones received the standard grade, indicating that he had the potential to make an adequate officer; few, if any, doubts would have been expressed. Nor, however, was he noted for stardom.

Three weeks later, 23675580 Officer Cadet Herbert Jones was duly enlisted at the recruiting office in Exeter as a private soldier. This was standard procedure – the status of an officer cadet is that of a private soldier – and H would have taken the oath of allegiance in the time-honoured way, facing a print of Annigoni's famous portrait of the Queen. With a Bible in his right hand, he would have declared:

> I, Herbert Jones, do swear by Almighty God that I will be faithful and bear true allegiance to Her Majesty Queen Elizabeth II, her heirs and successors, and that I will, as in duty bound, honestly

*Now Major-General Robin Searby.

and faithfully defend Her Majesty, her heirs and successors, in person, crown and dignity against all enemies, and I will observe and obey all orders of Her Majesty, her heirs and successors, and of the Generals and officers set over me. So help me God.

There are anomalies in H's Service Record Sheet. Although originally he had been medically assessed as fit only for the Royal Pioneer Corps, on 25 August 1958 he was enlisted in the Rifle Brigade (now subsumed into the Royal Green Jackets). On the military ladder of fashion and prestige, the former was perceived to be on a low rung and the latter highly placed. How did this occur? Two factors were probably responsible. First, the advent of contact lenses, with which H had recently been fitted, and which were now accepted as suitable for use in the front line. Second, the intervention of Lieutenant Colonel Gladstone, the Contingent Commander of Eton College Combined Cadet Force, and a Royal Green Jacket himself, who may well have arranged for that Regiment to sponsor H when he had passed RCB.

On 27 August 1958, Officer Cadet H Jones reported for duty at the Royal Military Academy Sandhurst, near Camberley in Surrey, to start his first term. Sandhurst, established in 1947,* was – and still is – a military academy of world renown. Generations of officers have passed through its portals, among them kings, princes, heads of state and several world statesmen. King Abdullah II of Jordan was commissioned in 1981, and before him his famous and widely admired father, King Hussein. The present Sultan of Brunei and the Sultan of Oman were officer cadets at Sandhurst, as were Sir Winston Churchill and Field Marshal Viscount Montgomery of Alamein – both, like H, late developers.

For the first twenty-five years after the war, the Sandhurst course

---

*RMA Sandhurst was formed that year by the amalgamation of the Royal Military Academy, Woolwich, with the Royal Military College, Sandhurst. The former, known as 'The Shop', was where officer cadets going into the Royal Artillery (Gunners), Royal Engineers (Sappers) and Royal Signals were trained. The RMC trained officer cadets predominantly going into the cavalry and infantry.

lasted two years* and was generally split into terms running parallel to the academic year. Very few cadets were university graduates, because at that time most young men went up to university after completing National Service. Certainly they would not have relished another two years' training on top of three or four at university. Nevertheless, there were features of the Sandhurst course that resembled a university, although the first or Junior Term was emphatically not one of them. That was a unique and never-to-be-forgotten experience.

The Junior Term was designed, like a shock therapy, to turn generally soft and immature schoolboys into fit, smart and alert officer cadets in the shortest possible time. For the first six weeks, Juniors were confined to the Academy. They had no peace, little sleep and enjoyed no privileges. They were not permitted to wear civilian clothes, or even their own pyjamas – the Army issue ones were de rigueur – until they had successfully 'passed off the square'.† Periods of drill were followed remorselessly by physical training (PT), succeeded by weapon training and fieldcraft. Then came yet more drill. H and his fellow cadets were permanently on the move, doubling or being doubled from one activity to another in different orders of dress to each of the far-flung corners of the vast Academy. But always in central focus was The Square, that sacred domain of ferocious drill sergeants.

In a sense the shouting, lack of sleep and unending kit and room inspections were totally unreasonable. The latter were destined to end in failure even before they began – the instructors and senior cadets in charge saw to that. But in other ways it was an entirely practical, and certainly effective, way of pulling together a diverse and uncoordinated group of individuals with different backgrounds

---

*The course was reduced to six months in 1972 to accommodate the increasingly large graduate entry. After numerous adjustments and experiments in the two decades that followed – not all of them successful – the course now lasts a year, with almost all the mainstream entry coming from university.

†A formal process to convince the Adjutant that the basic instruction so far had been successfully assimilated.

and abilities, and in quick time welding them into good military order. Everyone was treated the same, be he a prince of some realm whose experience of cleaning showers and lavatories was non-existent, or an inner-city cadet who had never been away from his family before and was feeling homesick.

The process developed, over time, a cohesion and pride that transcended class, colour and creed. All were united in one joint endeavour: to surmount the pressure, overcome the pain of aching body and limbs and get through the next hour, day and week as quickly as possible.

H was in Intake 25 in Alamein Company. This was one of four companies in Victory College, an ugly Edwardian red-brick building under the Academy clock, that arbiter of Sandhurst time. Inside were long green- and brown-tiled corridors that gave the impression of an immense public lavatory. H's platoon was a sixteen-strong mixture of ex-public school and grammar school boys, plus a few Army Entrants (those who had come through the ranks) and some Overseas Cadets. Lord Edmund Fermoy, the future Princess of Wales's uncle, was in H's platoon, as were Tony Marlow, later to be Conservative Member of Parliament for Northampton North; Prince Said Sudari of Saudi Arabia; and a fit young man from Northern Ireland named Paddy Dunseath, who was to become H's close friend.

The policy of mixing cadets together ensured that those of differing backgrounds shared rooms; indeed, this was the first time H had had to share since he had left St Peter's, six years earlier. Tony Marlow was soon to observe:

H was the only Etonian at Sandhurst at the time who did not give the appearance or impression of being an Etonian. He was distinctly unmilitary in the Sandhurst sense, and was not teacher's pet to the platoon sergeant, Larry Payne of the Royal Fusiliers, or to Company Sergeant Major Wynne, Coldstream Guards.[1]

Paddy Dunseath remembers that although H had had a good basic grounding at Eton in the College's Combined Cadet Force, he did not take to Sandhurst:

> He did not enjoy the necessary, but somewhat tedious, first-term cycle of drill, room inspections and PT . . . he was not naturally a tidy or smart individual, which hampered his turn-out. He lacked the precision and co-ordination to enable him to achieve the very high standard of drill that was demanded by our Guards instructors. As a result he was given numerous extra drills and minor punishments. H disliked much of the ritual 'bull' but he did enjoy the outdoor activities such as map reading, fieldcraft and minor tactics.[2]

Once H had passed 'off the square', life improved. Allowed out for the first time in weeks, he went straight into Camberley, where his prized possession, inherited on his father's death, was garaged. This was a magnificent red 1934 open-top 3.5-litre Bentley, with matching leather seats, which H had had completely renovated. The urge to take it for a spin was irresistible, although cars and driving were pleasures also officially denied to Junior Term cadets, and H succumbed, driving out of town and into the country without detection. He always drove fast – many would say recklessly, but he would insist skilfully – and Paddy Dunseath recalls travelling often with him after that first term:

> He used to drop me off at home on his way down to Devon. These drives on the old A30 were exhilarating, the open Bentley was very powerful and fast and H drove with elan. Heading west with the wind in our hair, the sun in our eyes and H driving flat out was exciting to say the least. There were occasions when I closed my eyes and hoped for the best.[3]

On his way back to Sandhurst one Sunday, H gave a lift to a hitch-hiker, who turned out to be a recently released – or perhaps recently escaped – ex-prisoner from Exeter Jail. The man was heading for

London, and rather than drop him off at Camberley, thirty miles short, H took him all the way. Moreover, when they got there, H emptied his wallet, gave all the notes to his passenger, and wished him well.

Sandwiched between weekends, life at Sandhurst continued at a brisk pace. Yet it was more enjoyable now with less emphasis on drill and more on physical challenges, such as the inter-platoon cross-country competition. This was one of several 'needle' events, taken most seriously, as the results determined where each company was placed in the keenly contested Sovereign's Competition.* The course was set to ensure all cadets had to get across the Wish Stream, a waist-high artificially improved watercourse between two Sandhurst lakes. H became stuck in the mud, losing a shoe, yet continued without it, finishing the race in good time without penalising his platoon. Such gritty displays of determination in the face of mishap went down well at Sandhurst and would have put H's 'Charlie George' – Character Grading† – up a few points in the minds of those watching. His instructors would have noticed, too, and so would the Commandant‡ and the Academy Sergeant Major, if they were present.

The latter was the legendary RSM 'Jackie' Lord MBE, Grenadier Guards, whom generations of officer cadets venerated. Immaculately turned out and ramrod straight at six foot two inches, with a neat military moustache, his was an awe-inspiring presence, modified only slightly, in lighter moments, by a twinkle. All good sergeant majors are part-actors, and Lord was no exception. He could project his personality and voice across the vast parade ground in front of the grey-stuccoed Old College so that all one thousand

---

*The winner of these aggregated competitions both sporting and military was declared the Sovereign's Company and enjoyed the privilege of going on parade last and marching off first. In practice the advantage was minimal, but symbolically it was important.

†An officer cadet's Character Grading helped to determine his place in the eventual Order of Merit.

‡The popular and admired Major-General 'Tiger' Urquhart CB, DSO.

cadets on parade could hear every remark, such as the famous: 'You are an idle little prince, sir. Get a move on your body!' to a future potentate from the Middle East. There was a long tradition in the Guards of such remarks to under-performers who might by their station imagine they were immune from criticism. One of Lord's predecessors is said to have bawled across the square at HRH Prince Henry of Gloucester, one of George V's sons: 'If your father saw your filthy boots, Sir, he'd . . . he'd . . . h'abdicate!'

Everybody knew that RSM Lord had been a prisoner of war, taken at Arnhem, and that he had been responsible for handing over his camp, Stalag XI b at Fallingbostel in Germany, in apple-pie order to the relieving Allies, who were dumbfounded to be greeted by an immaculate guard of honour with wooden rifles at the 'Present'. There was a rumour, never verified, that he had contracted tuberculosis at some stage and only had one lung. Whether or not that was so, his word of command on a still day could be heard a mile away in Camberley. He would introduce himself to new cadets on their first drill parade on the Square by saying: 'You will call me Sir and I will call you Sir. But *you* will mean it!' Belying the story, Lord considered it so great an honour to be the senior Regimental Sergeant Major of the British Army, and responsible for bringing on the next generation of officers, that he declined to accept a commission himself.

As the first year progressed, the course became more interesting, with less drill and increasing emphasis on infantry tactics, military studies and academic work. H enjoyed grappling with tactical problems, although he was not yet confident enough to express his views with the conviction he would later develop at the neighbouring Staff College. He maintained a keen interest in military history, spending hours in the library.

Sandhurst always had its lighter moments – sometimes by design, frequently by accident. When officer cadets travelled to distant events they often did so by bicycle, a method in theory both simple and economical. Heavy upright Army bicycles without gears were standard, and a journey out to the Barossa training area, a mile away, might start in the bicycle sheds. This would involve bicycle drill – that is, everyone mounting his bicycle on a given order and pedalling in pairs dressed by the left, in a column or 'snake' stretching back perhaps seventy-five yards.

The normal rules for paying compliments applied: in other words, officers were to be saluted at all times. Thus, if one approached, the bicyclists had to salute by giving an 'eyes right' (or left) and momentarily stop pedalling as the officer passed. This was awkward even on the flat. By the laws of physics, it was virtually impossible going uphill and downright dangerous going down. There was a further problem: many overseas cadets, especially from Africa and the Middle East, were unfamiliar with this mode of transport, so when they first arrived at Sandhurst, although they were given 'extra bicycling', some were still shaky in the saddle.

Thus, bicycle drill was relished by those who were adept at it, and dreaded by those who were not. Chaos lurked just around each corner as in the best of farces, and that was the attraction. Sometimes the leading cadets would divert the column in the hope of finding an officer to be saluted, occasioning wobbles among the unwary and, perhaps, a crash. This invariably provided much amusement for the cadets, whilst infuriating those in charge.

On one occasion H's platoon was to attend a tactical exercise without troops (or TEWT)* on Barossa. The only way to get there on time was by bicycle. H had been put in charge and was leading the column down a steep and narrow gully, at the bottom of which he lost his balance and fell off. A dozen cadets, many from overseas, unable to take avoiding action, promptly ran over him in a tangle of bodies and bicycles. As Dunseath recalled: 'Luckily pride was the only thing that was hurt. H was not allowed to forget it, and from then on people tended to avoid him when cycling – or driving!'

Incidents like this soon earned H a reputation as a platoon character – someone likely to enliven events – to the delight of his

---

*TEWTs avoid soldiers hanging around in the field while various tactical solutions are discussed.

peers. Their appreciation was not just because of the amusement he provided, but because the instructors tended to focus on him, and other equally hopeless cadets, rather than concentrating on them.

At the end of his first year, H's company commander, Major J de B Carey, described him thus:

> An immature cadet who is sadly lacking in common sense and a sense of responsibility . . . his personality, though charming, does not compensate for his lack of character. He has some initiative and plenty of dash but at the moment he is best described as erratic and unreliable . . . but he is a little less of a schoolboy than he was.

His 'Officer Qualities Grade' was 3 (out of 10) and he was placed in the First Year Order of Merit at 119 out of 133 British officer cadets. Officially, therefore, H was perilously close to the bottom of his whole intake and was only just holding his own. In the modern Sandhurst he would almost certainly have been back-termed.

The start of the second year was always a good time. By then, officer cadets knew the ropes and how to avoid trouble. They were not weighed down with any responsibility and the demands on their time were not great. The fourth term was mostly academic work, much of it deemed 'private study'. H's contemporaries were drawn to the bright lights of London with its shows, jazz clubs and pubs. But these were not his preferences and he seldom joined them.

Following his father's death, H had plenty of interests and responsibilities at home; whenever he had a spare weekend, therefore, he headed happily – and fast – for Devon and The Grange. As Paddy Dunseath observes:

> Being a loner, H was quite happy with his own company, and was not at all upset if he was not considered to be one of the boys. This did not mean he was unpopular or a poor team member. It was simply that his outlooks and interests were different.

In fact H's attention was part-occupied in another direction. Girls were becoming an interest. Two who had already entered his life at Eton were Ellie Kennaway and Blythe Munro. Through Blythe, the most important introduction in H's life was about to be made. One of her school friends was Sara de Uphaugh, the daughter of a well-known New Forest family. At that time Sara was in love with Tobin Duke's younger brother, Johnnie, and barely registered an interest in H, whose attention was focused anyway on Ellie and Blythe. Both girls were regularly mentioned in the quick scribbles he used to send his mother from Sandhurst. One rather perplexed letter recounted: 'Ellie has just written to me again. I wish I knew why. But, as usual, your eldest son is coming to heel like a good dog. Drat the girl.'

His relationship with Blythe seemed more established. According to her eldest sister Alison, who is adamant about it, in the first half of 1960 H flew to Norway, where Blythe was working as a nanny, and proposed to her. There is no collateral for this, and anyway, H would have realised that Sandhurst would have strongly disapproved of any officer cadet getting engaged. Among other things it would have ruined his chances of acceptance by a good regiment, as it was considered that a young officer should be looking after his men rather than being distracted by marriage. (Such an attitude was a widely accepted precondition of Army life until the early 1970s, although it may seem oddly old-fashioned now.) The matter was resolved anyway when Blythe turned H's proposal down.

For a time, H contented himself with driving his friends from one party to another. Sara remembers attending a Frankie Howerd show in Southampton with Johnnie Duke in what Johnnie almost had her believe was his own Bentley. She observed that 'poor H was there like a chauffeur – and a very shy one at that'.

Back at Sandhurst, at the end of his fourth term, and perhaps jolted by his poor showing so far, H had begun to make some impression on his Company Commander, who wrote:

He has worked well this term and has achieved good results. As far as his character is concerned he has really blossomed out; I was most impressed by his performance on the initiative exercise and

I now consider his OQ* rating to be 5. He is growing up fast.

Around this time under officers and cadet sergeants were being
selected for promotion from H's intake which was about to become
the senior one. Here were shades of Eton – the selection of those in
charge – but now the process was professionally handled, with all
the instructors being consulted as to which eight of the fifteen
remaining officer cadets – one had left voluntarily – should be
promoted.† H was chosen for one of the junior appointments –
cadet sergeant – which must have pleased him, as his first advancement in open competition with his peers.

Even though it was a relatively modest promotion, H's upward
progress had begun. It would have been helped by the Army's ready
acceptance that young men develop at different speeds, and the fact
that spotting and bringing on the late developer is something at
which it excels. It would be another fifteen years before H's
performance was earning consistent professional approval, but in
those days of abundant National Service manpower, the Army was
content to let young men develop at their own pace. A pool of
talented people, eager to fill the best jobs, was always available, so
there was little pressure on the late developer.

H now needed to take a crucial decision, one faced by all officer
cadets towards the end of their time at Sandhurst: to which regiment
or corps‡ to apply for a commission. The options were wide and
varied, ranging from the (then) numerous cavalry regiments to any
of the seventy-five infantry regiments, the Royal Artillery, Royal
Engineers, or one of the technical corps (not that H was qualified for
the latter). The aim was, and still is, to match unit to candidate to
the benefit of each. In other words, an officer cadet should be

---

*Officer Qualities, replacing the previous Character Grading.
†One senior under officer, four junior under officers and three cadet sergeants had to
  be found.
‡The distinction between regiments and corps is esoteric. As a rule of thumb, the
  infantry and cavalry consist of regiments and the remainder form corps, except in
  the case of the Royal Regiment of Artillery.

commissioned into a regiment or corps that best suited his, or her, talents and circumstances.

This system does not always work perfectly, and it is different to that adopted by the other two Services, which commission their officers directly into either the Royal Navy or the Royal Air Force as a whole, rather than a particular part. But despite endless changes and modernisations, the Army rightly holds dear its regimental system, which is fundamental to understanding the ethos and traditions of its constituent parts. The system's ramifications were to feature strongly in H's subsequent career.

Arguably, one of the few drawbacks to the regimental system can be the initial selection or 'matching' process. Not all officer cadets have the necessary knowledge or experience to know which regiment or corps would best suit them. Equally, regiments want to feel that they are securing their share of the most able people. This may pose difficulties when too many regiments chase the same cadet. Market forces may work for commodities but are not a good basis on which to construct an officer corps.

In the late fifties the process was much less competitive and more leisurely. Cadets approached, or were gently put in touch with, suitable regiments with a view to obtaining a commission in them, but on H's showing there would have been no scramble for him. He wished to join the infantry, as he had indicated on enlistment when he had recorded a preference for the Rifle Brigade. But they did not offer him a place, and at some stage he must have made contact with his own county regiment, The Devonshire and Dorset Regiment, known colloquially as the Devon and Dorsets. In the 1950s nearly every county in England had its own regular infantry regiment, and recruited almost exclusively from within its borders. For instance, there were the Norfolks, the Worcesters, the Royal Sussex, the Glosters, the Royal Northumberland Fusiliers, the King's Shropshire Light Infantry and many more. Some counties even had two regiments, such as the East Lancashires, and the South and North Lancashires (The Loyals). The Army List of 1958 shows forty infantry regiments associated by name with an English county.

The Devon and Dorsets would have been interested in any potential officer with a bona fide county connection, such as residential or educational links in either county, or some family association through a relative with service in the Regiment. This might appear unduly selective, even exclusive, but there were, and are, good reasons for it. Almost all soldiers in the Devon and Dorsets came from one or other of those two counties (ninety-seven per cent in 1982, according to a survey)[4] and so it was a prerequisite for acceptance that their officers had a proper appreciation of, and interest in, the counties from which their men came. The same criteria would apply to any county regiment.

Hence H, with his love of Devon, borne of having lived there all his life, was a natural potential officer for his County Regiment. Whether he would be acceptable depended, at the start of his second year at Sandhurst and in the wake of his company promotion, almost entirely on one man, the Colonel of the Regiment – the titular head of the regimental family.

This honorary appointment is unlike any other. The Regiment chooses its own Colonel from among those it considers will best represent its interests. He is not appointed from above but is chosen internally* on the basis of soundings taken among wise and experienced members of the Regiment – past and present. It is, therefore, a unique and singular honour – indeed, the greatest honour a regiment can bestow on any officer.

When H applied for a commission, the Colonel of The Devonshire and Dorset Regiment was a distinguished, well-decorated retired officer, Major-General George Woods CB CBE DSO MC, affectionately known to his friends and acquaintances as 'Mothballs'. His was not an onerous task on this occasion, for one so shrewd and good with people. He needed only to satisfy himself that young Jones would 'fit' in his Regiment, that he was fully committed to it, and that he had something worthwhile to offer.

---

*The appointment is promulgated however in the normal way by the Queen on the recommendation of the Defence Secretary.

Since H was applying for a regular, not just a three-year short-service commission, the Colonel would have looked especially for evidence of character and long-term potential.

To advise him was the regimental representative at Sandhurst, Major Tony Lewis, H's College Chief Instructor, and a legend in his own right. In the early 1940s, Lewis had been appointed, aged only twenty-three, to command No. 6 Commando, and had remained with them throughout the war. His distinguished command, including leading the last bayonet charge of the war, at the River Aller crossing, had been recognised by both the DSO and the Croix de Guerre avec Palme. Monty always referred to Tony Lewis as 'my Boy Colonel' because he was the youngest lieutenant colonel ever to command a combat unit in the British Army, a record never to have been broken.

After the war, many such gallant commanders had to revert two ranks and accept an appointment far below their abilities and previous responsibilities. Invariably they did so with good grace, and certainly Tony Lewis seemed entirely content at Sandhurst training the next generation of officers. He was a good judge of character as well as a brave officer, and having spotted H's long-term potential, he commended him to 'Mothballs' Woods. Following a successful interview with the general, H was accepted for a regular commission in his regiment of choice. Now all he had to do was to steer clear of trouble until he completed the Sandhurst course on 22 July 1960.

Sandhurst's Sovereign's Parade is always a moving and spectacular occasion. It is held in front of the Army's top generals and the Colonels of Regiments and Corps of the cadets being commissioned, together with all the Academy instructors; and the parents and friends of those on parade. The Queen's Representative that day was The Right Honourable Harold Macmillan PC DCL MP, who was, he declared, the first Prime Minister ever to take this great Parade on behalf of the Queen. He concluded his address by saying: 'I am privileged to be here today as a symbol of the reliance which the whole country places on you. I know you will be worthy of that trust.'

The Parade then moved to its climax. In the tradition founded over a century before, H and all those being commissioned marched, in slow time, up the steps of the Grand Entrance to Old College to the tune of 'Auld Lang Syne', followed finally by the Academy Adjutant on his white charger. At midnight, Second Lieutenant Herbert Jones was commissioned into The Devonshire and Dorset Regiment and a new chapter of his life began.

CHAPTER FIVE

'Primus in Indis'*

The arrival of a newly commissioned subaltern† is a significant event in any regiment that is small enough to notice and intimate enough to care. The Devon and Dorsets were, and still are, such a Regiment, and H's arrival was akin to any new member joining a family. Everyone wanted to meet him but no one wanted to appear too eager to do so – after all, the Regiment had been around for nearly three hundred years.

The origins of the Devonshire Regiment go back to 1685, when the Duke of Beaufort's Musketeers helped repel the Duke of Monmouth, who had landed at Lyme Regis in Dorset to raise the West Country against the Catholic King James II. Within a month the rebellion had been crushed and Beaufort's Musketeers were properly established, becoming eventually the 11th Regiment of Foot and subsequently the Devons.

Colonel Coote raised the Dorsets in Ireland in 1702 during the War of the Spanish Succession. His Regiment became the 39th when the size of the Army was doubled, and infantry regiments were numbered, to take part in the Duke of Marlborough's campaigns on the continent of Europe. A further expansion of the Army was necessary prior to the Seven Years War and so, in 1755, the 54th Regiment of Foot was raised. In due course the 39th and the 54th

---

*Motto of The Devonshire and Dorset Regiment.
†Subalterns are officers of the most junior rank, i.e. second lieutenant and lieutenant.

became the 1st and 2nd Battalions of the Dorsetshire Regiment.

The history of both regiments can be traced through the conflicts of these centuries. Soldiers from one or other of the regiments, and sometimes both, fought at Dettingen in 1743; and they were the first government troops in India – hence their motto 'Primus in Indis', inscribed on their cap-badge – where they distinguished themselves with General Clive at the Battle of Plassey. They served in the War of American Independence and the Napoleonic Wars. They fought at Salamanca with Wellington; and they campaigned in the Crimea in 1854–5. In the Boer War both regiments were active, with their 2nd Battalions present at the Relief of Ladysmith in February 1900. In the Great War the Devons and the Dorsets provided respectively twenty-five and eleven battalions, whilst in the Second World War they fielded thirteen and nine to fight in every theatre of operations. Altogether, it is an extensive and distinguished catalogue of service to the Crown.

In the late 1950s and early 1960s, a substantial reduction in the Army occurred as National Service was phased out. The Devons and the Dorsets, still separate regiments, were a natural choice for amalgamation in view of their geography and intertwined history. Sensibly, they retained their county identity by emphasising their local roots. The historic bonds and titles, forged over the centuries, were incorporated into the new Regiment, so that on 17 May 1958, The Devonshire and Dorset Regiment was formed. It proved to be a happy and successful amalgamation, with both counties demonstrably stake-holders in the new Regiment.

By September 1960, 1st Battalion The Devonshire and Dorset Regiment* was in the last twelve months of a three-year tour in Cyprus, which had earlier involved counter-insurgency operations against EOKA terrorists. That phase of the EOKA campaign for Enosis,† in which a hundred British soldiers were killed, had been

---

*1st Battalion is always a regular battalion; and when H joined there were two Territorial Army (TA) battalions, one in each county.
†Union with Greece.

successfully defeated, and with the Emergency over, those units remaining on the island moved into permanent garrisons and reverted to conventional peacetime roles.

The Devon and Dorsets were in a tented camp, Kitchener Lines, at Polemidhia outside Limassol, with views in one direction over the deep blue Mediterranean and in the other to the distant Troodos Mountains. However, when H reached Cyprus on 3 September 1960, the Battalion was in Libya on exercise. In those days King Idris afforded Britain extensive facilities in his country. The Royal Air Force had a major strategic air base at El Adem, near Tobruk, the Army had garrisons in Tripoli and Benghazi, and large tracts of the desert were allocated to training. This was long before the bloodless coup that toppled King Idris whilst he was on a state visit to Greece in December 1969, and which brought Colonel Gaddafi to power.

H was posted to B Company, one of three rifle companies of the Battalion, each around 140 strong,* deployed in company locations in the desert. The Battalion was shortly to start a major exercise against another regiment, and so this was a good time for H to arrive and gain experience. The evening before the exercise began, B Company, under their able and ambitious Company Commander, Major (later General) John Archer, invited the rest of the officers of the Battalion – about thirty of them – over to their Mess before dinner. It was here that his brother officers met H for the first time.

They were not impressed. He was wearing a pair of voluminous khaki shorts from which emerged a pair of white knees and thin, hairless legs. He looked pale, puny and out of place compared with the fit, bronzed officers who had already been in the desert for several weeks. Furthermore, he was wearing a monocle and had a surprised, shy smile on his face whenever officers went up to introduce themselves and welcome him to the Battalion.

'What's your name?' they would enquire kindly.

'H,' he replied.

'H what?' they pressed.

---

*This high figure reflected the National Service strength of the Battalion.

'H Jones. I prefer just H.'

'But what does H stand for?'

'Herbert, but I don't like being called that, actually.'

'Ah,' they said, and after a few cursory remarks, duty done, would take themselves off to talk to a friend, muttering probably about the apparent deterioration in the quality of young officers. It was not a good beginning.

The monocle was a puzzle. No one in his company at Sandhurst remembers H wearing an eyeglass, and it is hard to believe that on joining he produced it for effect. He might have been emulating Guy Crouchback, in Evelyn Waugh's *Men at Arms*, who adopted a monocle to improve his marksmanship; but H was not given to affectation, and his new Regiment was not the kind to be impressed by it. The more likely explanation lay in its proper purpose: to assist his defective short-range vision in one eye; but there was a suspicion – later proved unfounded – that the lens was neutral. Whatever the circumstances, a monocle on a long desert exercise seemed impractical and out of place.

The next day the twenty-year-old Second Lieutenant Jones was given command of 6 Platoon, consisting, like all rifle platoons at the time, of about thirty-six soldiers – National Service and regular – split into a platoon headquarters and three sections of ten men each. In preparation for the exercise, H's platoon were doing work-up training, which involved, among other things, digging and occupying a defensive position. All began well, and in a relatively short time 6 Platoon had dug a series of interlocking slit trenches within a company layout. By nightfall the position was complete, and a hot evening meal was brought forward in containers to a distribution point a couple of hundred yards behind the trenches.

Those were the days before the Army used hexamine solid-fuel cookers, or gaz burners, which nowadays enable defenders to cook in their trenches. The procedure then was that after dark each platoon in turn went back to collect their food in mess-tins, leaving sentries behind to safeguard the position. Although this sounds straightforward, its successful accomplishment depended upon the person in charge moving his men from their trenches to the supply point and back again with the minimum of noise, lights and fuss. This was normally the job of the Platoon Sergeant, but because H was new, the sergeant tactfully suggested that he himself should remain on the position in case of attack at this vulnerable time.

H led off with his men, and with hot food in their mess-tins, 6 Platoon prepared to return to their trenches to eat. Half an hour later, the Platoon Sergeant rang Company Headquarters, which was meant to co-ordinate such things, on a field telephone to check that all was well and that his Platoon was on its way back. He was told that they were. He rang again fifteen minutes later and reported that 6 Platoon had still not arrived back; nor had they thirty minutes after that. By now the Company Commander had been apprised of this unwelcome development. He called H on the radio that every platoon carried, but communications in the desert are notoriously unreliable. There was no reply.

About an hour after that, H called in on the old '88 radio set' then in service, which his signaller must have nudged into action, and confessed that he was lost. John Archer, suppressing his irritation, asked H if he could see the two red tail lights of his Land Rover, which his driver was switching on and off. H, with relief in his voice, confirmed that he could. 'Well, march on them,' barked his Company Commander.

But thirty minutes later, 6 Platoon had still not returned. This was worrying because the desert is a dangerous place in which to be lost, by day or night. More radio messages followed; H confirmed he was still marching on the two red lights. Another hour went by, but now radio signals were fading. H's last faint message asked whether Company Headquarters had moved on to a hill. 'I can see your lights but they are above me and we don't seem to be getting closer.'

Dawn breaks quickly in the desert, and with it came the revelation that 6 Platoon were indeed approaching two red lights. But these were on a pair of tall radio masts outside Derna, some twenty miles away from the original position. In the crystal-clear desert air, H and his Platoon had been marching on them all night.

News of such an event spreads quickly through a unit and provides much amusement for anyone not directly involved. Those listening to the exchanges on the radio between H and John Archer would have mischievously enjoyed the latter's irritation that one of his officers had publicly made B Company look inept. Nevertheless, soldiers are tolerant of the early mistakes of a young subaltern, and 6 Platoon would not have held this against their new Platoon Commander. As for H himself, instead of being some new arrival whose name and form would remain unknown for months, he became identified overnight – not very flatteringly perhaps, but nevertheless, his name was widely recognised by the end of his third day.

His boyish enthusiasm and zest for his first experience of active soldiering only six weeks after leaving Sandhurst is clear in his first letter home to Sara de Uphaugh, who was by now his established and serious girlfriend. Revealing, too, is his admission that getting his platoon so badly lost was a frightening experience.

We've had a series of most exciting exercises, the last one of which lasted 5 days and took us 100 miles down into the desert and then up again, fighting the Welch Regiment* all the way. Most exciting, especially when I wanted to attack a fort with my platoon, which was later attacked by the whole battalion. Bloody silly, if you ask me; if they had let me attack it I reckon I could have captured it, with 1,000 less men, six hours earlier. I nearly did my nut!

Eventually, we did a dawn attack on the fourth day, during which the umpires got fed up with me trying to finish the exercise a day early by charging off at 400 mph! So they told me I had a double fractured jaw, and so I had to hand over to my Platoon Sergeant and go off to the hospital, where I stayed about five hours before they let me go. Apart from that however, all has gone

---

*Subsumed into the Royal Regiment of Wales in 1969.

quite well, except that I spent my first two nights in the field (platoon training, early on) completely lost, wandering around the desert. Most unnerving – well to be frank, I don't think I have ever been so scared in my life. I only hope I never get lost again.

At the end of the exercise, the Battalion flew back to Cyprus. By now H had established a rapport with his Platoon; he felt comfortable and at home with them, their West Country ways and their gentle burr. Almost half of his Platoon were Plymothians; some were from Torbay, a couple of them from Paignton; and the mother of one, from Brixham, called Payne, had worked for H's family up at The Grange. This is the appeal of a county regiment with its easy comradeship based on strong local bonds and loyalties. By now H's soldiers had shrewdly summed up their new Platoon Commander. One of them, Graham Woodward, now aged sixty-three and a retired British Rail technical officer, remembers H well:

> Mr Jones was often in trouble with Company Headquarters and he got things wrong, but he joined in everything and did his best to protect us from the 'powers that be'. We never doubted that he had our best interests at heart.[1]

A fellow subaltern in B Company, Andrew Scrivener, remarked that H's soldiers mothered him. 'They could see he was eccentric, yet they knew he was genuine.' The point is amplified by one of them, Barry Davis, who recalls:

> . . . he was very well liked by 6 Platoon. Speaking for myself, it was an honour – and a good laugh – to have served under him, even though he did charge me for sand up the barrel of my Bren gun! . . . There was never a dull moment when he was around.[2]

By late autumn the Cyprus heat had subsided, and as soldiering was over by lunchtime, the afternoons were used for sports, such as swimming, water-skiing, go-karting – at which H excelled – or whatever else suited individuals. H bought a Mini Cooper on hire purchase and drove it so fast and aggressively that he only got five thousand miles from a set of tyres. His evenings were spent either in the Officers' Mess, or at some private party, or in Limassol at one of the open-air Greek or Turkish tavernas, clubs or cabarets which proliferated once the EOKA campaign had ended and before the island became partitioned after the Turkish invasion of July 1974.

Life in the Army abroad was generally agreeable as Britain slowly divested herself of her overseas responsibilities. The work was not onerous and there were more than enough people around to share it; most of the senior officers had fought in the war and had a relaxed, almost disdainful, attitude to peacetime soldiering. There was a dislike of bureaucracy and petty restrictions and young officers were encouraged to get out of camp with their men. 'Work hard; play hard' was the watchword and spirited young officers abided by it.

All regiments have a tradition of 'dining-in' new officers and 'dining-out' those leaving, in some cases on retirement. These are invariably happy, sometimes nostalgic, evenings, with the music of the Regimental Band adding to the atmosphere and grace of the occasion. Whilst hair will always be let down as the evening wears on, the standards, traditions and customs of the Regiment are maintained. The Devon and Dorsets had many of these, some of them unique.

One was the 'Puja ceremony', a harmless enough initiation of all subalterns on joining. It had been inherited from 1st Dorsets, the first British regiment in India. Traditionally a young officer was not considered to be a full member of the Mess until he had been Puja'd. (Puja is a Hindu term, describing a religious or mystical initiation, such as Sherpas observe before an assault upon Mount Everest.) Within the Regiment, the ceremony was a rite of passage anticipated with some trepidation. Those who had already been Puja'd declined to talk about it; hence mystery was deliberately fostered.

In fact, most of the evening was no different from a normal regimental dinner. All officers, dressed in their scarlet mess kit with green facings, dined off magnificent solid silver bequeathed by the

Dorset Regiment on amalgamation. The Queen's Colour and the Regimental Colour were displayed uncased behind the Commanding Officer's chair, and on the walls hung the portraits of the Colonel-in-Chief, former Colonels of the Regiment and the VC holders. H's portrait hangs there now.

At the end of dinner three toasts were proposed and drunk. The first was to The Queen, and the second to the Colonel-in-Chief, who was, at that time, HRH Princess Marina, Duchess of Kent. Last, and uniquely for a British infantry regiment, came the toast to the French Army in recognition of France's award to the Regiment of the Croix de Guerre, her highest decoration for gallantry. This was won by 2nd Battalion The Devonshire Regiment at the Battle of Bois des Buttes, an action to save the French left flank from a German onslaught on 27 May 1918. It cost the Devons dear; they lost their Commanding Officer, twenty-two officers and 528 non-commissioned officers and men. But the French line was saved.

After dinner, with the formalities over, the Puja ceremony began. Those being initiated – H and another on this occasion – were blindfolded. In a darkened anteroom they had to crawl, one at a time, through a double row of officers who were muttering disapprovingly. On a 'throne' at the end sat the Second-in-Command robed as the 'Grand Puja', silhouetted by flickering candles. In front of him was a solid silver sphinx, as emblazoned upon the Regiment's cap-badge, with Marabout underneath, derived from their gallant action in Egypt against Napoleon. After due obeisance, the young officers had to recite a passage, which they should have learned by heart, requesting admission to the Regiment. Each said:

> Oh wise and venerable Puja, I seek admission
> To the Honourable Company of the Sphinx.

If the young man had not fluffed his words, the Grand Puja replied gravely:

> You are a miserable and worthless creature!

> Your lineage is as unimpressive
> As your credentials are uninspiring.
> But we accept you under sufferance
> Into the Honourable Company of the Sphinx.

At this point H was handed a regimental cocktail – one matching the old Dorset regimental colours of red, yellow and green.* Custom required that this should be downed in one. This done, H had to crawl back through the row of officers who, because he had performed his part correctly, would now be making noises of mild approval.†

The whole thing was hardly an ordeal, and H did not find it one; indeed, his 'dining-in' seems to have meant a great deal to him.‡ On completion of the Puja ceremony, regimental songs, mess rugger and other games began. H wrote to Sara a couple of days later describing it all, and his growing sense of well-being. He felt now, perhaps for the first time in his life outside his own family, that he was part of something with which he could readily identify and to which he was proud to belong. Notwithstanding an unfortunate injury sustained that night, he wrote from the RAF Hospital in Akrotiri on 2 November:

> I really have an incredible amount to tell you since I haven't written since El Adem . . . and I am feeling absolutely bung full of happiness. Last Friday I was officially 'Dined-In' by the Regiment, which involved getting very, very drunk and doing

---

*Considerable skill was required by the Mess Colour Sergeant to get the colour match right: cherry brandy, advocaat and crème de menthe were used in various proportions.

†A fuller account is found in *Officers' Messes – Life and Customs in the Regiments* by Lt. R J Dickinson.

‡All such initiation ceremonies have since been officially banned by the Army, on the basis that what might be an amusing and harmless occasion among friends in an officers' mess could not easily be differentiated in principle from bullying and other unacceptable initiation practices in a barrack room.

several rather foolish things, with the full approval of the Colonel and all the other officers. After the 'ceremony' we played Mess Rugger and during the game a large subaltern . . . picked me up and dropped me head first onto the floor and then jumped on me. During all this there was a splintering crack, and Jones gave a yowl. Net result: one dislocated collarbone!

The trouble was that I was the only person who really realised it, as everyone else was too drunk (it was really a splendid party) and I felt too ill to do much so I was led, vomiting, to bed and the binge went on. At about 4 a.m. the pain roused me from my stupor, but I could not get up, of course (you can't with a broken collarbone), so I lay there and shouted until I woke up the chap I share the tent with, and another officer three tents away. Anyway, they got me into the car and up to the Medical Centre, where I was strapped up and sent back to bed after being sick again. Woke up at 8. My Company Commander arrived and started asking awkward questions about my platoon's training programme. At which I was conveniently sick again! Saved.

Eventually, they got me to hospital here, X-rayed me and prepared to operate only to discover that the bloody bone had gone back after all. At this they gave up and put me into bed. I don't think they thought much of my drinking habits!!

So there we are. All most exciting. And most painful. Since then I have just lain here, occasionally reading, if my headache wasn't too bad, but mainly just thinking, about England, home and beauty. And under the heading of beauty I think I included both you and the Bentley, so you're highly honoured, my sweet!

The first things that were brought along to me were photographs of you and the Bentley, so I had nothing to do but gaze at them and dream. So much for my illness, exciting though it has been and still is, drat it. I must say I am happier in the Army than I had thought possible, especially as my brother officers are extremely good chaps.

. . . One of the things I like about it is the chance to be up and doing things, which is more than I would if I was stuck in an office somewhere . . . and I reckon that the privilege of being able to do something for the country is well worth not making a fortune. End of speech!

H's separation from Sara seemed to strengthen their relationship. His prolific letters* were light and full of news – often highly exaggerated. He could be nostalgic and sensitive and seemed better at describing his feelings and emotions in writing than face to face, as his account of transferring his allegiance to Sara illustrates:

I remember the day I finally decided that I'd had enough of being mucked about by her [a previous girlfriend]. I was still at Sandhurst, the summer before last, and I went to see her near Salisbury, where she was bloody-minded and dead bolshy, so I drove off in disgust, feeling miserable, and drove down to Brockenhurst, where you were ill in bed. I spent the rest of the evening with you, and instead of feeling bored or miserable when I left you, after just sitting and talking to you, which normally would have bored me stiff with any other girl, I just felt tremendously happy, and I decided then and there that whilst you had the power to make me so ecstatically happy (which power you still possess) I would have nothing to do with a girl who just made me miserable.

In early 1961, H was detached to Dekhalia with his platoon to guard a key military installation. The strategically important and mysterious Royal Signals monitoring station at Ayios Nicolias was nearby. (Mysterious, that was, until it was unmasked as an intercept station during the trial of the convicted spy Michael Bettaney.) Alone and with little to do, H's thoughts turned nostalgically to

---

*He wrote, for example, twice on 20 December 1960; twice again on the 23rd; on the 24th before and after tea; and on the 27th, 28th, 29th and 30th; as well as on New Year's Day 1961.

home and to his late father. He wrote to Sara:

> I've started writing this because I'm having one of my infrequent
> bouts of the 'blues'. It's an absolutely glorious summer's day, the
> sun beating down out of a cloudless sky, but still with enough of
> spring left for the countryside to be quite green still, instead of the
> dreadful brown it becomes later on. The sea is very calm and blue,
> and from my window I can see couples strolling along the water's
> edge. Some of them, soldiers out with their girlfriends, or
> families, but mostly just walking in pairs, wishing, no doubt as I
> do, that they were back in England.
>
> The bay the Mess overlooks could almost be on the South
> Devon coast, between Dartmouth and Torquay, and it could
> almost be the height of summer there.
>
> On top of all this, the tape recorder is playing a tune my father
> used to be very fond of and if I close my eyes I can imagine myself
> to be sitting on the terrace outside the living room at The Grange
> with the gramophone playing inside, and my father sitting in the
> sun reading a book. One of the times I wish I could turn the clock
> back four or five years. But you never knew my father, so all this
> must sound a lot of rubbish to you. I'm sorry; but I have got to
> get it out of my system and if I wrote it to my mother, I know it
> would only make her start remembering, and then she'd feel
> miserable too.
>
> I wish you'd met my father sometime. I'm biased about him, of
> course, but to me he will always remain the dominating figure in
> my life. He seemed to have done everything there was to do, and
> he had certainly been almost everywhere there was to go. He's the
> only poet who brings tears to my eyes every time I read some of
> his poems, and he was the cleverest and kindest man I have ever
> come across. If only he hadn't died when he did I'm damned sure
> that I would be more worthy of my commission.
>
> But I'm starting on the sob-stuff now, and that is hardly fair to
> you, so I'll stop. Thank you for listening, though there's not much
> else you could do!

A few months later Sara's relationship with Johnnie Duke was waning and H, two thousand miles away, sensed an opportunity. Desperate to see her – Sara was now on a secretarial course in Oxford – but without any proper leave in prospect, he decided to fly home over the Whitsun weekend. This was unheard of: the distance was vast, the piston-engined flights slow and infrequent, and the cost prohibitive. Troopships were the normal means of military movement, and low-cost air travel was decades away. Undaunted, H found and boarded a flight leaving Nicosia after work on Friday and returning on Whit Monday.

The two lovers had a glorious forty-eight hours, including a romantic dinner at the French Horn in Sonning, and entirely satisfied that it had been worth every penny, H flew back to Nicosia. On arrival he rang the officers' mess to see if there was any transport available back to camp and was told that there was none in view of the holiday the next day. 'What holiday?' he enquired. 'The one in lieu of the Queen's Birthday, when we're all on parade,' replied the Orderly Officer. 'Right then, I'm going straight back to London,' shouted H down the telephone and caught the same aircraft back to England.

News of this made an impact, even on those who were normally indifferent to what subalterns did in their free time. It indicated, first, that H must be desperately smitten by whoever he was flying to and fro to see; and second that he must be unusually wealthy – and perhaps a little crazy. Until then he had done nothing extravagant and most of his brother officers were unaware that on his father's death he had inherited a substantial legacy. That apart, it was generally considered vulgar in those days to talk about money in the Mess.

The temptation to react to the news of H's second flight home was irresistible, and the Adjutant sanctioned a hoax telegram declaring him absent without leave (which, technically, he was, as his second trip had not been authorised). Sara remembers the telegram, with black edging, arriving even before H's flight reached London, saying: 'For 2nd Lt. Jones. You are absent without leave and should return to your unit immediately.' This did not detract from their further twenty-four hours together, and he returned, as he had planned, in time for first parade on the Wednesday.

By now there was beginning to be a perceptible shift in how H was viewed in the Battalion. Despite its size, the Devon and Dorsets was a close-knit community. As in any large family, certain members stand out and develop personae and reputations of their own. From the beginning, H had been considered mildly eccentric. The Warrant Officers and Sergeants' Mess, that barometer of regimental life, had already nicknamed him 'Monocle Jones'. The soldiers referred to him among themselves as H; but initially he was too new and junior to count for much. Now, a year into his commission and following his latest exploit, his standing rose. From being considered merely unusual and high-spirited, he had become someone of much greater consequence – a regimental character. There are probably no more than a dozen of these in any major unit: that is, people – rank is immaterial – who are widely known and talked about, whether positively or negatively. H was now one of them. His contentment was apparent in his letters to Sara:

It's rather strange to think of people dreading Monday morning. I haven't done so since I joined the Battalion, but I can well remember how I used to loathe it at Eton and Sandhurst . . . I may feel differently back in England but I don't think I'll ever loathe it as I used to.

The camp at Polemidhia was in two halves, and the Devon and Dorsets' neighbours were 2nd Battalion, The Parachute Regiment, known as 2 Para. Units stationed in the same garrison, let alone the same camp, frequently fall out, and turf wars often erupt, particularly in the local clubs and bars. The Parachute Regiment's reputation is not good in this respect and they are normally unwelcome neighbours. But that was not the case here. Both battalions got on well at all levels, and respected each other. Each had an excellent commanding officer who set the tone, and the natural competitiveness of the units was channelled into healthy directions, such as sport and military events, where the honours were about even. Furthermore, the old 12th Battalion Devonshire Regiment (The Swedebashers, as they were affectionately known) had been a successful airborne unit in the war. So the Devon and Dorsets, unlike some regiments, invariably encouraged suitable officers wanting to undertake a tour of duty with the Special Air Service, Parachute Regiment, Army Air Corps or other specialised units, to do so.

A number of friendships among the officers of the two battalions had formed; one of these was between H and a subaltern from 2 Para called James Emson. They had a notion to drive back to the UK on leave via Moscow, an unusual proposal and one which the local Brigade Commander had surprisingly endorsed. However, the War Office vetoed it, so they determined to go via Belgrade instead, for which permission was granted. The circumstances of the trip and H's friendship with Emson were to be significant, and formed the genesis of a later decision which was to alter H's life.

When H and James reached Istanbul in mid June on the first leg of their journey, they heard, on the Overseas Service of the BBC, that 24 Infantry Brigade Group were being flown from Kenya to Kuwait to protect it from a threatened invasion by Iraq. In what turned out to be a forerunner of Saddam Hussein's operation thirty years later, the then President of Iraq, General Abdel Kassem, had suddenly moved his tanks down to Basra near the Kuwait border. More significantly for James, 2 Para were to fly in from Cyprus to reinforce the Brigade Group, commanded by Brigadier Derek Horsford,* who had already arrived in Kuwait.†

James rang his Battalion at once, only to be told he was not needed – disappointing for a man hoping for some action. He

---

*Later Major-General D G T Horsford CBE DSO.

†The deterrent effect of Britain's quick reaction worked. Iraq withdrew her forces from the border and, after four and a half months, 24 Infantry Brigade returned to their original bases, and the Arab League assumed responsibility for security in the area.

remembers, however, that the incident caught H's imagination, and as they drove across Europe, taking in the delights of Trieste, Venice and finally Paris, they discussed various options for secondment.* It was probably this, coupled with the good relationship between the two units in Cyprus, which first caused H to consider volunteering for service with the Parachute Regiment three years later.

When they reached their destination, covered in grime and exhausted from their long drive, Emson recalls H remembering that his grandfather might have left a small deposit in a Paris bank, just in case any member of the family should find themselves stuck there one day.

'I think we *are* stuck, James, don't you?' said H. Whereupon somehow he acquired the account number and bank details and emerged shortly with a hundred pounds, a princely sum in 1960.

Other essentials had been provided too: guidance on the best restaurants and sights. Having smartened themselves up, H and James dined at Pruniers and went on to the Folies Bergère. Emson reflects: 'At that age it was the most expensive and memorable evening I had ever had.'

Next day, H insisted they visit the Musée de la Marine, in view, he said, of his keen interest in naval history, of which Emson was previously unaware. The Musée has a remarkable historic collection of ship models whose glories their eager private guide began proudly to describe. Before he could shepherd them on from the magnificent *L'Orient* to the next exhibit, H politely added:

'*L'Orient* was anchored in Aboukir Bay on the First of August 1798, when Nelson arrived on the scene, and during a battle lasting from six p.m. to four o'clock the following morning, she was destroyed in one of the biggest explosions ever experienced at sea. The French line was reduced to dismasted hulks.

'Unfortunately,' he added, 'the British allowed the *Guillaume Tell*

---

*A two-year secondment to another unit was something most officers did on completion of their first tour of 'regimental duty'.
†The figure denotes the number of guns.

80 and the *Generaux 74*† to escape.'

The guide was somewhat taken aback, and even more so as H continued to amplify the Frenchman's explanations as their tour progressed. However, according to Emson, 'The manner of H's interjections did not engender any annoyance or animosity – just, perhaps, a grudging respect for this young Englishman's familiarity with French naval history. As for me, I was mighty impressed and full of admiration!'

At some stage the two young officers must have gone their separate ways, as H had arranged to meet Sara in Paris. She had booked into their prearranged hotel in the Quai d'Orsay, and gone up to her room to await H's arrival. But she fell into a deep sleep and H could neither raise her nor get into her room. So, in the dark, he climbed along the window ledge and entered through an open window. Next morning Sara remembers looking out and discovering to her horror that her room was three floors up and the ledge only a few inches wide.

Meanwhile the Devon and Dorsets were about to sail home to Plymouth in the troopship *Nevasa*. Although Plymouth was in the Regiment's heartland and the soldiers enjoyed being back at home, garrison life in Plymouth was militarily dull. For H this was doubly appealing: he was able to see Sara regularly, and he could take up motor racing seriously. He determined to combine both, but first he was required to attend two mandatory Young Officers' Courses at the School of Infantry.

The first was at Hythe in Kent, where young officers were instructed in the use of small arms.* This was a six-week course that many found tiresome because the instruction was repetitive and the students were tested endlessly and competitively. What was acceptable for recruits and officer cadets soon wore thin with young officers. But H had forgotten his basic training and was about to be exposed by the passing-in tests. He was invited to strip and assemble a rifle in the dark, load a magazine in fourteen seconds

---

*Weapons used at platoon level.

and rectify a stoppage on the Bren light machine gun. He failed each test. When he was told to assemble and fire the 3.5-inch rocket launcher, he put the rocket in the wrong way round. But it was not until he prematurely pulled the pin from a 36 Mills hand grenade that the patience of his instructors finally snapped. He was thrown off the course – in the Army's euphemistic parlance: 'Returned To Unit' (or RTU'd). Suitably chastened by the disgrace, he had to attend a later course, which he passed with credit, but not before he had had another brush with authority – this time with the Royal Navy.

The Dartmouth Commissioning Ball was an annual summer event with which H, as a resident of Kingswear, was familiar. But the 1961 ball was different. His brother Tim was coming to the end of his first year at the Britannia Royal Naval College and Johnnie Duke, Sara's former boyfriend, was passing out. Mrs Jones threw a large dinner party at The Grange for Tim and his friends prior to the ball. H was home that weekend – as was Bill – but they were not invited to the ball, and so during dinner, out of Tim's earshot, various plots were hatched to liven up the occasion. A plan duly emerged: to open the fire hydrants and let water spray over the wardroom, and its revellers, at the end of the evening. It was thought that the Captain of Dartmouth and most senior officers would have left before then and only the newly commissioned midshipmen, deemed to be fair game, and their partners would be standing to attention on the ballroom floor as the National Anthem concluded proceedings. In terms of traditional inter-Service College rivalry, this scheme was conceptually no worse than Dartmouth diverting the A30 traffic through the grounds of Sandhurst and across RSM Lord's beloved drill square, or painting Queen Victoria's statue dark blue.

At the appointed time the conspirators climbed on to the wardroom roof and rolled out the fire hose. On the opening bars of the National Anthem, Bill Jones opened the stopcocks and H sprayed the water through the skylights. All might have been different had the hydrants been recently tested; but they had not.

Instead of fresh water, filthy rusty liquid cascaded down, staining and ruining the ball-gowns of the ladies and the new mess-dress of the midshipmen.

Outside, H and Bill should have been making good their escape. Climbing down from the roof, H leaped into his car and prepared for a fast getaway, but Bill, who was only sixteen and somewhat out of his depth, was cornered. H reversed to help but this only enabled some alert cadet to take his car number. With Bill in custody and H's car identified, a major row now erupted. The opprobrium was visited initially upon Tim who, despite being blameless, was presumed to be the perpetrator. Although H owned up straight away, poor Tim remained under suspicion for many years. However, H, instead of being contrite and conciliatory, made matters worse by telling the Navy that the damage would have been minimal had they had clean water in their hydrants – as would any half-decent Army unit.

A stiff letter of complaint about H's behaviour and attitude was dispatched to Sandhurst, on the erroneous assumption that this was another inter-College prank in bad taste. Sandhurst replied sniffily that 2nd Lt. Jones was no longer their responsibility and forwarded the complaint to the School of Infantry at Hythe. But H, having been RTU'd, was not there either. Although they held no brief for H, the School of Infantry felt the Navy's letter was slightly hysterical and certainly pompous. So they made haste slowly and passed it routinely to H's Battalion in Plymouth.

By now at least a fortnight had elapsed, and when the Adjutant got round to briefing H's notably wise and unflappable Commanding Officer, Lieutenant Colonel Peter Willcocks, a sense of proportion had been restored. It had all happened whilst H was at home; full financial recompense would be paid; no one had been hurt, and the reputation of the Regiment had not been harmed – indeed, Dartmouth seemed unaware that it was anything to do with the Devon and Dorsets. H was given a few extra orderly officer duties, the standard minor punishment for subalterns, and sent on his way with a flea in his ear. But he had been lucky; in different circumstances, under a different CO, such irresponsibility and arrogance, on the heels of his failure on his first professional course, could have cost him his commission.

H's behaviour may have exasperated his seniors but he was earning the trust and friendship of his brother officers. He was spontaneously loyal and generous to his friends, as one of them recalls. Lieutenant John Andre, a fellow subaltern with H in Plymouth, is a direct descendant of the famous Major John Andre* who was hanged during the American War of Independence for spying for the British, and has many of his forebear's engaging qualities. Andre recounts how he had flown into RAF Lyneham in Wiltshire from Norway, where he had been canoeing, to find that the RAF had lost his baggage. With only the clothes he was standing up in, he rang the Battalion for help and luckily found H in the Officers' Mess. Without hesitation H jumped into his car for the three-hour drive to Lyneham to collect John. Such spontaneous, friendly acts are what brother officers remember, and with H there were scores of examples. However, his name and reputation cropped up everywhere, and past misdeeds could not be laid to rest. Many months after the incident at Dartmouth, the College invited the Devon and Dorset officers to an official function, but unwisely added that Second Lieutenant Jones would not be welcome. The Mess replied that they did not accept conditional invitations.

Much of H's free time was now being devoted to motor racing. He bought the second Lotus 'Super 7' ever produced in kit form, assembling it in a shed at The Grange with Colin Armstrong who had learnt his mechanics in the Royal Navy before working for H's father. H joined the British Racing and Sportscar Club and, accompanied by Sara, started doing the rounds of race circuits. They entered the Lotus most weekends in the season wherever they could find a meeting that accepted novice drivers. Thus H competed at

---

*Major Andre was thought to be the first British spy. He was executed aged thirty-one on 2 October 1780 at Tappan, New York, and because of his charm, dignity and sense of honour has become a cult figure among American military historians.

Snetterton, Goodwood, Silverstone, and at Brands Hatch, where he had to put a large black X on the rear window to indicate that he was a beginner. He proved to be a talented amateur who caught the eye of at least some of the motor-racing fraternity and commentators, with *Autosport* recording from Snetterton in his first season: 'The small GT event saw a walk-away win for Herbert Jones and his Lotus Elan.'

Encouraged by his early success and the thrill of it all, H bought another racing car, a Lotus Elan, with a higher specification than the 'Super 7', which he sold. However, continuity is all-important in motor racing; a driver must clock up points and needs race experience to make progress, and for H, clashing military duties often got in the way.

Rushing back to Plymouth in the Lotus from a race meeting late one Sunday, H approached the 'drop barrier' at the entrance to Plumer Barracks. He had taken care to measure it beforehand, and raced towards it now as if it were the finishing line at Silverstone. The startled sentry raised the alarm and frantically tried to wave him down, but H drove at, and clean under, the barrier, scattering soldiers everywhere. Many more extra orderly officer duties were to follow, which curtailed for several weekends his chances both of racing and of seeing Sara. She was furious and started subtly to rein H in. His friends noticed that slowly he was succumbing to her influence.

For her part, Sara was falling in love. What attracted her increasingly was that H was different from other boyfriends, and that he was 'playing it long'. 'I had been going out with Johnnie Duke for ages,' she explained, 'but I was later to discover that H had taken to me straight away. However, because Johnnie was around, H bided his time, which was quite clever.'

There was an aura about the Joneses, as Sara explained:

They lived down in Devon, they had a big house, their father had been an American, it was all just a little bit different from what I was used to. H was very good-looking in a way, even with his large nose. He was appealingly shy in many ways, and slightly eccentric. He'd been to Eton, then was in the Army; he had a lovely car and was now motor racing, which was quite a macho thing.

All this created a romantic image; he adored poetry, which he would read to me, and he would buy me nice clothes, which was a bit unusual for a military man. He was pretty tactile too, and if he had had his way, I would be dressed in boots, a nightdress and a fur coat. Those were his favourite items of clothing.

He could also be quite rude but, taken in context, it was harmless enough and actually quite amusing. He would say outrageous things – I remember him once coming to collect me for a party and I thought I looked the bee's knees. He said something like: 'Did you put that on with a trowel?' But I thought it was funny because I knew it was a front. He was trying to be extremely confident but one only had to scratch the surface to find that he wasn't in the least bit so. In fact he was rather vulnerable.

On 26 May 1962 the Devon and Dorsets were presented with new Colours* on Plymouth Hoe. This was the first event to which H, who was proudly in front of No. 3 Guard, invited Sara and her mother. Sara loved the pageantry and glamour of the occasion, with the Hoe crowded with thousands of well-wishers and curious holidaymakers. The introduction of a serious girlfriend to one's regiment is a matter to which most officers give thought. They want their choice to be admired by their brother officers, but also want her to feel at ease and enjoy herself, even though under scrutiny. In H's case there was no need to fear on either count. Sara, undaunted by the royal occasion – Princess Marina was presenting the Colours – made a favourable impression from the start, and she in turn responded to the warmth of the Regiment's

---

*Every infantry regiment carries two Colours on parades when the Queen, or her representative, is present: the Queen's Colour and the Regimental Colour. On them are emblazoned the Regiment's battle honours. About every twenty years infantry regiments of the line are presented with new Colours.

welcome and the splendour of the occasion.

Despite such highlights, Army life in England was often uneventful, and so in mid 1962 H was pleased to hear that he was to command a composite platoon of Devon and Dorsets sent to reinforce 1st Battalion, Royal Welch Fusiliers, on exercise in Canada. Representing your Regiment when attached to another is a task that a wise commanding officer gives only to someone who is professionally competent, and likely not to let the Regiment down. Peter Willcocks, knowing H's promotion to full lieutenant was due shortly, would have seen the need to give him a challenge, and being a far-sighted and confident CO, he was prepared to take a chance.

It is no easy task to weld a disparate group of individuals into a composite platoon, because each individual is accustomed to the procedures and practices of his own sub-unit. But H, ably assisted by his Platoon Sergeant, Colin Walters, made a great success of it, and the Royal Welch Fusiliers regarded him highly.

H's enthusiasm and his pride in his soldiers were very apparent to the Welshmen. One evening, at a company 'smoker' around a campfire under the bright stars of the Canadian prairie, they challenged H's platoon to sing. This was akin to an English pub visitor being challenged by the locals to darts, or whatever they do best. Although vocally inferior and outnumbered, H's platoon responded magnificently, countering 'Men of Harlech' with 'The Farmer's Boy', and then swapping West Country songs – such as 'Widdecombe Fair' and 'Where be Yon Blackbird To?' – with the Welsh favourites all evening. Eventually, as empty beer cans were piled high, H was challenged to sing a solo. Singing – let alone solos – was not his forte, yet if he refused it would have been an embarrassing loss of face. At such times inspiration can come unexpectedly to a condemned man, and H broke, hesitantly at first, into 'The Eton Boating Song'. This caught the Welshmen's imagination; they recognised the well-known tune and took it up eagerly. But only H knew the proper words, so he ended up leading the much-vaunted Welsh choir. Honour satisfied, the party continued happily into the early hours.

Before he went to Canada, H had applied formally to his Commanding Officer for permission to marry Sara, because by now there was no doubt in either's mind that they were right for each other. But his application was turned down flat, on the basis that, at twenty-two, he was too young. The Army did not officially recognise marriage until an officer was twenty-five (at which point an Army 'quarter' would be provided and a marriage allowance paid). It was made clear that if H did get married, he would be required to find another regiment, and this despite Peter Willcocks being a tolerant, generally enlightened commanding officer. He liked H, could see his potential, and had no doubt that Sara would make him an excellent wife but, on the matter of subalterns marrying too young, he was unshakeable.

Such a tough line may seem inexplicable today, but then it was normal. The liberalisation heralded by the 'Swinging Sixties' had not yet had an impact upon the Army and would not alter such attitudes for many more years. Willcocks was not unusual in believing that young officers' first priorities were to their soldiers and that life in the Officers' Mess would be impaired should they 'live out'. His view prevailed, and neither H nor Sara challenged it. Indeed, Sara confided later that she was rather pleased to have to wait because she had just secured a good job as a secretary in the House of Commons and did not want to leave London.

The Battalion's two-year tour in Plymouth was nearing completion, with the Devon and Dorsets due to be posted to Holywood in Northern Ireland. H had been promoted Lieutenant and now wore two pips on each shoulder. He would shortly hand over his rifle platoon and start to specialise, but first came a final exercise on Salisbury Plain. It was the normal two-sided battle against an enemy using blank ammunition. The details are not remembered, except that H was there.

In August 1963, with extraordinary prescience, the Regimental Journal, which records for posterity all major events over the previous four months, described the concluding battle of the exercise with the words: 'Several of the platoon commanders won posthumous VCs during the day.'

It was meant as a light-hearted reference to the spirit and dash that H and others had displayed. It turned out to be a chillingly accurate prediction.

CHAPTER SIX

Wider Horizons

For most of the 1960s, Northern Ireland was what soldiers called a 'plum posting', and to be stationed there was most agreeable. In July 1963, 1st Battalion, The Devonshire and Dorset Regiment took up residence in Palace Barracks, where they were due to remain for the next two years. This was one of only four regular Army barracks then in the Province, and was generally considered the best. Situated about three miles outside the city, on the outskirts of the respectable town of Holywood, it had sweeping views across Belfast Lough to the Antrim shore. The Harland and Wolff shipyard and Belfast Docks were thriving, and from H's large room in the comfortable red-brick Officers' Mess, vessels of every size and nationality could be seen plying the Lough.

New arrivals were struck immediately by how friendly everyone was – full of greetings and smiles – and it was an unexpected pleasure to serve in a place where soldiers were popular. Local girls queued at the barrack gate hoping for admittance to the weekly NAAFI dances; and young officers were welcomed into many homes, especially where unmarried daughters had not already gone to London or, having gone, had returned disappointed.

The countryside was lush and green, and when the rain fell, as it did most days, it did so softly. Dublin was readily accessible; the border was of no practical account, and going down to watch a rugby international at Lansdowne Road was part of a normal weekend. There was sailing on Belfast and Carlingford Loughs;

excellent golf nearby; salmon fishing on the Bann; walking in the Mournes and swimming from the fine beaches of County Down. Everything one could reasonably want was on the doorstep, and by air even London was only ninety minutes away.

Membership of Her Majesty's Forces conferred many privileges in Ulster society. Goods and services were often discounted for the Army and, if caught speeding by the Royal Ulster Constabulary, the production of a Service identity card would elicit not a summons but a friendly: 'That will be all right this time, Soor. Only just don't do it again!'

The notion that anything was fundamentally amiss in such a haven hardly occurred to H or to his brother officers. Occasionally an officer was surprised to be asked how many Catholics there were in the Mess; to which the honest answer was that he neither knew, nor cared. But there were few other indicators that the community was deeply divided, or that so massive and fundamental were the resentments on both sides that within six short years the tranquillity of Northern Ireland would be shattered, never to be restored again in the twentieth century.

Few predicted the significance of the Northern Ireland Civil Rights Association marches of July 1969, and none the consequences to flow from them. The virtually autonomous Government of Northern Ireland at Stormont knew of the grievances of the Nationalist minority, but was so bigoted and unresponsive that it failed to do anything effective until it was too late. Her Majesty's Government had hoped, with some justification since Partition in 1922, that the 'Irish problem' had gone away, but was caught hopelessly unprepared when they discovered it had not. The British public did not understand 'Ulster'; and the intelligence community, who did, and whose duty it was to monitor and assess these matters, was found to be lamentably wanting. Many years were to pass before they got on top of it – if, indeed, they have yet done so.

In the Battalion, of course, everyone knew of the IRA: that was why the police were armed. Yet it was still a shock to arrive off the Liverpool ferry and find a policeman with a rifle at the bottom of the gangplank. Likewise, Battalion teams would be intrigued, when playing local rugby sides, to be told with a knowing wink that the massively built opposing front row were 'all good B Men' – in other words 'B Specials'.* The security of armouries had always been taken seriously in Ulster over the years, following various IRA break-ins, but otherwise duty there was little different to that in other garrisons in the United Kingdom. It was, however, a great deal more fun. Even the Republican pubs and clubs of Belfast, such as Kevin Barry, were haunts where soldiers who were not quarrelsome could safely down their pints and perhaps join in the singing of rebel songs.

H had now risen a notch in the military hierarchy. He was the Battalion's Mortar Officer, responsible for the task of providing integral fire support from six 3-inch mortars. He was soon as proud and protective of his burly soldiers – they had to be strong to hump the ammunition – as he had been of 6 Platoon. Providing fire support is a specialist task that brings the Mortar Officer, as adviser, into close contact with his Commanding Officer.

Lieutenant Colonel John Randle had recently assumed command of the Devon and Dorsets and was to play an important part in H's future professional and domestic life. Randle had been commissioned into the famous 10th Baluch and had won the Military Cross as a company commander in the Burma campaign. Shortly before the Partition of India in 1947, he had, along with many other officers, transferred to the British Army, leaving behind a most agreeable country and way of life. It was a heart-breaking and uncertain time. But Randle's acceptance into The Devonshire Regiment proved to be a happy transition. He was an officer of high principle and integrity, and although his values and judgements had been forged in a different army, he admired and understood universal concepts, such as duty, loyalty and obedience. He was less comfortable with too much discussion, he disliked being challenged, and felt that flexibility could be overdone. But no one

*A tough, armed paramilitary reserve branch of the RUC generally loathed by the nationalist community.

doubted that at heart he was a kind, compassionate and proud Commanding Officer doing his best at all times for his officers and men. Moreover, he liked H and H's friends, although he was not entirely at ease contemplating what they might be up to next.

This was understandable in view of an earlier incident. Shortly after assuming command, he received a letter from H informing him that while back in England on his mortar course (on which, incidentally, he achieved a high grading), he had been stopped by the Plymouth police. H reported, as was required, that he was to be summoned for being drunk in charge whilst driving out of the Naval Dockyard after dining aboard his brother's ship. After expressing his regret at the embarrassment caused, he added: 'But do not be too concerned, Colonel, I am engaging one of the best counsels in London, who is confident of establishing my innocence.' This was years before the advent of the breathalyser. 'No one was more relieved than I,' recalled Randle, 'when H's confidence proved to be justified. The eminent QC convinced the court that H's indisposition was due entirely to some bad fish that he had eaten at dinner in the wardroom. Initiative of a high order, perhaps with quite a bit of luck thrown in.'[1]

The Irish Sea did not inhibit H and Sara from seeing each other. The flight to London was quicker than H's notoriously rapid drives up from Plymouth, and Sara would meet him at the old Cromwell Road Air Terminal, in the West End. They spent most weekends together in the family flat at Whitehall Court, notwithstanding the wife of H's Jewish godfather, Arthur de Tiel, being a neighbour. She made her disapproval of their cohabitation clear to H's mother, but Dia was indifferent to the news. She approved of Sara, and in any case she knew that, but for the Army's old-fashioned attitude, her eldest son would already be married.

Sara remembers these blissful weekends nostalgically. They would dine in Beauchamp Place at Fiddlers Three, and H's favourite pastime, she recalls, was seeing cartoons (in the old Loony Tunes cinema at Waterloo Station), or cowboy films. Another recreation, perhaps surprisingly, was buying Sara's clothes. 'He loved shopping and often, even though I would be dying to go home, he would say: "Just try *that* on!"'

H also continued motor racing, and Sara spent much of her time in the House of Commons, where she was private secretary to Grenville Howard,* arranging entries and pre-positioning cars for the next weeks' races. By now H was racing seriously: and he even enthralled the Easter Monday crowds at Brands Hatch in 1964, according to the *Motor*: 'The second REDeX Trophy event was equally thrilling . . . a fantastic fight between the eventual winner, H Jones (Lotus Elan) and two others . . . had the crowd on its collective toes.' Sara thoroughly enjoyed it too: 'It was huge fun – and a great fraternity. We used to sit in the pits with a board of three stopwatches that you pressed down – one for time lap and so on. Oh, it was great stuff!'

H raced his father's old Bentley as well, and this too was written up in specialist magazines, one of which recorded:

A large field of Vintage and PVT† cars assembled for the start of the second 4-lap handicap. Interesting cars included Christopher Mann's 1914 French GP winning Mercedes . . . Mann stayed ahead from limit until the last lap, when 'Aitch' Jones' [*sic*] 1934 Van den Plas 3.5 Bentley just managed to squeeze past to take the flag by 0.2 secs.

Posting results such as these was no mean achievement for an amateur living on the wrong side of the Irish Sea, without back-up or the continuity needed regularly to compete with success at a high level.

In mid 1963 H again sought permission to marry. Matters were moving inexorably forwards; he was now eighteen months older and would be twenty-four by the time of the wedding – one year short of the Army's permitted age. Moreover, he and Sara had now known

---

*Then Conservative Member of Parliament for St Ives.
†Post Vintage Thoroughbred

each other for five years. Ideally, John Randle, a traditionalist, would have preferred H to wait. However, as luck would have it, his wife had been at the same school as Sara and she put in a word. It helped too that H was proving a proficient mortar officer of considerable value to his Commanding Officer. In his annual confidential report, which all officers receive – and have to sign off as read – Randle recorded:

Jones is a first class officer of character and ability who has had a successful year . . .

He is an individualist with iconoclastic views on many of the shrines of military thought and custom. These views, combined with intelligence and a pleasantly relaxed manner, produce a refreshingly unorthodox approach to life, with something always in reserve for an emergency.

He has a wider knowledge and interest in the broader aspects of the Army than most of his contemporaries. He will fight with determination and even vehemence for what he considers to be the best interests of his platoon and his men – but is equally loyal to accept an adverse decision. These qualities, combined with his lightness of touch, make him an excellent leader of soldiers and his platoon is well trained and possessed of high morale.

Bad sight prevents him from playing some games, but he takes part with enthusiasm wherever he is able. He is also a racing driver of some talent.

The upshot was that H was given permission to marry. He and Sara promptly went down to Kingswear and, after a romantic dinner dance at the Royal Dart Yacht Club, at which Sara remembers wearing a very smart green dress, announced their engagement to Dia and their friends.

Dia was not a demonstrative person and Sara recalls that she did not easily show her affection. 'I was rather frightened of her at first. When you were leaving and kissed her goodbye you could tell that she wasn't used to anybody doing that.' This was the famous 'Jones reserve', with which H's family and friends were familiar. The Jones men had a distaste for outward demonstration of personal feelings. H was romantic and passionate in private, but shows of public affection were reserved for his black Labradors – of which there was a succession, all named 'Jimmy'. This was one of those peculiarly British characteristics, baffling to most foreigners, whereby family members are addressed by proxy through a pet. When H returned from work, Jimmy would be covered in affection, and having been patted, fondled and probably kissed, might be asked: 'What's Sara got for dinner, then?'

H and Sara's hope of a smooth passage from engagement to marriage were now torpedoed by what the Army terms the 'Exigencies of the Service'. Their wedding was planned for 20 June 1964, but on 22 May the Devon and Dorsets were ordered to deploy their 'stand-by' company at once to British Guiana, with the rest of the Battalion to follow in seventy-two hours.

British Guiana (now Guyana) was a small colony on the northeast corner of South America where disturbances had erupted between the two main communities – those of East Indian and of Negro* extraction. In mid May, serious rioting occurred in Mackenzie on the Demerara River; two hundred East Indian homes were set on fire by malcontent Negroes and two thousand Indians fled the area in the wake of what today is termed ethnic cleansing. The Governor sought immediate military reinforcement from Britain.

For the Devon and Dorsets the prospect of action 4,500 miles away was just what soldiers relish. In normal circumstances H, too, would not have wanted to miss a skirmish overseas, but at this particular moment it was most inconvenient with his wedding less than a month away. Duty called, however, and there was never any question of his remaining behind to catch up later. So discussion was confined to two alternatives: to postpone the wedding until the Battalion's return, whenever that might be; or to hope that H might

---

*The terms of classification in the British Guiana census.

be released once the Battalion had settled in. Unexpectedly the second option hit the buffers. The Commanding Officer felt it wrong to allow H to return to the UK without everyone else in his situation being treated the same. No one disagreed with that in principle; but the practical difficulty was that scores of soldiers had recently become engaged to the beguiling women of Northern Ireland, and John Randle could not contemplate a reduction in his fighting strength just when a crisis might develop. Therefore he put a blanket ban on all leave.

Sara and her mother were remarkably stoical about these developments, but they cannot have been easy to accept, particularly as Sara's father had recently died and Mrs de Uphaugh was having to cope on her own. But luckily she was a remarkable lady – calm, elegant and capable – and well able to handle the uncertainty. Nothing much fazed her; after all, she had taken in her stride one of H's most preposterous remarks: 'I thought you might be nouveau riche,' he said soon after they first met, 'but I've since discovered that you are neither!'

The de Uphaughs were indeed neither. They were an old, distinguished and at one time wealthy family. One ancestor, Dr Brian Duppa* (1588–1662), had been in turn Bishop of Chichester, Salisbury and then Winchester. Another had been tutor to Charles II, and a third, Sir Thomas Duppa, was said to have been the first Gentleman Usher of the Black Rod. Sara's father, Francis, born in 1898, had enlisted under age in the Royal Fusiliers for the Great War and been wounded three times, once seriously, on the Somme. Like so many veterans of that war, he was deeply scarred by his experiences and suffered thereafter periodically from nightmares and acute depression. It was a trauma that alcohol was able to ease. This would now be diagnosed as serious 'post-traumatic stress disorder', but then it was not even acknowledged as battle fatigue.

After the war, to add to Francis's woes, an unsympathetic father disapproved so strongly of his son's desire to join the Forestry

---

*The name Duppa later became the present de Uphaugh.

Commission – rather than go up to university – that he cut off every penny of his allowance. Thus Sara's family existed on a relatively humble salary from the Forestry Commission. Her mother's side were named Watkins, originally an Anglo-Irish family from Navan in County Meath. But Sara's maternal grandmother seems to have been as profligate as her paternal grandfather was unsympathetic, and so no financial help came from that quarter either. Nevertheless, by 1950 the de Uphaughs had settled into an attractive Victorian house in the New Forest, before later moving into the comfortable bungalow to which H was first welcomed. Sara's father died of muscular dystrophy early in 1964 but not before he had met H, of whom he thoroughly approved.

On 26 May 1964, three weeks before the wedding was due to take place, H flew out to British Guiana with the main body of the Devon and Dorsets. It was a tedious thirty-hour journey with RAF Transport Command, crammed initially into Argosies for the short haul from Belfast to RAF Colerne in Wiltshire, and then in large Britannias from Lyneham to British Guiana, staging through Gander in Newfoundland and Bermuda. H's heart must have sunk as he looked down over his barren and undeveloped destination before landing at Atkinson Field, which was no more than an airstrip in a large clearing with a control tower on stilts in the middle. He must have wondered how he would get back to England from this distant outpost, as he had promised Sara. It was a promise that he was in no position to keep, but taking him at face value, Sara and her mother were going serenely ahead with the arrangements.

H's mortarmen, formed into a support platoon, were placed under command of A Company, based initially in the capital, Georgetown, and living on a sugar plantation at Diamond on the southern outskirts. Although the situation was tense after the communal rioting and murders at Mackenzie, it stabilised with the arrival of the Battalion. Extensive patrolling along the interfaces between the two communities soon restored confidence, and searches for suspects, arms and ammunition took the pressure off the beleaguered local police. It was clear to even the most cautious that the situation was under control and unlikely to deteriorate significantly. So, as a great concession, H was granted seventy-two hours' leave to return home – at his own expense – to marry. But his honeymoon would have to be foregone, at least for the time being.

On a showery June day, H and Sara were duly married at St Nicholas's Church in Brockenhurst. Tim was H's best man, and Sara's brother, John, gave her hand in marriage. Dia came up from Devon with all those who worked at The Grange, and some of H's American relations sent messages from the United States. It was a happy occasion marred only by the absence of a honeymoon and most of H's brother officers, although that undoubtedly made it a more sober and ordered affair. After the reception, in a large marquee in a neighbour's garden, husband and wife drove in the Bentley down to Devon, where they stayed for three heavenly days before motoring up to London for H to catch the plane back to British Guiana. Sara remembers their last night, at the Ritz; it was not a great success. They were late booking and only got a room with two single beds – and a pneumatic drill outside the window roused them early next morning.

After Sara had seen H off, Tim thoughtfully took her to dine in a Greek restaurant where she remembers being given inedible squid. The strain of the weekend and their cancelled honeymoon in Corfu caught up with her; missing H, and frustrated by what she saw as the Army's sheer unreasonableness, she burst into tears. 'I just cried into my plate throughout the meal with Tim, poor chap, who has had to pick up the bits so often, trying to be bracing and splendid!'

Back in British Guiana, H's absence had hardly been noticed. Nothing had changed, except that a properly funded leave scheme had now been authorised which would benefit all those to follow. Such are the irritants and quirks of Army life which wise soldiers learn to shrug off; however, that particular news rankled greatly with Sara. H now embarked on a prolific and loving correspondence with her, ticking off the days until November when they would take their delayed honeymoon in nearby Antigua.

Meanwhile there was work to be done. A Company, with H's

support platoon still attached, was moved across the Demerara River to the township of Leonora on the west coast, where the situation was much more challenging. Three policemen had been shot dead in an ambush, and several sugar-cane cutters murdered in the Demerara sugar estates, so platoons were based there to protect the workers and patrol between the conflicting communities. For young platoon commanders to be on their own in this way was excellent training, and H and his fellow subalterns thrived on their independence.

H's Platoon Sergeant was David Gigg, who remembers that it was something of a culture shock when H took over the platoon: 'Here was a man who wanted things done his way, but he never expected anyone to do anything he could not do himself.' Gigg also recalls H's concern for his soldiers, and his inherent generosity. In an age before videos and CDs, reading material was prized, but it was in short supply through the usual Army channels. So H, privately and without letting it be known, arranged to buy books, magazines and newspapers from Georgetown for his whole platoon every week. Such thoughtful gestures are still remembered at reunions nearly forty years later.

The months ticked by with little action or excitement, and soon the main enemy became boredom. This often occurs when the original aim is achieved and the Army imposes an uneasy co-existence on a community. By early December 1964, Sir Richard Luyt, the Governor, considered the situation to be sufficiently restored and calm for elections to be held. The protagonists were the ruling left-inclined People's Progressive Party (PPP), led by the Prime Minister, Dr Cheddi Jagan, whose supporters were from the East Indian community, and Forbes Burnham's predominantly black People's National Congress (PNC). The United Front (UF), a mixed-race party, held the electoral balance. When the votes were counted, the PPP had collected three more seats than the PNC, but six seats were held by the UF. So Forbes Burnham invited the UF to join him in coalition and was thereby able to form a government.

One of the military implications of the election was that the

Devon and Dorsets had to remain in British Guiana until mid January 1965. H and Sara's first Christmas as a married couple was therefore spent apart. In the event, under the watchful eye of the security forces, ninety-six per cent of the electorate were able to vote and not a single ballot box was lost. The outcome was deemed a success in the sense that peace endured from then until independence* eighteen months later.

It had been an interesting nine months. British Guiana's hesitant path to independence did not attract world attention, and unlike Aden, where soldiers were under frequent attack, the operational risks were slight. Nevertheless, the Battalion left in mid January 1965 with the satisfaction of knowing a good job had been done.

By the time H got back to Northern Ireland he was considering the next stage in his career. He had reached the age when infantry officers are encouraged to spread their wings and broaden their experience. One of H's friends was applying for Special Air Service (SAS) selection, another did the US Airborne Ranger Course in America and a third was to be seconded to the King's African Rifles. H set his sights on an attachment to the Parachute Regiment, which in those days still relied for many of its officers on volunteers from throughout the Army.

This migration of keen young officers to and from airborne units was considered to be of mutual advantage: the Parachute Regiment benefited by drawing on a wide pool of experience, and as a result were well regarded and supported across the Army. Equally, the Army gained from the cross-fertilisation of ideas and the high standards of personal fitness and training which officers carried back to their parent units.

Having discussed the future with Sara and explained the various implications, H formally applied to volunteer. In this he was strongly supported by the Devon and Dorsets. H's application was accepted and he reported to Aldershot in early May 1965 for the start

---

*British Guiana became independent on 26 May 1966 and is now Guyana, a 'Co-operative Republic'.

of the rigorous two-week selection course, called Pre-Parachute Selection, or just 'P Company'. Provided he passed, this would be followed by three weeks' parachute training with the RAF at Abingdon in Oxfordshire.

H had taken the sensible precaution of getting fit before arrival, for there was no period of grace for officers to settle in gently. Bill Sanders-Crook, then of the Lancashire Regiment* and a fellow motor-racing enthusiast, who had known H in Plymouth, was one of those encouraging him to second to the Paras, as he himself had done. He helped H to prepare temperamentally for P Company, for the course was more a mental than a physical challenge for a fit officer. Its purpose was – and continues to be – to test not just a candidate's physical fitness and powers of endurance but his mental robustness as well. Everyone who wants to serve in the Airborne Forces, irrespective of age, rank or background, has to pass P Company. It is a great leveller and a bonding experience.

Bill recollects that candidates arrived on a Sunday and were off on a two-mile timed cross-country steeplechase first thing on the Monday. H, being wiry and lean, had no difficulty with this, but there were a dozen more challenging tests ahead, of which four stood out. The first involved a gruelling ten-mile route march in combat kit, helmet and boots, carrying a rifle and thirty-five-pound pack; this had to be completed in one hour fifty minutes. It could not be achieved without running for at least half the distance, and officers were expected to assist those who fell behind. This test also suited H's physique admirably and he had no difficulty. On its completion, and whilst still exhausted, trainees were confronted with a series of confidence tests on a 'trainasium' – a vast scaffolding trelliswork reaching forty-five feet above the ground. Although not difficult in a technical sense, this was designed to test and eliminate those who were frightened of heights. It, too, posed few problems for H, who sprang gazelle-like from one piece of equipment to another,

*The Lancashire Regiment (Prince of Wales's Volunteers) later to become the Queen's Lancashire Regiment on amalgamation with The Loyal Regiment.

bellowing as required his name and number while balanced precariously at the apex.

The start of the second week was known as Black Monday, when bloodthirsty and demanding tests of courage and commitment took place. 'Milling' was a one-minute slogging match – boxing is too elegant a term – wearing sixteen-ounce gloves. Trainees were expected to face each other and deliver sixty seconds of continuous controlled aggression, whilst sustaining an equally ferocious onslaught. H's prowess at boxing at Eton under the Queensberry Rules was irrelevant here. He was required to 'mix it', which he did with determination and spirit.

The climax of P Company came on the final day with the notorious Log Race. Its purpose was to eliminate any candidate over whom the instructors still harboured doubts, and those who were insufficiently strong and robust. Because H lacked brute strength, this was the event he dreaded most.

Teams of eight carried a 130-pound log, attached to each trainee by a toggle-rope around the wrist, over a one-and-a-half-mile course of sandy hills and ravines. The race could only be successfully completed if all eight men worked together. Invariably someone would slip or drop back, thereby adding to the others' burden. It was a classic lesson in teamwork, and those suspected of not pulling their weight were subjected to sustained verbal abuse from the instructors. There is no record of where H's team came – he and the others would, in any event, have been near to collapse at the end – but their relief at completing the race, and the course, would have dulled the pain. Now they waited tensely for their results. H had passed. Despite the threats and personal abuse he had received throughout the fortnight, he had never looked like failing. It would have been unusual if he had, for officers on secondment rarely failed P Company.

On 17 May H joined Course Number 619 at the RAF Parachute Training School at Abingdon in Oxfordshire. The atmosphere here was much more relaxed and enjoyable. The RAF instructors were dedicated to getting students through the course, rather than failing them, as the Para instructors seemed intent on doing at Aldershot.

There were good reasons for this new approach: parachuting is inherently stressful, so confidence-building and encouragement were needed rather than hassle.

The course progressed systematically over three weeks through the assimilation of basic skills and drills – mostly landings and rolls – to balloon jumps, and then the real thing: descents from ageing Hastings aircraft. Like most students, H mastered the basics easily and by the end of the fourth day he was ready for his first jump. This was on to a disused grass airfield at Weston-on-the-Green, near Oxford. A hydrogen barrage balloon, with a metal cage under-slung, containing four students and their instructor, was winched to 800 feet. It is cold and still at that height, and noises from the ground are eerily muffled.

As the officer and leader, H was ordered to stand at the open gate first and then step purposefully into the void. This is an unnerving experience, and most parachutists confess to hating their first balloon jump. When exiting from an aircraft, the slipstream whips the parachutist sideways, thus lessening the falling sensation, but from a balloon he falls like a stone with a sickening sinking feeling. Once the parachute deployed – which it does automatically – H would have experienced a feeling of peace and elation before being jerked back to reality by the disembodied voice of his instructor on the grass, far below, shouting orders through a megaphone. The ground rushed up at him, and despite his best endeavours to remember his landing drills, he hit it with an undignified *crump*. But he was still in one piece.

After two successful 'balloons', six further jumps from the Hastings aircraft followed. These became progressively more diffi-cult as students graduated from jumping in threes without equip-ment to jumping at night with, on the final descent, a heavy equipment container strapped to the right leg. Bad weather and high winds, which so often limit military parachuting, imposed delays towards the end of the three weeks, but eventually forty-eight of the fifty-seven trainees completed the course. Of the nine who failed, eight were from injury; only one had refused to jump.

Looking back on this and his subsequent experience, H claimed never to enjoy parachuting. It was not so much the actual jumping, or the landing, but the prospect of imminent mid-air collision that worried him. Parachuting is only a means of getting there, after all, and in this he reflected the attitude of most members of the regiment in which he was about to serve.

Proudly wearing his maroon beret, with his coveted wings on the right shoulder of his smock, Acting Captain H Jones reported for duty with 3rd Battalion, The Parachute Regiment on 15 June 1965. He was disappointed to be posted to this battalion, because in October they were going to British Guiana for six months, whence he had just come. He had pointed this out at Regimental Headquarters, where such decisions are made, expressing a preference for either of the other two regular battalions, but to no avail. New to the Regiment, he was in no position to argue and was sent where the need for an officer of his age and experience was greatest. He was appointed initially as Second-in-Command of one of 3 Para's rifle companies in Aldershot. It was not a demanding job.

Sara was probably more disappointed with these developments than H. Whilst H was in British Guiana, she had happily settled into the Devon and Dorset regimental family in Holywood as a 'newly wed'. Now she faced the prospect of another six months on her own in an Army 'hiring' near Aldershot, trying to make new friends among the wives of an unfamiliar regiment. Considerations such as these bear more heavily on the wives than on the men because the latter can quickly immerse themselves in their new work and fresh surroundings.

This was what H did. He went on exercise to Kenya with his company shortly after arrival, and he made new friends. One of them was Second Lieutenant Rupert Smith, years later to become one of the Army's most internationally distinguished and respected generals as the senior UN commander in Bosnia-Herzegovina, and later as DSACEUR.* H and Rupert were together in British Guiana

---

*Deputy Supreme Allied Commander Europe, one of NATO's top appointments.

when H returned there. For part of that tour they were based up-country on an old hutted cattle station near Tacama, a village on the Berbice River. After the day's work was done – H was Battalion Mortar Officer by now – they lay on their camp beds in the sweltering heat, reading and quoting to each other from *The Complete Works of Kipling*, which Rupert had with him, and from Wavell's anthology *Other Men's Flowers*, which was H's favourite.

It was here too, on the savannah, that H received the wonderful news that Sara was pregnant with a baby due in June the following year. The Battalion returned to Aldershot in February, and so H had a period of relative stability at home, which was especially convenient in view of Sara's approaching confinement. On 13 June 1966, to their intense joy, David Francis Herbert Jones was born in the Louise Margaret Military Hospital in Aldershot, fulfilling H's strong sense of dynasty and his oft-expressed wish to Sara for 'one son at least, but preferably more'.

A month later H was about to make national news, but of the wrong kind. He had organised a live firing exercise on Dartmoor for his mortar platoon. There are few ranges in England where it is permitted to fire heavy mortars but Dartmoor was one, and it had the added advantage of being near H's home. So at the end of the exercise, rather than face the long journey back to Aldershot in holiday traffic, he arranged for the platoon to spend the weekend camped at The Grange.

Considerate as this was, soldiers want bright lights on Saturday nights, not singsongs round a campfire in a wet field. So, as the evening wore on, H's Paras found their way down to Kingswear and across the river to Dartmouth in search of entertainment. Some found it at the youth centre in Duke Street, which had a disco that Saturday organised by the youth leader from the Royal Naval College, Petty Officer Lyons. At around ten o'clock, Lyons found one of his young members scuffling with a Para who, apparently, objected to paying the four shillings entrance fee. He managed to separate them but the Para allegedly swung round while being escorted out and punched Lyons on the jaw. The Petty Officer saw the situation getting out of hand and ran to the nearby Seale's Arms to ring the police. Unluckily for him, other members of H's platoon were already there. When they heard that one of their mates might be in difficulty they went to his aid, as soldiers instinctively do. In such circumstances Paras tend to fight first and think later, which in this case resulted in several of the youngsters ending up in hospital, and the youth centre being extensively damaged.

When police are called and ambulances summoned, the press are seldom far behind. Furthermore, any story about the Parachute Regiment is potentially newsworthy, and one reflecting un-favourably upon their behaviour seems to be irresistible. First the *South Devon Chronicle** ran the story, and then, on 17 July, it made headlines in the *Sunday Express*.

H was up at The Grange at the time and was not directly to blame. However, they were his soldiers, and his responsibility whether he was present or not. His reputation locally had not yet recovered from the various escapades of his youth; moreover, influential ex-Service residents – and the neighbourhood was full of them – take a dim view of bad behaviour on their doorstep, for by association it rubs off on them.

Further away, in various military headquarters and at the War Office, reaction was equally hostile. Reports were called for and conclusions reached that H's platoon had behaved deplorably. Bad publicity for the Parachute Regiment, which reflects badly on the Army generally – particularly when self-inflicted and prevalent – is viewed with disfavour, and frosty letters went to Aldershot.

The repercussions were still rumbling months later when Major Keith Spacie† arrived at 3 Para to take command of Patrol Company, which had recently been created and to which H had been transferred. The concept of a patrol company, consisting of twenty-four four-man patrols specialising in reconnaissance and observation, was a recent innovation, and one that led eventually to

*Of 15 July 1996.

†Later to become a major-general, and Commander British Forces Falkland Islands from 1983–4.

the formation of close observation platoons in Northern Ireland. These were later to become one of the most successful military assets in the fight against terrorism; and H was in at their inception.

Keith Spacie recalls that H joined him in the spring of 1967:

> He came to me under something of a cloud following an incident with his platoon in Devon, but he fitted in very well in terms of the personality required for our type of operation, which was rather special, and he formed an elite group.
>
> The work was challenging, physically demanding and every-thing that he enjoyed. He was impatient, not least with the 'system' and with bureaucracy, and he had unbounded energy plus the capacity to react rapidly to a new situation.
>
> He had a warm personality, a good lifestyle and an interesting background with a lot of money. But he did not flaunt his wealth. He had style, and soldiers like style, so there was absolutely no problem at all with him from their point of view.[2]

H had moral courage too. During a Mess party one night, he found his Commanding Officer, who had a fondness for pretty women, married or otherwise, dancing too close to Sara for his liking. H was furious when, to Sara's obvious embarrassment, the officer became increasingly intimate, and he leapt up and strode across the dance floor, seizing Sara away and saying loudly: 'That's quite enough, sir, you have had a fair crack of the whip!' Junior officers do not lightly upbraid their CO in public about his behaviour, and the incident gives an insight into H's personal standards and strength of character.

Six months later, with his present tour nearing completion, H had to consider his next posting. Some difficult decisions were needed: should he apply to transfer permanently to the Parachute Regiment, or should he return to his own? It is a problem that faces every officer towards the end of his time with another regiment; it can be a crucial decision made even harder if not all the cards are on the table. Two out of H's last three confidential reports had been B grades; in other words he was assessed to be in the second batch of officers of his rank and service. This was still an above-average grading, but the reports contained a couple of less than favourable passages, such as:

> He is highly strung; this sometimes leads to the loss of temper over some minor irritant or to a hasty decision better taken after some consideration. He knows of these weaknesses and the dangers into which they can lead . . .

Would the Parachute Regiment offer him a permanent commission, and what appointment would the Devon and Dorsets have for him, if he went back? Opportunities and ambitions had to be assessed, loyalties to his own Regiment and to the Paras considered, and Sara's preference discussed. Ultimately the Army would decide, but at least H had now reached the age where his views were sought.

Rupert Smith, who was by now a firm friend of both H and Sara, remembers H discussing the problem with him. The Devon and Dorsets had moved to Osnabruck, where they had an interesting role as a mechanised battalion in the 1st British Corps.* H was wanted as their adjutant, which was an excellent appointment and career move. What, if anything, the Parachute Regiment were offering was not clear. Keith Spacie, with whom H had worked well and happily, had handed over Patrol Company by now and was not involved in the decision-making. Rupert Smith's recollection is that being adjutant of a mechanised battalion in Germany, then the shop window of the Army, seemed a better prospect to H than an unspecified appointment in the Parachute Regiment. H chose accordingly, and Sara was happy that the matter was settled that way.

The decision was to be a turning point in H's career. Adjutant of a front-line unit was, and still is, a key post. The Adjutant is the chief executive to the Commanding Officer, and acts in his name and

---

*1st British Corps was then the British Army's major contribution to the NATO alliance. It no longer exists.

with his authority. He is known to all ranks above and below him and he sets the tone of the unit. If he is wise, he controls all access to the Headquarters, and he should know exactly what is going on at all times. He is both a weathervane and a barometer; and he must be a good communicator whilst remaining discreet. Potentially, therefore, the adjutant is more influential than anyone other than the commanding officer himself. A good adjutant can carry an indifferent commanding officer for many weeks, whilst a bad one can destroy unit morale in a morning, however brilliant his boss may be.

H's overall performance and reputation, up until now, had been somewhat inconsistent. He was seen as a character and he was certainly fun to have around. He was energetic and enthusiastic, but he could be a bit of a loose cannon and get himself into scrapes. He was liked by his soldiers and, despite being argumentative and increasingly opinionated, was popular with almost all his peers. Although no one doubted his flair or his potential ability, some did wonder whether it could be harnessed effectively in such a crucial job.

What most observers missed was Sara's increasing influence on H, and the effect of parenthood. He was growing less shy and awkward, and in one of his letters he acknowledged Sara's part in building up his confidence. He greatly enjoyed being a father and took the responsibility seriously. He had a better focus and sense of purpose, and the sparks of ambition, which had rarely been evident before, were now being ignited by his new circumstances.

Much was hanging on H's next job. There was keen anticipation at how it would work out – for both him and his Regiment.

CHAPTER SEVEN

Increasing Responsibility

Speculation always accompanies the return of an officer to his Regiment. When a new adjutant arrives, the interest is intense, particularly amongst those most affected – the subalterns. Lieutenant Colin Pape, a fit, keen twenty-four-year-old anti-tank platoon commander of the Devon and Dorsets, was one of them. In July 1968 the 1st Battalion had deployed on exercise to Larzac in the unspoilt Central Massif of France, where, in caves adjacent to the rugged training area, the famous Roquefort cheese is matured. Pape clearly recalls Captain H Jones's return:

I first met H when he rejoined the Battalion as Adjutant, and his reputation had preceded him. My first sight of him was on exercise where he was the umpire attached to my platoon. He exploded on to the scene dressed in para smock and umpire's white armband. He seemed to be everywhere at once, bringing the exercise to life. Everyone went up a gear so affected were they by his enthusiasm, drive and energy.

The first half-hour was all go and we sweated and gasped for air as H galvanised us into action, lifting our performance beyond anything we were used to. Finally, the position won, H debriefed us with clarity and professionalism and I remember how pleased we felt when he told us how well we had done. And then suddenly he was gone as quickly as he had arrived. It was as if a hurricane had passed through the exercise and all was quiet again.'[1]

H's new Commanding Officer was Lieutenant Colonel Adrian Rouse, an officer of great ability who, like John Randle, had transferred to the Devons from another Indian Army regiment, the Jats. An uncompromising disciplinarian, he knew what he wanted, but was having difficulty getting it. In his new Adjutant, Rouse was to find exactly what he needed.

Rouse could be formal and austere on duty, although at home he was a most generous and charming host. His officers tended to keep their distance, unless they were on sure ground, as mostly he knew their business better than they did. By contrast, H was informal and unconventional, and would no more be intimidated now by his Commanding Officer than he had been by the Library at Eton – not that Rouse wanted to intimidate him, and still less would he want a sycophant in his outer office. He was too wise for that.

Colonel Rouse had spotted H's potential years before, and was not disappointed:

> I had known H first in Cyprus where, although he was not in my company, he stood out at once as a character undaunted by convention – his monocle and his H 1 registration plate was evidence of that – and he had obvious originality. I therefore had no hesitation in selecting him as my Adjutant.
>
> His arrival was a relief. He was quick and efficient and got on with things without a fuss.
>
> His presence was a great assistance to me, and that alone made my life so much easier.[2]

However, it was not all plain sailing. Behind closed doors there were disagreements on priorities, and indeed on the most appropriate way to run a busy mechanised battalion in the hothouse of BAOR. As often happens, little irritants became more troublesome than major issues. For example, Rouse felt that his young officers were scruffy, particularly out of uniform, and he determined to change this. He directed that in future when out of barracks they would wear a jacket with collar and tie, together with a hat. This was not

H's style at all. He always dressed down when off duty, and in the late sixties hats were unfashionable. He urged the Commanding Officer to allow them to relax when not working, but to no avail, so H decided the best way was to keep a low profile and turn a Nelsonian blind eye should problems arise.

One did, on a Saturday morning. Some subalterns wearing ties and hats were shopping in the NAAFI when H entered, dressed, as usual, in jeans and ragged sweater. Greetings were exchanged and H explained sheepishly that he had only popped in briefly to buy something for his car, on which he was working. So far, so good. But then in walked Adrian Rouse.

H froze behind a bookstand. The Commanding Officer greeted his neat and tidy officers and then asked the question they were dreading.

'Didn't I see the Adjutant's car outside? Is he in here?'

'I don't *think* so, sir,' they replied.

H had already secured the loyalty of his subordinates. Meanwhile Rouse, delighted that his instructions were being followed at last, turned round and left, making a mental note to thank his Adjutant on Monday.

Opinions in the Army varied about serving in Germany. Some soldiers and their families disliked the predictability of life in BAOR and the distance of most garrisons from home. They felt claustrophobic in their isolated English communities in a foreign land, where some were stationed for ten years or more. Others – the more imaginative – enjoyed the opportunities afforded at the heart of Europe where life was improved by various allowances and concessions, including tax-free cars and petrol.

Furthermore, Rhine Army was professionally rewarding. As the principal operational component of BAOR, 1st British Corps had the latest equipment and the most challenging role. The brightest up-and-coming commanders were in charge – and the threat was real. A visit to the fortified 'Inner German Border', as the artificial barrier between East and West Germany was termed, demonstrated the sinister presence of Warsaw Pact Forces, poised less than an hour's drive from Hanover and only a few hundred miles from Bonn. The threat may seem over-exaggerated now, but it was real enough at the time; indeed, the Soviet invasion of Czechoslovakia in May 1968 violently made the point. H arrived in Osnabruck only a couple of months after this formidable demonstration of Soviet capability and intent.

Most of H and Sara's friends liked being in Germany and, as they were not going to be there for long, they determined to enjoy it. An added, joyous bonus was the arrival of Rupert Timothy Herbert, their second child, born in the British Military Hospital in Munster on 29 April 1969.

Professionally H was in his element. The autumn exercises were on a scale he had not experienced before, with hundreds of tanks, guns and other armoured vehicles moving freely across the North German Plain once the harvest was in. It was an amazing sight: tanks drove over private land, convoys stretched for miles and even stretches of autobahn were temporarily closed to facilitate the mass autumn migration of armoured vehicles and trucks. At that time German farmers positively welcomed the Army on to their land, thanks to the generous compensation they received. Besides, they were far more conscious of the Soviet presence than were any other Western nation, and they found these annual demonstrations of NATO solidarity reassuring.

H's Commanding Officer was an excellent tactician and a good trainer. H, who ran Rouse's Headquarters on exercises, was right at the centre of things and learnt a great deal from him. This was good preparation for his forthcoming Staff College Examination – the major competitive hurdle facing all regular officers in their early thirties. It involved detailed study in an officer's own time, long after most civilian contemporaries had completed their professional qualifications. Paradoxically, most of these officers' careers would end at fifty-five, a decade ahead of their civilian counterparts. It was hard, although not impossible, to reach high rank without attending Staff College, so success in the examination was a watershed. For H, preparation under Adrian Rouse's tutelage was a distinct benefit.

Another was the posting of the Devon and Dorsets in January 1970 to Malta, one of the Army's most attractive backwaters. This was a perfect place to study for the exam because, unlike BAOR, there were so few pressures on an adjutant's time. However, things seldom work out quite as expected, and the turn of events about to unfold was extraordinary.

The Devon and Dorsets settled down to enjoy a carefree first summer in Malta. The island was steeped in history, fine architecture and tradition. The work was undemanding and over by lunchtime; the sea was warm and very blue, the beaches clean and unspoilt – mass tourism was unknown. H and Sara lived in an attractive Army 'hiring' near Mosta, and there was an active social life built around the visit of Royal Navy ships.

Typically, H could either be spontaneously good fun among friends, or awkward, shy – even sullen – if he felt ill-at-ease attending some dreary social duty. On such occasions he would remain on the fringe of the gathering, seemingly tongue-tied, often nervously biting his finger-nails. In contrast when the atmosphere was right and he felt at ease, fortified with a stiff drink, he could be the life and soul of a party. The attractive young wife of a fellow officer described him as 'extremely good fun. Sometimes he would do or say outrageous things, as if attention seeking. I concluded he must have been starved of approval and love in his youth. He was physically attracted to pretty women, whilst always behaving properly towards them.'

The only shadow across an otherwise delightful posting was Dom Mintoff, the leader of Malta's opposition party, whose election manifesto pledged to remove from the island within a year the local NATO HQ and all British Forces, including the closure of the famous naval dockyard. It was a radical agenda designed to turn this George Cross island* into a non-aligned republic, and was largely stimulated by the proximity of Gaddafi's regime in Libya, plus

---

*Malta was awarded the George Cross for her resolve and bravery during the Second World War.

Mintoff's wish to break the influence of the Church. Mintoff faced bitter opposition, including that of many dockyard workers, and in any case the election was some way off, so those who cherished the island's links with Britain and the West optimistically believed that he would not get elected, and even if he did, they imagined he would not implement his pledges.*

The unexpected turn of events was not in Malta, however, but in Northern Ireland. By early 1970 the situation there had deteriorated in the wake of the Northern Ireland Civil Rights Association (NICRA) marches in Londonderry the previous summer. Disturbance and tension had risen throughout the Province and events were being watched closely in London, and in Dublin too. In Belfast, as spring turned to summer, ugly scenes of sporadic inter-communal rioting emerged. The burning and looting of Nationalist homes was attributed to the so-called 'Loyalist' paramilitary thugs based on the Shankill, an area of run-down shops and squalid houses near the centre of Belfast. It was followed, predictably, by retaliation against areas where Protestants were in the minority. What is now called ethnic cleansing was rife in a capital city of the United Kingdom, and the Labour Government in London was fast losing confidence in the ability of Stormont, the provincial, Protestant-dominated government, to handle the situation. Several batches of Army reinforcements had already been dispatched to support the hard-pressed Royal Ulster Constabulary – the B Special reservists had been disbanded in March – but still more soldiers were required.

As the 'Twelfth of July' approached, all available units in the United Kingdom had already been drafted into the Province. A hundred thousand Loyalists were expected to take part in this annual celebration commemorating the victory of the Protestant King William of Orange over the Catholic James II by raising the

---

*Mintoff was duly elected in June 1971 and the NATO HQ went by August; the withdrawal of British Forces was not far behind. He was re-elected in 1976 and again in 1981.

(*Above*) Loe Kann (1885–1944), Herbert Jones's first wife.

(*Above right*) H's grandfather David Benton Jones (1848–1923).

(*Right*) H's father, Herbert Jones (1888–1957), as a young man.

(*Below*) Pembroke Lodge, Lake Forest, Illinois. Herbert Jones's family home.

(*Above*) The view from The Grange across to Start Bay, Devon.

(*Right*) H at The Grange aged 12.

(*Below*) Family group. (*Left to right*) Herbert Jones, Bill, Tim, Dia, 'Jimmy' and H.

St. Peter's, Seaford

(*Above*) St Peter's, Seaford, Sussex, H's preparatory school.

(*Left*) Children's tea party just after the war. H with back to camera; his mother, Dia, stands by the fireplace.

(*Below*) H (*second from left*) with members of Brocklebank's in their Boating Colours.

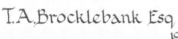

T.A. Brocklebank Esq —Boats Choices—

19 57

| N.D. Tinne | H. Jones | M.A.E Tennyson-d'Eyncourt | R.T Williams-Bulkeley | G.V Cooper |
| Prince of Wales | Alexandra | Victory | St George | Prince of Wales |

(*Above*) Regular Commissions Board, July 1958. H is number 25.

(*Below*) Alamein Company Intake 25 in front of Victory College at Sandhurst. H is seated front row second from right. Tony Marlow is standing centre in the boater, and H's friend Paddy Dunseath is directly behind Marlow.

(*Above*) Summer holidays afloat. Sara de Uphaugh (later to marry H) on *Duckling* with Tobin Duke, H's life-long friend, at the helm.

(*Right*) H in Cyprus as Orderly Officer wearing his monocle.

(*Right*) 2nd Lieutenant H Jones in Tropical Service Dress, Cyprus, 1960.

(*Below*) Sara and H at their wedding reception at Brockenhurst on 20 June 1964.

(*Top*) H racing his Bentley at
Oulton Park, 17 June 1967.

(*Above*) H at Whitehall Court
after his first win at Brands Hatch
in his Lotus Elan, March 1964.

(*Left*) H at the helm of *Romanel.*

(*Above*) Sara with Rupert (*left*) and David with The Grange in the background. 'Jimmy' is in the foreground.

(*Right*) H with David (*on his left*) and Rupert in Paphos, Cyprus during H's 1975 tour there.

(*Below*) H and Sara on *Romanel* leaving for the Spithead Review 1977 (David is standing in the cockpit).

siege of Londonderry in 1690. To the Loyalist Orange Order, their Province-wide marches were legal, licensed and represented an important tradition. To the Nationalist community, especially those living along the route, they were seen as a humiliation, a provocation and a threat. Little has changed over thirty years; this absurd 'exhibition' remains as alien and mystifying to the British Army as it is to television audiences at home and abroad.

In London the Ministry of Defence desperately sought further reinforcements, searching as far as Hong Kong for uncommitted units. In the end they found them in Malta. The United Kingdom, faced with an insurrection at home, was about to be reinforced from British garrisons abroad rather than the other way round. This in itself was unprecedented since the first months of the First World War.

The Devon and Dorsets were duly put on stand-by to deploy shortly before the Twelfth. But a weekend of rioting in mid June caused that to be brought forward, and they were now wanted as soon as possible. Emergencies always seem to occur over a weekend, and weekends in Malta for those off duty were spent on the beaches, or at sea. The British Forces Broadcasting Service put out recall broadcasts summoning soldiers back to camp, and H and others toured the island with megaphones making announcements wherever soldiers might be. British soldiers respond magnificently in a crisis, and the Devon and Dorsets duly arrived in the grey gloom of Belfast on 28 June, looking tanned and fit.

Those living in the Nationalist ghettos, particularly in the exposed Falls and Ardoyne, were initially delighted that the British Army was being interposed to protect them from their malign neighbours. But at heart they had little confidence in the durability of any arrangement that was ultimately in the hands of the distrusted Stormont government. So they took out an insurance policy with the IRA as guarantors of their protection. This gave the IRA standing – lost in the fifties and sixties – in the eyes of the Nationalist community, which was precisely what they needed to recover their credibility.

During the late afternoon of Friday 3 July, while the Devon and Dorsets were settling in to their new base in the vast Ulster Hall on the outskirts of the city, a platoon of another battalion, acting on a tip-off, discovered a mass of arms and ammunition in a house in the Catholic Lower Falls. This sparked spontaneous reaction. Angry crowds formed and buses were commandeered, overturned and set on fire as barricades. The soldiers, assailed by missiles and petrol bombs, were in danger of being encircled. Reserves were rushed in to extricate them, and as the full extent of the fury and intentions of the mob became clear, all units in Belfast were brought to immediate notice.

Within minutes the Devon and Dorsets were ordered to take up positions along the Grosvenor Road, one of the main arteries of the Falls. One company was launched against a mob at a key crossroads and similar actions began in surrounding streets. The aim initially was to restore free movement for the security forces, but resistance was violent and intensifying. Petrol bombs, grenades and missiles were hurled at the soldiers and sniping from upstairs windows began. The Battle of the Falls, as it became known, was under way, and relations between the Nationalist minority and the British Army – who went to Northern Ireland originally to protect the Catholics – would never again be the same.

With the Second-in-Command, H had been held in reserve at Battalion HQ in Ulster Hall. He was not pleased. A recently introduced infantry reorganisation, small in itself, decreed that each battalion should appoint a separate officer, an Operations Officer, to help the Commanding Officer run his command post. This had previously been the Adjutant's task, but it was reasoned with some justification that with the intensity of modern battle, he would be over-stretched.

H was furious when his new Commanding Officer, Lieutenant Colonel Douglas Lovejoy, implemented the measure. He fundamentally disagreed with the concept of transferring the most interesting and important part of his job to another man. So when Lovejoy took his Operations Officer, rather than H, along to

Brigade Headquarters to receive his orders, H seethed. His frustration and irritation might have blown over had events not escalated. But they did.

A showdown between the Army and the mob was now unavoidable. Brigadier Peter Hudson, who was responsible for all military operations in Belfast, could not accept that an area of the city should be denied to him. (An identical situation was later to have serious repercussions in Londonderry, when the security forces allowed the Bogside to become a 'no-go area'.) As resistance to the free movement of the security forces intensified, as casualties started to mount, and finally when snipers opened fire on his soldiers, the calm and able Brigadier Hudson acted, mounting a full cordon and search operation on the Falls, half a square mile of mean housing into which a thousand Catholic families were crammed. To accomplish this, twenty-seven company-sized sub-units under the command of six battalion HQs (in total around 3,500 men) were deployed into the area for three days.

This was no mean feat technically. H's redefined job was to assist the process, as it applied to the Devon and Dorsets, from a safe and secure Battalion Headquarters from where he could keep in touch with everyone involved, including Brigade Headquarters, and monitor progress at one remove from the events on the ground. Meanwhile his Commanding Officer was forward in his Tactical Headquarters (known as 'Tac'), sited where he could best see and hear what was happening.

Soon after Tac was established on the edge of the Falls Road, they came under sniper fire. At the time Lovejoy was in a telephone box talking to Brigadier Hudson (this was improvisation at its best, before mobile telephones) and the Operations Officer* was speaking to H on the radio. The sound of firing and rounds ricocheting off the kiosk could be heard over the radio. When H realised that Tac was under attack, he reacted in a way which no one present will forget.

---

*The author.

With him in Battalion Headquarters was Major Gerald Blight, the Second-in-Command, who was the Battalion's senior major and the Commanding Officer's deputy. It was he who would take over if anything happened to Lovejoy. Blight was a loyal regimental character and a down-to-earth officer of the old school. A veteran of Malaya, Borneo and Syria, he had fought with the Parachute Brigade at Suez. He was experienced, unflustered and unambitious. Already thirty-nine, he knew he would not get command of his Regiment, but he was proud and happy to be serving with them once again after a series of dull staff jobs. From the safety of Battalion Headquarters, Blight witnessed the chain of events that was about to unfold:

The 'First Eleven' all went off and I was left out of battle with H in the Ulster Hall. H sat listening to every wireless communication. Meanwhile, away from the constant cackle on the radio, I found a nice little niche where everybody knew I was if I was wanted.

All went well for a while until a message came in asking for something mundane, like more sandbags. H came to me and said, 'The Battalion needs sandbags and I must take them down.'

I said, 'Send a corporal with them. He has only got to go straight down the road and he can't get lost.' So H looked grumpy but did what he was told.

Then the telephone went again and this time it was something more serious, like a demand for flak jackets. H said they were so important that he would deliver them himself.

I said, 'Look H, I have explained this to you once, and I'll do it once more. You and I are left out of battle. This is our job. We are not skiving; we are here for various reasons, one of which is to remain uncommitted so that if anything goes wrong we can take over. Tomorrow we will go forward when the battle is over and the excitement has died down and the CO and Ops Officer are exhausted. We will then handle all complaints that will surely come that churches have been desecrated, schools ransacked and women raped. It will be up to us to sort out all the messy bits whilst the rest get their heads down. *That's* our job.'

H said, 'I don't think that's right.' And I retorted, 'OK, H, but that's it, I'm telling you; now leave it alone.' At that stage I turned in and went to sleep.

Suddenly I awoke to hear H shouting, 'The CO is being fired at – he's in a telephone box. I can hear the rounds ricocheting off it. I must go down there at once. You must get on to the CO' – he was almost ordering me – 'and tell him I should be sent for. I *must* get down there.'

By now fully awake, I was getting testy – very testy. I said, 'Shut up, H, I'm going back to bed. If you wake me once again I am going to put you in that store room and lock you in there until morning!' As I said this, I felt sorry for him because I had been on operations in Malaya and Borneo and been fired at in Suez, whereas H had not been in action before. He had missed out on all the little wars that had gone on, and he resented missing this small action too.[3]

Another officer put it more strongly: 'If H had been shot at properly when he was about twenty-two, and had earned himself an MC,* there would have been none of that.'[4]

Also present was the Regimental Signals Officer, Captain Paddy King-Fretts. He is adamant that the exchange was more highly charged than described, recalling an irritated Blight shouting: 'Go to fucking bed, H. Your turn will come sooner or later and you will either get killed or win the VC.'

Whichever version applied, there was nothing very terrible in it. It did not impede the ongoing operation and only a few signallers and clerks would have heard the exchanges. Blight handled it as an

---

*Military Cross.

exasperated father might upbraid a son who was being impetuous and tiresome. As he pointed out:

> I liked H and admired his ability. I loved his enthusiasm, and I could see in him a bit of what I would like to have been. I never had his intelligence or brains yet I knew that, although he used to imply that I was some old relic from the past, he was jealous, not of what I was, but of what I had done.[5]

The significance of this incident – and there were others similar to it – was that it created, among those who knew H well, an expectation of how he would react in such circumstances. Undoubtedly he was attracted to the sound of battle; danger was a stimulant and gunfire acted as a magnet. Historically this is not uncommon among soldiers. It was General Sir Garnet Wolseley, the great Victorian Commander-in-Chief of the British Army, who once declared:

> The first business of any ambitious young officer is to try and get himself killed . . . All other pleasures pale before the intense, the maddening delight of leading men into the midst of an enemy, or to the assault of some well defended place.[6]

This is one of the reasons why those who knew and understood H well were not surprised to learn, twelve years after this episode in Northern Ireland, that he had been killed in action, or the circumstances of it.

By the autumn of 1970, the Devon and Dorsets had returned to Malta after their peaks of exhilaration and troughs of boredom in Belfast. As Gerald Blight had predicted, a number of complaints arose from the 'Falls Road Curfew'. Two formal investigations were routinely convened, one by the Army's Special Investigation Branch and one by the Royal Ulster Constabulary. H, as Adjutant, was the interface between the Battalion and the investigators, but there were no complaints lodged against the Devon and Dorsets collectively or individually. The record showed that over 1,000 weapons, 21,000 rounds of ammunition and 250 explosives were found in the Falls over the thirty-four hours of the curfew (apart from a two-hour break on Sunday for Mass). Five civilians had been killed and sixty injured; fifteen soldiers were wounded.[7]

H now immersed himself in final preparation for the Staff College Exam, which he sat in Malta in December. Under a traditionally tough marking regime, candidates needed to average 50 per cent overall to pass, with no less than 40 per cent in any single paper – and there were eight of them. H obtained a very creditable 59.1 per cent overall, doing well in the three tactics papers, where he averaged 64 per cent, and in military law, where he obtained 76 per cent. Least successful was his current affairs paper, with 41 per cent – only just a pass – and the three-hour administration and morale paper, for which he was awarded 45 per cent.

Even though he had passed the qualifying exam, H now had to be 'nominated' to attend the Staff College. This additional selection process, which sometimes came a year or more after the exam, whittled the candidates down still further. Nominations were made first on the basis of confidential reports, particularly in respect of the long-term potential of a candidate; and secondly according to which part of the Army the candidate was in. There was a fixed allocation for infantry officers, for example, and as a rule of thumb only about one third of those eligible to sit the exam actually entered the Staff College.

To improve H's chance of selection, he was posted to a challenging captain's appointment at Wilton, then the Headquarters of Strategic Command, three miles outside Salisbury in Wiltshire. It meant another move for H and Sara, but this was a small price to pay for so good a job in such an attractive area.

His appointment was as a Grade 3 Staff Officer – the junior grade – in the operations and planning branch of that large Headquarters. It was a job he relished and for which he was well suited. One part of it involved the mundane process of preparing and updating contingency plans for operations around the world, and H, being quick and accurate on paper, soon mastered this. The other aspect, which he much preferred, was acting rather as a licensed 'ferret' in the Headquarters, penetrating dark and sleepy corners where work got bogged down, and nipping idle ankles.

His immediate boss was Major Richard Rockett of The Green Howards, a distinguished Yorkshire family regiment similar in outlook to the Devon and Dorsets. Richard, tall and upright, unflustered and conventional, enjoyed having a bit of a maverick on his team. He recalls that:

> H relished being at the centre of a crisis. At times he had to be restrained from taking charge of the whole business. More than once I had phone calls from other branches, asking me 'to control your young man'. Indeed, at one point I said to him, 'H, I'm getting confused about whether you are the Grade 2 officer, or I am!'[8]

However, in the mostly good-natured jousts with other staff branches, Rockett recalls that H was invariably in the right. He did not suffer fools gladly and he 'wrote off' those he considered to be 'grey men'. No one could ever accuse H of greyness. No opinion was expressed in pastel colours – his views were black or white. He never sat on fences, and none of his friends can ever recall him replying: 'It all depends' or 'I'll need to think about that' to any question posed. Rockett's memory of his thirty-year-old subordinate is clear:

> A cynic might describe him as an 'adrenaline junkie' with his zest for speed and his love of challenge. But from my own point of view, admiration and amused affection were the feelings he inspired in me most. His moral courage was as great as his physical courage, if not greater. He had all the qualities of a G A Henty hero, a Bulldog Drummond or a Richard Hannay. Without doubt, he would have distinguished himself equally well at Waterloo, Omdurman or Rorke's Drift.[9]

H did not have long to wait to learn of his nomination for the Army Staff College at Camberley. Unusually for a 'small' regiment (that is, a regiment having only one battalion), two others from the Devon and Dorsets were nominated too. On the one hand this indicated that they had talent in depth, but on the other, and of greater practical significance, it flagged up problems for future command. Those three officers, aged within three years of each other, could not all command the Devon and Dorsets, so as early as 1972, a future 'bulge' was evident – and with it, hard choices ahead.

The Army takes its command and staff training seriously. Staff deficiencies causing soldiers much unnecessary suffering were first properly recognised in the Crimea. At the instigation of Field Marshal HRH The Duke of Cambridge, then the Commander-in-Chief, the Army Staff College was established in 1858 to rectify the problem. Further impetus came from the mistakes of the Boer War, and staff training in the Army has been given a high priority ever since. Just off the A30 at Camberley in Surrey, the Staff College until recently* occupied an imposing Victorian building in large, attractive grounds shared with the Royal Military Academy Sandhurst. This was where H reported, in January 1973, for Army Staff Course 7.

For many of the 125 British students attending the year-long course it was their first reunion since they passed out of Sandhurst a decade or so before. Old acquaintances and friendships were renewed and the physical changes wrought by the passing years were noted with jocularity. Many a svelte twenty-year-old officer cadet had become a balding thirty-two-year-old captain with an expanding waistline, a wife and two children. Yet although reactions might not be quite as quick, heads were wiser; whereas ambitions were no longer so idealistic, they were better focused. After all these officers had invested heavily in time and effort to get to Camberley and they knew that only a step away a fast career escalator was waiting. Almost all the top generals of the twentieth century – Montgomery, Alanbrooke, Robertson, Slim – had passed this way,

---

*The Army Staff College, and the RN and RAF equivalents, have been incorporated into a Joint Service Staff College at Shrivenham in Wiltshire.

and Staff College unashamedly espoused excellence in all things.

The course lasted a year, excluding a preliminary military science course, and prepared students to assume greater responsibility both in command and on the staff.* The syllabus covered all the procedures and practices required of these officers, and included tactical doctrine and training. For example, exercises were set involving the notional deployment to, and maintenance of, a force in a distant undeveloped country. But most valuably, the course afforded the opportunity to explore ideas, widen horizons and assess priorities. Moreover, it was a year in which lasting friendships were made and networks formed.

Academically Camberley was hard work, with reams of paper to assimilate overnight in preparation for discussion in syndicate,† or for exercise the next day. But it was memorable socially. A vibrant community still in touch with their youth found themselves together for a whole year, free of external military commitments and without any routine responsibilities, except to themselves. The student body was strengthened by a handful of officers from the Royal Navy and Royal Air Force – H's brother Tim was one of the three RN representatives – and about forty allied and overseas students. Groups for golf, tennis, croquet and amateur dramatics thrived; parties – formal and informal – proliferated, and there was an annual ball.

H now turned to sailing for recreation. He and Tim had recently bought a Nicholson 35, *Romanel* (named after the title of one of their father's books of poetry), and as H became more experienced under Tim's expert hand, he sailed frequently along the South Coast, and across the Channel. His love of Devon and The Grange took him there regularly, and on occasion inspired poetry:

---

*The distinction is between command of soldiers in units and working in a staff job in a headquarters directing and serving those units.
†A group of about ten officers.

Off Berry Head

Summer in the Channel
The waves are sliding by,
Not one ship around us,
The sun is hot and high.

The spinnaker is flying,
It's white and blue and red,
The wind, alas, is dying,
It's almost like the Med.

My sweetest Sara's steering,
A wine glass in her hand;
David and Rupert peering,
But not a sight of land.

The sound that breaks the silence
Is only wind and sea;
The clatter of the halyards
The waves beneath our lee.

The perfect day is ending,
Look! High above the haze,
The Devon Coast is wending
The Landmark shows the way.

The Mew Stone slips beside us,
The main comes sliding down;
Newfoundland Cove has spied us,
And Points Field green and brown.

Our bow turns in to Mill Bay,
All eyes are on The Grange;

The jib slides down the forestay,
Our foghorn wakes the Range.

That's my idea of heaven,
A black dog on the shore,
Our boat, you three, and Devon.
How could I ask for more?

H was better prepared and suited for the Staff College than most students. He had just come from his demanding staff job at Wilton, where he had shone. He was quick to absorb the mass of précis and other papers that filled students' pigeonholes several times a day, and he was a widely experienced infantryman. However, he was unusually restless for someone on such firm ground and he seemed unable to sit back and relax, as almost everyone else did once they had the measure of the course.

His argumentative streak had free rein because there was plenty to argue about in syndicate discussions, but whereas most students would debate an issue up to a certain point, H, compelled to prevail, would flog it to death. Hints from his close friends that this was becoming tiresome were ignored.

Inevitably he caught the eye of the Directing Staff (DS). Lieutenant Colonel John Waters, who would one day become Commandant of the College,* and under whose command H would shortly serve, was one of them. According to Waters:

H was sufficiently unusual for all the DS to know who he was – which was itself uncommon. He was viewed as extremely ambitious and, in spite of having other members of his Regiment, as well as his brother, on the course, he was absolutely 'the cat that walked by himself'. It was as if he had erected around himself a carapace or an invisible electric shield. You could get so close but no closer, not that he was in any sense dour, unfriendly or hostile.[10]

---

*Retired as General Sir John Waters.

The officer who was the next rung up on the College's military ladder was H's Divisional Colonel, Bob Richardson, a craggy and measured Scot. His job was to assess and guide the sixty students in his Division. His reports were shrewd and candid – the more so because, unlike the usual annual report, they were 'unseen'. Of H he wrote:

> Jones began the Course just a little too enthusiastic and brash. As a result he tended, at the start, to overrun everything and everyone around him. He is intelligent with a quick and incisive mind but he is not an intellectual. He works hard, has an abundance of self-confidence and determination . . . but is not much liked outside a small circle of friends. Tact and charm do not come easily to him . . .
>
> He has tended to dominate each syndicate he has been in. In full spate he interrupts other speakers and is deaf to all counter argument. When checked he is genuinely contrite and makes a serious attempt, albeit of short duration, to mend his ways.

The highlight of each course was the legendary Battlefield Tour to Normandy, on which those who had fought, on both sides, described to students their experiences on D-Day and in the weeks following. One such guest speaker, to whom H and every student listened particularly intently, was Company Sergeant Major Stan Hollis VC, of the 6th Battalion, The Green Howards. His modest and moving account, delivered in a flat Yorkshire accent, of the two separate actions for which subsequently he was awarded the Victoria Cross – the only VC awarded on D-Day itself – was acknowledged as one of the year's most memorable experiences. Like many of the other distinguished speakers, including Colonel Hans Von Luck, formerly of the Panzer Grenadiers,* he described the confusion, fear, determination, exhilaration and sacrifice implicit in battle.

By the end of the tour vital lessons had been assimilated, some subliminally. First, that even the best-laid plans do not survive the

---

*He commanded the Panzer, Grenadier Regiment of 21st Panzer Division.

first shot of battle. Next, the eventual outcome is largely determined by the initiative and the actions – or inactions – of individuals or groups. Third, in good units the officers and senior non-commissioned officers always take a disproportionate share of the casualties.* The final lesson came directly from Hollis, although other speakers echoed it. When asked – as he always was – why he had undertaken such a seemingly suicidal assault on a German pill-box over open ground in broad daylight, he replied quietly and with humility: 'Because I was a Green Howard.'

That was all that needed to be said. His audience understood at once that CSM Hollis's instinctive loyalty to his Regiment, and to all those wearing his cap-badge, meant that any lesser action would have been unthinkable at that moment. This was *esprit de corps*: the most powerful ingredient of the regimental system which was, and still is, despite many recent changes, the cornerstone of the British Army.

The Battlefield Tour experience made a profound impact on H. On the way home – he sailed both ways in *Romanel* – he discussed and analysed earnestly all he had seen and heard with his friend and crew, Paddy King-Fretts. Paddy, a fellow Devon and Dorset student, who had done a tour with the SAS when H was serving with 3 Para, remembers waiting in Braye Harbour in Alderney for the tide to turn, pondering at length with H the actions of men like Hollis when under fire. They concluded that there were moments when the pendulum of battle can be swung decisively one way or the other by an individual determined enough to exert his influence on events.

After the tour, and summer leave, students handed in their offerings for Commandant's Essay – a military dissertation. H won the prize. Then followed the simulated indoor exercises termed 'telephone battles'. These were testing occasions, partly because of the realism of the battles (they were fore-runners of today's battle simulators) and partly because the students realised they were being

---

*Between D-Day and D+34 twelve of 50th Division's Infantry COs had become casualties – an attrition rate of 133% as some were already replacement COs.

assessed for appointments after graduation. There were about a dozen key posts each year for the ablest officers, and these carried considerable prestige, so H was determined to shine. His best opportunity came when he was nominated the exercise 'Corps Commander' – a notional Lieutenant-General and the most senior appointment on the exercise. He wound himself into a frenzy in the preparatory phase and Tony Holt, his 'Commander, Corps Royal Artillery', remembers him being 'unnecessarily cross' with a number of fellow students who were not taking the exercise as seriously as he was. Like some highly strung prima donna, H was thoroughly tiresome backstage before the opening night, but emerged coolly efficient and impressive once the event began. His ability, never in doubt, was demonstrated to a wide audience, although his excitability and driving ambition were also widely noted.

Most Staff College students had healthy ambitions – certainly the able ones had their sights set high – so H was no exception, except that his aspirations were much more transparent. In the Services, the team comes first and the individual second; hence naked ambition is viewed with suspicion. A fair appraisal would be that H, while undoubtedly gifted, often appeared too keen and overbearing. All this was reflected in his final report, in which Colonel Richardson graded him B: Well Above Average. (Few students earned Bs and none was graded A that year.) Richardson concluded:

> Jones is a young man of considerable potential. His failings are obvious but they are outweighed by his many virtues and obvious ability. He and I have talked about his arrogance and tendency to ride roughshod over others. I think he realises that there may be times when he could have difficulty in getting the best out of people.[11]

The popular and highly respected Commandant, Major-General Pat Howard-Dobson (who needed no lessons about competitiveness, especially on the sports field or croquet lawn), endorsed what Richardson had written and recommended H for a brigade major's appointment – the *crème de la crème* of all post-Staff College jobs.

Twelve years previously, H had been an awkward officer cadet lucky to be commissioned into a good regiment. Now he was emerging from Camberley on the crest of a wave. He had exceeded the expectations of all those who knew him at Sandhurst and in his early years in the Army. Certainly he had had some luck – although no more than most of his contemporaries – but that alone did not account for his progress. He was a late developer, and certain regiments are good at identifying latent talent and nurturing it under careful leadership. The fact that H had been allowed the luxury to develop in his own time and mature in the warm atmosphere of his Regiment was arguably his best piece of luck – and the Devon and Dorsets' skill.

Now, having already completed one staff job, he was to return to 'regimental duty'. He would go back to a battalion for two years as a company commander; but with which battalion? He was eligible to return either to the Devon and Dorsets, or to a battalion of the Parachute Regiment. He applied for the latter. Why he was reluctant to return to his own Regiment is not clear. Perhaps he could see ahead the blockage for future command in the Devon and Dorsets, or perhaps he simply wanted more of a challenge than he thought they could offer; at the time the Devon and Dorsets were in a potentially humdrum Home Defence role based at Gillingham in Kent and, not knowing the Commanding Officer, he felt no obligation to return.

Whatever the reason, his decision did not create a good impression, because he appeared unduly manipulative – even selfish – at a time when his Regiment needed him. Not for the first time, his preferences were overridden, and he was posted back to the Devon and Dorsets in Gillingham. As it turned out, however, the next couple of years were to be far from humdrum. His future was about to be shaped decisively.

CHAPTER EIGHT

The Watershed

The rank of major covers a wide spectrum of age and ability. Some struggle to reach it and will then spend the next twenty years there before retiring on a modest pension. Others – the ablest young Staff College graduates such as H – will be majors for perhaps six or seven years before sweeping onwards and upwards. These fast-track officers are kept under discreet scrutiny, not only in their relation to current jobs, at which it is anticipated they will excel, but also with their possible next appointments in mind.

A major commands a company (or the equivalent squadron or battery)* of around 120 men. A company commander has considerable responsibility and authority; he is normally in immediate charge of three platoons, and is answerable for everything that happens in them. He has certain summary powers of jurisdiction over his soldiers, each of whom he must know well. His is the smallest sub-unit that can fight independently for any length of time, and even then it needs the support of other elements to do so successfully.

The company commander's relationship with his commanding officer, and vice versa, is crucial. The CO should exercise his command through his company commanders, however tempting it may be to short-circuit the system and take personal control

---

*Batteries are artillery sub-units; squadrons are Royal Armoured Corps sub-units, and some logistic sub-units.

whenever a problem arises. COs can – and sometimes do – do this, but other than as an exception it leads to muddle, duplication of effort and loss of confidence.

The normal tour for a company commander is two years, and during his time H was to have three different commanding officers, two of whose patience he was to try. When he returned to regimental duty, the 1st Battalion, The Devonshire and Dorset Regiment was based at Gillingham, one of the Medway towns in Kent. Regardless of where the Battalion went, the families remained in Army married quarters there; and with the children now at school, Sara hoped for a little stability.

The boys were at an interesting age. Not content merely to let nature take its course, H actively encouraged their development, stimulating their young minds and treating them almost as adults. On one occasion H had David attend one of his company conferences, taking notes as if he were a platoon commander. David had just started at his preparatory school – following H to St Peter's – and Rupert, aged five, attended a local day school.

These were but fleeting moments together, because in 1974–5 the peripatetic life of infantry battalions – endemic now – was just beginning. It was the start of a hitherto unprecedented period of Army turbulence in peacetime, and the attendant separation hit the Devon and Dorsets and their families hard. (In those days there was little recognition of the complex problems arising from enforced separation, and support from a proper Unit Families organisation was rudimentary.)

When H and Sara arrived in Gillingham from Camberley, the Battalion was back in Northern Ireland and halfway through another emergency tour – their third in as many years. H was at once dispatched to take over Support Company.* His area of responsibility was the Turf Lodge enclave of Andersonstown, another Catholic ghetto of, at the time, run-down housing, high

---

*Normally of mortar, anti-tank and other support platoons used as an extra rifle company in Northern Ireland.

unemployment and incipient discontent. On arrival, he found that Colin Walters, his old Platoon Sergeant and friend from his tour in Canada ten years before, was now his Company Quartermaster Sergeant. This is one of the attractions and strengths of the regimental system: H found old friends in the Warrant Officers' and Sergeants' Mess, and elsewhere in the Battalion, to welcome him. Many of them had recently been promoted, as had he. They knew him and understood his ways; former relationships were soon re-established and adjustments made to suit his style.

H's reputation had preceded him, and he quickly stamped his mark on his new Company. His Second-in-Command was a young captain called David Shaw. Unruffled, loyal and super-efficient, Shaw was a most conscientious subordinate. He can still recall the adjustment that was necessary.

On the first night of H's new command, all was quiet, and he went to bed at midnight. An hour later a body – a victim of paramilitary execution – was found in the open at Milltown Cemetery. Shaw instigated the usual checks to ensure it was not booby-trapped, then called the police and other agencies which, under the protection of the Army, dealt with the formalities. It was all horribly routine for Belfast, and the incident was quickly sorted out. Under H's predecessor, Shaw had been used to dealing with such events on his own, but thoughtfully he remained on duty until 0730 to talk the night's activities through with his new Company Commander.

H listened intently to every word of the patrol debriefing. At its conclusion he offered no comment other than to thank the soldiers present. He then indicated to Shaw the privacy of his office next door, and a one-sided conversation ensued: 'David, I am the Company Commander here. This was a serious event in the area for which I am responsible. I expect to be informed of all such incidents and I will be the one who decides whether they warrant my attention or not. Do you understand?' Shaw replied that he did. 'Fine,' said H. 'Well done; now let's go and have breakfast.'

On a more personal level, late one evening H called Shaw aside and conspiratorially told him that if he was to be called out in the middle of the night, he was to be given as much notice as possible. Shaw was puzzled: this hardly needed saying, since the only reason for getting anyone out of bed fast was that something unexpected had occurred. When he asked for elucidation, H confided that he was wearing a new set of contact lenses and it was taking him about five minutes to get them in properly. Without them he was blind and useless, but he was not going to admit this to anyone else, as he was anxious never to be seen wearing the glasses he hated. His monocle had long since been discarded as impractical.

H's tour in Belfast was short and, in a period of relative calm before the collapse at the end of May 1974 of the Power Sharing Executive brokered in the Sunningdale Agreement, historically uneventful. But no sooner was he back in Gillingham with Sara and the children than the Battalion were off to Kenya on a training exercise. It was here that the high regard H's soldiers had for him gave expression. One of them, Corporal Stan Underwood, a massively built Plymothian, and one of the Battalion's more popular and engaging characters, remembers H devising the most realistic exercise on which he had ever been.

H's Company were in a tented camp in northern Kenya preparing for a live firing exercise.* Suddenly one of the signallers rushed out of the command post shouting for Major Jones, who was wanted immediately on the radio. H, having been found, re-emerged looking anxious yet purposeful. He gathered his Company quickly around him and said: 'I have just heard that ten thousand Somalians have crossed the border into Kenya and are heading this way in civilian trucks. We have been ordered to delay them right here until the rest of the Battalion arrive. They're on their way, so prepare defensive positions now!'

Corporal Underwood and Support Company were galvanised into immediate action, and under their platoon commanders

*An advanced training exercise on which live ammunition is fired on an open range, as opposed to on an enclosed one.

gathered their weapons and as much ammunition as possible and hastily dug interlocking trenches covering the road. After about an hour the dust of several trucks appeared in the distance and Underwood remembers thinking: 'This is it!' Final orders were shouted, arcs of fire and range cards checked, and they waited until the trucks closed up. Just as Corporal Underwood was about to open fire, the RSM appeared at his side, as if from nowhere, and ordered him to unload, explaining that he was an umpire arranged by Major Jones and that the whole episode was preliminary preparation for the field firing proper which was about to follow. As Corporal Underwood later confessed: 'H had successfully fooled us all. It was brilliantly realistic and it motivated us more than any other exercise I remember.'

Underwood's response was typical. Although H was shortly to run up against superiors, his soldiers never had any doubts about his commitment and professionalism. Even those he found dull and unresponsive – and he could be casually dismissive of weak links – knew that he had their best interests at heart. Soldiers will sometimes say they would follow a certain officer anywhere, even, some add, if only out of curiosity. It is far more unusual to hear the compliment: 'I know that officer would do *anything* to help me if I had a problem.' But that was the reputation H had amongst his own men.

By early 1975, the Devon and Dorsets were on the move again. Following the Turkish invasion of Cyprus, they were unexpectedly sent there on a six-month unaccompanied tour, to protect the Eastern Sovereign Base Area (SBA) at Dhekelia. H was now commanding B Company, one of the Battalion's three rifle companies, and a new commanding officer had arrived.

Lieutenant Colonel Colin Shortis was a dynamo of a man, eclipsing even H for sheer energy and sense of purpose. He was greatly honoured to find himself in command of his Regiment, and devoted the next two and a half years exclusively to it. Initially, until everyone got used to a very different regime, this did not make for a particularly comfortable time. Cobwebs were blown away, compulsory early morning runs were instituted – even for a shocked Quartermaster and his staff – and every soldier in the Battalion was kept on his toes. Within a short time a fitter and more alert unit did not exist in the Army.

Although neither probably appreciated it – much less admitted it – Colin Shortis and H were temperamentally similar. Both were highly professional, energetic, argumentative and unconventional. Perhaps each had a degree of insecurity or uncertainty buried deep in his psyche, obscured by an apparent firmness of resolve and clarity of purpose. Whatever their make-up and chemistry, they could have disliked each other profoundly but, thanks mainly to Shortis's deft handling of his subordinate, they did not. Equally, H could not fail to admire a superior every bit as dedicated as himself. However, none of this prevented him expressing his irritation with his new Commanding Officer in his letters home to Sara: 'Over dinner the CO and I disagreed violently yet again; I sometimes wonder if we can agree about anything . . .' And three weeks later: 'The CO is being as bloody as ever – I got a bollocking this afternoon about the Mess.* Ah, well, can't be helped, and I am sure mortification is good for the soul!'

H in turn must have tried Colin Shortis's patience sorely. On one occasion, for example, as PMC and de facto host, he opened his briefing for an official Beating Retreat and cocktail party by declaring: 'Let's face it, this whole thing is going to be an indescribable fucking bore!' As he later reported to Sara: 'The poor CO nearly died of shock.'

The truth was that H had almost complete disregard for the usual Army conventions of loyalty, whereby subordinates support and carry out the lawful orders of their superiors as if they were their own. However, there was no denying that sometimes he achieved remarkable results his way. One day, all companies were ordered to

*H had been appointed President of the Officers' Mess Committee (PMC) and was hence responsible for its smooth running.

erect a barbed-wire barrier in front of their sector of the Sovereign Base Area perimeter. H did not think this at all a good idea and remonstrated with Colin Shortis. Losing his argument, he returned to brief his soldiers.

'The CO has had one of his crazy ideas,' he said openly. 'He has told us to put up a bloody stupid fence between us and the Turks. It's ridiculous. But as we are B Company and the best, our fence had better go up quicker and higher than the others. Now, let's get cracking!' It worked. His soldiers went at it furiously and B Company's sector was erected well before the rest. Somehow, H could get away with it; time and again his superiors would turn a blind eye to his idiosyncratic ways. Shortis, practical and shrewd, observed:

> I would put it like this. H had a very personal leadership style which made him bond with whoever he was commanding, and they with him, by saying: 'We are the only people who can do this.' This by definition rather implied that everyone else was hopeless and there were idiots up there giving the orders. But he did not see that. He could not admit it was disloyalty – which it was. But I felt H's positive qualities far outweighed that and, anyway, I was well enough established in command not to worry unduly.

What concerned Lieutenant Colonel Shortis more was H's tendency to be dismissive of people, and casually thoughtless sometimes to those he felt did not matter. Often this was due simply to his inherent social awkwardness and dislike of small talk; but generally people are not readily prepared to accept that excuse in a thirty-five-year-old officer, and it caused unnecessary affront, often to H's own detriment.

During the long and largely tedious months in Cyprus, H felt keenly the enforced separation from his family. He resented not being with the boys, particularly for their holidays. Just before Easter, he wrote to Sara:

Thinking about you and David and Rupert off skiing together really depresses me. One really is hostage to fortune if you love people, aren't you? Life really is hardly worth living without you. I do hope you all enjoy yourselves. I'm sure you will if you set out to; but don't be silly and stint yourself over money, will you? Or the boys. You all deserve something nice for having to go off on your own.

Unaccompanied tours can cause problems even in stable marriages. One was apparent in another of H's letters home to Sara. It seemed that Sara had had an unusual and disturbing dream, such as can occur when husbands are away for months at a time. She told H she had dreamed he had met and gone off with someone else. In reality nothing could have been less likely, as H was strictly faithful, and he responded:

Poor darling having such a horrid dream. You needn't worry though, as you very well know – you're the only girl I love, and you always will be. I'm not the sort of person to get involved with anyone else – my dislike of socialising isn't only shyness, I'm also very much aware that discretion is the better part of valour, and that chatting up birds . . . can do me no good whatever, and could easily do harm. So don't worry! This quite apart from the fact that there's no one on this poxy island who's a patch on you in any way; but even if there were, it wouldn't make any difference. I made my choice nearly 15 years ago, and I won't be changing it now!

Guarding the Sovereign Base Area was not very stimulating, and neither was keeping the Greeks and Turks apart. However, occasionally there would be the odd highlight for H to write home about, as he did on 15 April 1975:

On Sunday, there's this damned 'Women's March Home' to Famagusta; apparently it's to be 100,000 Greek women led by

Jane Fonda and Vanessa Redgrave protesting about the Turkish occupation of Famagusta. We're not sure yet what effect they'll have on us, as they are not supposed to come into our part of the SBA. Still we'll see, it could easily be a major nausea as the Turks have said they'll treat them just like men and that nobody will be allowed past the wire.

It must have passed off peacefully as no more was heard of it, and anyway the Battalion's tour in Cyprus was nearly over.

Within months of H's return to Gillingham, however, another overseas emergency blew up, in British Honduras (later Belize), where A and B Companies of the Devon and Dorsets were flown in the autumn of 1975. Their mission was to reinforce the infantry battalion already there – the 'Glorious Glosters' of Korean fame, and a valued sister West Country regiment.

Commanding the Glosters was Lieutenant Colonel John Waters, one of the Directing Staff at Camberley, who remembered H clearly from his days there. He was delighted at the arrival of his reinforcements, as he had a predicament. Two months into the Glosters' tour, Guatemala, to the south and west, whose animosity towards Belize went back a hundred years to a dispute over boundaries and a road, had become increasingly belligerent towards her neighbour. Further, Guatemala boasted a large conscript army of many thousands, including a parachute capability, and there were indications that she was about to invade Belize. This had not been anticipated by the Foreign Office or the Ministry of Defence, and Waters recalls that 'Something not far short of panic ensued.'[1]

In response, a large number of reinforcements arrived – Harrier jump jets, helicopters, air defence assets and a frigate, as well as the two companies of Devon and Dorsets, who flew in direct from England in lumbering Hercules aircraft. To prevent incursions, the Glosters had already been positioned on the border, so John Waters immediately sent one of the reinforcing companies to Belmopan, the capital, to protect the seat of government and provide a force reserve. He ordered the other, B Company, under H, to secure Belize

International Airfield against what seemed the most likely threat – *a coup-de-main* operation to seize it.

Waters recalls H's arrival:

> He came out of the aeroplane looking as if he wished personally to shoot somebody on the runway immediately! Within a very short time he realised, quite rightly, that he had arrived in a place not geared up, mentally or physically, to fight a war, although there were masses of plans in all directions. Those responsible for them, he felt, had clearly never seen a shot fired in anger, and never wished to do so. H made his disdain immediately and totally apparent.

Indeed, during the next few days H managed to upset the Force Commander (a full colonel who was in overall command), the Senior Royal Air Force officer, the High Commissioner, the airport manager – and almost everybody else he met. However, his new Commanding Officer could see that what H was saying was logical and extremely sensible, although the manner in which he was saying it was not. He explained:

> H was urging upon all these worthies plans which he considered to be appropriate in the worst case to defend the airport against any eventuality. But what went wrong was the manner in which he presented his case and his obvious disdain – even contempt – for people who pointed out, inevitably, that his proposal was going to inconvenience seriously the day-to-day users of the airport.

This was not an easy situation for even the able Waters to handle. On the one hand he knew operationally that H was correct, and he was mightily relieved to have a no-nonsense infantryman on the airfield for what could be an ugly situation if the Guatemalans tried to seize it. On the other, Waters had three vulnerable companies of his own up on the border and he could not afford to be distracted by having to smooth feathers that H was ruffling further back. Additionally, having soldiers from another cap-badge under command is never easy when their leader is being awkward. So it was hardly surprising that Lieutenant Colonel Waters viewed H's presence as a mixed blessing.

Seen through H's eyes, his soldiers had drawn the short straw. They were protecting the airfield, yet those who lived and worked there would not address the situation seriously. Furthermore, the sight of off-duty RAF aircrew splashing about in the swimming pool while his soldiers dug trenches around them in the sticky heat infuriated him.

Throughout his service, H's neuralgia point was his soldiers' welfare. If he felt they were being misused or unfairly treated, he would react sharply – some would say overreact. Here he had no redress to hand, although Waters himself spent hours with him trying to alleviate the situation. For a man who liked a tight, obedient ship, Waters was extremely patient with H – indeed, his own officers marvelled at his tolerance. Ultimately, however, the hard truth could not be avoided. B Company had been ordered to do a vital job and H must now accept the situation and get on with it, or he would be relieved of his command.

In the middle of this unhappy situation Brigadier John Randle – H's Commanding Officer at the time of his wedding – arrived in Belize. Randle was now Commander Overseas Detachments at Headquarters, United Kingdom Land Forces, at Wilton. His agreeable duty was to fly round the world on the Commander-in-Chief's behalf, checking that British soldiers in the Command's farthest outposts were properly administered, trained and led. His anticipation of a relaxing few days in Belize was to be disappointed.

The Force Commander, Colonel Duncan Green MC, and the Glosters' CO met him off the aircraft, and Randle soon sensed that all was not well. He recalls Green telling him in no uncertain terms:

This chap Jones, in your Regiment, is being a bloody nuisance, moaning and groaning and generally being disloyal. He is causing a lot of difficulty here, and it's being widely commented upon by the RAF and everybody else. The situation is adversely affecting morale, and so I do hope you can sort it out.[2]

The reminder that John Randle and H were in the same Regiment was felicitous. When perhaps all other avenues have been exhausted, the regimental system can almost always be relied upon to sort out problems informally – which was what now happened.

In private, over a drink, Randle made it clear to H that he was jeopardising the Regiment's fine reputation for co-operation and making things work, whatever the difficulties. H in turn made the point that he thought B Company were getting a raw deal and that if he, as Company Commander, did not stand up for them – which Randle as a good regimental officer would, of course, understand – who else could? After half an hour, the air had been cleared and H felt that at last he had got everything satisfactorily off his chest.

But it was not the end of the story. The Guatemalan threat soon subsided and so the infantry reinforcements could be released. Both A Company, who had not put a foot wrong throughout the tour, and B Company were flown home. H's prestigious new appointment as Brigade Major of 3 Infantry Brigade in Northern Ireland was promulgated, and after Christmas he handed over his Company and moved to the Province. No reference to his Belize tour was entered in his confidential report book, where a gap is shown from 20 August to 31 December 1975. Officially it was as if he had never been in Belize.

Whether this was by accident or design is not clear. In one sense it hardly mattered, because there was never any doubt that H would command a battalion – a man of his ability obviously would. But in another it did, as H had now jeopardised, at least in John Randle's eyes, his prospects for command of his own Regiment.

The Devon and Dorsets were in a fortunate position regarding future commanding officers. They had three aspiring ones to cover the period 1980–5, when only two would be required. In the parlance of the Military Secretary's Branch* – the arbiter of such things – one of the three would have to be 'offered' elsewhere. The senior of them was fifteen months older than H† and had already been pencilled in for command first – for two and a half years from late 1979. This left either H, or a younger brother officer, Major Paddy King-Fretts, to fill the next vacancy, in mid 1982. A decision on the 'regimental choice' would be required by 1980 at the latest, so an internal debate amongst a select few senior Devon and Dorsets began shortly after H took over B Company, and continued sporadically but with increasing seriousness over the next five years.

The regimental choice rested with the Colonel of the Regiment, John Archer, now a Major-General and shortly to be Commander British Forces in Hong Kong. He consulted John Randle, as Acting Colonel of the Regiment whilst Archer was abroad; and Colin Shortis, H's Commanding Officer. Their principal concern was what would be best for the Regiment in both the short and long term, and this included the effect of their choice on the whole regimental family, including wives.

John Archer had had H as one of his company subalterns fifteen years previously, and he knew Paddy socially but not professionally, except by repute. John Randle knew both H and Paddy well, as they had both been subalterns under him. Colin Shortis, on the other hand, knew H extremely well, but not Paddy latterly.

The difficult debate continued, but the clock was ticking and eventually a decision would have to be made. For one of the candidates it would be unpalatable, as every serious regimental officer's keenest wish is to command his own regiment. Furthermore, Paddy's father had served with distinction in the Dorsets at Kohima during the war, and continuity is instinctively valued in family regiments. Meanwhile, anticipating a blockage in the Devon

---

*The Military Secretary, then a three-star general, was responsible to the Defence Secretary for the selection for promotion of all officers above the rank of major, and for the proper management of their careers.
†The author.

and Dorsets for at least one talented officer, the SAS and another regiment put out feelers about King-Fretts's availability. The Parachute Regiment followed suit with regard to H's.

Against this background, Brigadier Randle's visit to Belize was timely and significant. With typical honesty, Randle recorded what happened next.

> I left Belize with an impression lodged in my mind that, whatever the rights and wrongs may have been, there were question marks over H's judgement. Now, if you project that forward to a commanding officer in that position – being awkward and not accepting orders – it could do a battalion untold harm. So, when asked for my advice, that was what I said.[3]

Lieutenant Colonel Shortis's advice was the opposite, yet it was consistent with the confidential report he had written on H in Cyprus: 'Overall Major Jones has had a most successful year . . . He is an officer of high calibre who I strongly recommend for promotion and for command of a regular infantry battalion . . . now.' Confidential reports often contain coded messages, and there was one here. An infantry battalion technically is distinct from an airborne battalion. So Lieutenant Colonel Shortis was recording formally that he believed H should not command a parachute battalion but, by implication, the Devon and Dorsets. He had made this view clear whenever he was asked, and so he was not just hiding behind the esoteric conventions of confidential report writing. He felt strongly that H, supported so admirably by Sara, would be the right choice for future command of the Devon and Dorsets, and better than any alternative.

H was unaware that this discreet debate was going on, although he and King-Fretts had long known the matter would have to be concluded one day. Right now he was far more concerned with his new job.

A brigade major (or BM) is to his brigade commander as an adjutant is to a commanding officer, but on a higher level and broader canvas. The strong personal relationship and trust between the two is just as important. The main difference is that a brigade headquarters has integral staff branches, which include intelligence, operations and administration. A brigade major's principal role is to translate his commander's policy and orders into co-ordinated action and direction by the staff. In a good headquarters, staff officers remember that they are there ultimately to serve the interests of the soldiers and the units on the ground, not the other way round. H never let his headquarters forget it.

HQ 3 Infantry Brigade, then based in Lurgan,* in County Down, was responsible for all military operations in County Armagh and County Fermanagh, as well as most of County Down and County Tyrone. It was the largest of the Tactical Areas of Responsibility (or TAORs) and arguably the most difficult to manage because it took in almost all of the border with the Republic of Ireland.

The very existence of the border is a bone of contention with the Nationalist communities. On Partition in 1922, what had previously been just a county boundary became an international frontier. Republicans who involuntarily found themselves in the newly formed Northern Ireland refused to recognise the border or give allegiance to the state. To complicate matters, the border (of over 210 miles) divides villages, parishes, farms and in some cases buildings. Intersected by a network of roads leading to the Irish Republic, it makes no sort of military sense. However, to many Ulstermen, particularly in the seventies, it became an important symbol giving substance to the Union and defining the geographical and political entity of Great Britain and Northern Ireland.

A side effect of Partition was the development of a major smuggling industry that in turn developed guile and native cunning, priceless advantages to the terrorist. Smuggling and racketeering became endemic, even entering folklore in part of an old Irish ballad:

---

*It moved to a newly constructed Mahon Barracks, in Portadown shortly after H arrived.

> From Carrickmacross to Crossmaglen
> There are more rogues than honest men.

Many Unionists consider that most of the people living along that part of the border are traditionally lawless and violent simply because the authorities have never consistently pursued tough law enforcement, including the physical closure of what they refer to as the 'frontier'. As so often in Ireland, the argument is never settled.

Into this cauldron of opposing views – often held at the highest levels – came H and his family after Christmas 1975. They took over a modern four-bedroom quarter in Bocombra, a small protected Army housing estate outside Portadown. When they had unpacked all their belongings, H promptly knocked a hole through into the roof space upstairs and set up the children's model train set. In truth, he enjoyed playing with it even more than they did.

He tackled his work with equal gusto. A number of talented young staff officers were already there, eager to work for a new brigade major with his wits about him. Captain The Hon. Philip Sidney* of the Grenadier Guards was the desk officer responsible for operations and plans, and Captain Martin Edwards of the Royal Regiment of Fusiliers was the GSO3 Ops/Air.† They were attracted at once to H's commitment, his direct approach and his willingness to listen. The latter was almost the exact opposite of the impression he had created only weeks before in Belize. Both men remember that he was right on top of his job. He was quick and thorough, his in-tray was cleared effortlessly and his office was always tidy. They recall too that, although H did most of the written work himself, he always invited their input and gave them encouragement and credit. Others would pick the brains of their subordinates and serve up the ideas as their own.

H's first boss, Brigadier David Anderson, was also delighted with

---

*Then heir to Viscount De L'Isle VC KG; and now succeeded to the peerage.
†The General Staff Officer Grade 3 dealing principally with operations relating to helicopters and flying.

his new Brigade Major. He found him particularly good at getting round the units of the Brigade – the turnover was rapid as battalions came and went, with over 24,000 men passing through the Brigade in his two years. H also regularly joined patrols, even in the most exposed areas.

Relations with the Royal Ulster Constabulary were just as important as good military relationships within the Brigade. In early 1976 'Police Primacy'* had not yet been established, and the Army led on all counter-terrorist matters. This was shortly to change and when it did, the ramifications of that decision were to last for at least two decades. However, this was a policy matter well above H's level; he simply went ahead and established excellent relations with the brave RUC officers in 3 Brigade's area, as the only sensible working arrangement. Thus it is not surprising that he is still well remembered by policemen such as Michael McAtamney,† then Chief Superintendent of H Division, based on Newry, as a man of boundless energy and deep commitment.

A brigade major's day starts early. First, the overnight situation reports (sitreps) from units need to be compiled, absorbed and dispatched to Headquarters Northern Ireland (HQ NI), 3 Brigade's superior headquarters, at Lisburn, outside Belfast. Here they digested the sitreps from across the Province before signalling a consolidated summary to hundreds of addressees around the world. This was how appropriate ministers, ambassadors and military Commanders were routinely updated on the previous day's events.

Next, at 0800, was 'morning prayers', at which the Brigade Commander and the heads of each staff branch were briefed on the past twenty-four hours' activity, and what was in prospect for the day. Then came the co-ordination of visits to and from the HQ. There was seldom a day without a visit from some senior visitor or

---

*The term given to the concept of returning the lead in counter-terrorism to the RUC.

†The popular and much-respected McAtamney became the senior Roman Catholic in the RUC, rising to be the Deputy Chief Constable.

other. Some scoffed at what they termed time-consuming 'military tourism', but not H. He could see the importance of ensuring that the people who had to make the decisions were fully in the picture, be they from HQ NI, from Stormont – from where direct rule, imposed in 1972, was exercised – or from Whitehall. He saw it as particularly important to ensure that senior visitors left reassured that the increasing number of soldiers being sucked into the border area were being used to good effect. Meanwhile, H's profile and reputation were enhanced by his impressive briefings.

Superimposed on everything were 'incidents' both major and minor which would come without warning or pattern. Brigade HQ would monitor each unfolding situation and ensure that the units in the area had the necessary resources to cope. Even before H had been there a week, two particularly unpleasant events occurred. On 4 January 1976 Loyalist terrorists burst into a house at Whitecross in County Armagh and opened fire on the occupants, killing two brothers and wounding a third, who died later in hospital. The next day, in retaliation, ten Protestant workers were ambushed outside the small town of Newton Hamilton on the County Armagh border and murdered in their minibus.

This atrocity became known as the 'Kingsmills Massacre'. As the facts emerged – and they never did quickly – the outrage became intense both locally and nationally. In no time the political temperature was at boiling point. Demands came for the closure of the border – the assailants clearly had crossed it and fled back to the Republic after their murderous attack. Calls followed for more soldiers to be drafted in, especially the SAS, and for internment to be re-introduced – it had only been suspended the previous month. Finally, there were the usual demands for ministers' resignations.

The operational brunt of all this was borne by HQ 3 Brigade, and within it by H. He relished it. To him responsibility and challenge were stimulating, and now at last he was at the centre of things, holding all the cards, and the initiative. No more was he reacting to the judgements and decisions of others with whom he often felt at odds. Both of the brigadiers he served as BM during his tour approved wholeheartedly of H's positive approach. The second, Brigadier David Woodford, who ran H on a loose rein, remembers: 'I barely had to hint at something and he'd set about it in exactly the right way. I may add that he *never* overstepped the mark, or misused my authority, although he knew he had my complete trust and confidence.'[4]

Always at the top of H's in-tray would be initiatives to improve intelligence-gathering along the South Armagh border, using both human resources and technical means. It is a fundamental tenet of British military doctrine that all counter-terrorist operations should be based on intelligence. In its absence, operations must be instigated to increase the flow of information which, when analysed, provides the straw to make the bricks of future intelligence. Thrashing around to no good purpose in an area in which the Army is not welcome is counter-productive and to be avoided.

Two days after the Kingsmills Massacre, Prime Minister Harold Wilson authorised the first operational deployment of the SAS into Northern Ireland. The decision on where, when and how to use these specialists within the parameters and rules of engagement laid down was delegated to the appropriate senior army commander at HQ NI. Nevertheless, H was involved almost immediately in the practicalities of their deployment within 3 Brigade's area.

This was sometimes fraught. SAS operations are afforded the highest level of secrecy, not so that they may be conducted without legal constraint – as many like to think – but primarily because their work revolves round intelligence emanating from the best sources, the protection of which is critically important. However, this secretiveness and mystique tends to make all Special Forces un-comfortable bedfellows when they are working in a battalion area. Commanding officers are held responsible for their 'patch' and so they wish to be aware of everything that goes on in it. Hence, a CO's annoyance is understandable when the first he knows of a Special Forces operation in his area is the presence of a gorilla of a man, dressed in coveralls with no badges of rank, saying:

'Hello, Boss. I'm Rus. We're here on a job but I can't tell you any more. I'll be next door on my radio if anything comes up.'

Of course, the furious Commanding Officer would at once pick up the telephone to H and demand to know what was going on. H would be practical, refreshingly open and unbureaucratic. He had already established mutual confidence with the local SAS commander and, as a good intermediary, was usually able to placate all concerned. One departing squadron commander wrote to him:

> It made an enormous difference to the Squadron, and to me personally, having at least one sympathetic, yet objective, party with whom I could discuss the problems and options with complete confidence in the sure knowledge that I would get informed and balanced advice. Knowing how busy you inevitably were, the time and patience you expended on the SAS were particularly appreciated.

In May 1977, well into H's second year as BM, a deeply shocking incident occurred which was to have international repercussions. Irrespective of political or any other persuasion, the abduction and murder of Captain Robert Nairac and the disposal of his body were horrific.

Nairac, born in 1948, was the scion of a well-established and close Catholic family from Gloucestershire with its roots in the south of Ireland. He had been educated at Ampleforth, where Dom Basil Hume, later to be Cardinal Archbishop of Westminster, was the Abbot, and his headmaster. Robert, an unusually popular and delightful boy, made a favourable impression on all those with whom he came into contact – staff, pupils, friends and even casual acquaintances. He was a happy, enthusiastic teenager – good at games, competent at his work and a young man of integrity and honour. He went up to Oxford in 1968, read history at Lincoln College and won a Blue for boxing. He was commissioned into the

Grenadier Guards and joined their 2nd Battalion in May 1972, having first completed one of the Graduate Entry courses at Sandhurst.

Early in his service he went to Northern Ireland, as did almost every young infantry officer. He showed a particular aptitude for soldiering there, possessing a natural flair for chatting easily and informally to those he met casually, for he was genuinely interested in them. Accordingly, he volunteered for special duties and was accepted for one of the specialist intelligence units. As a brother officer put it: 'Robert was definitely not entirely happy as a ceremonial soldier. He wanted something more and was considering taking SAS Selection.'

Unlike P Company, which is aggressively macho, Selection involves self-reliance and individual performance. To pass requires unusual aptitude. Candidates discover their own limitations and after failing to make, for example, an obscure rendezvous or meet a punishing deadline, they leave the course, often of their own volition, without any rancour.

Contrary to mythology, Nairac never put himself to this test. With his personal qualities and magnetism, he was encouraged to volunteer for one of the other intelligence-gathering units in Northern Ireland. In its way this was just as demanding as Selection but, open to women as well as men, it did not require the same general war capability and pronounced physical endurance that the SAS required. He passed with flying colours.

With Nairac's Catholic faith, his knowledge of Irish history and his instinctive understanding of Republicanism – not that he was of that persuasion himself – he could identify and communicate easily with many of the young men drifting towards the extremes of the movement. He once coached boxing in a club in the Catholic Ardoyne, and his fund of Irish stories and rebel songs gave him a cult status in young Republican circles. In the Army it earned him a mixture of respect and some bewilderment. Only a few senior Army officers knew his true identity and role. Elsewhere he was accepted as an officer with unusual gifts doing his best to improve, not before time, relationships between the Catholic community and the Army.

In the late summer of 1976, following a previous tour in Belfast, Nairac volunteered for an appointment in South Armagh as a liaison officer between various Army agencies, such as the SAS and intelligence units, and the RUC and HQ 3 Infantry Brigade. This encouraged him to see what he could achieve in that notoriously close-knit border community, where even before the 'Troubles' any stranger was an object of suspicion. In this role Nairac was essentially engaged – as he had been latterly in Belfast – in 'talent spotting'; that is, identifying anyone who might be persuaded to provide the security forces with information.

The IRA call this 'touting' – an offence traditionally punishable by death after interrogation for anyone caught working for the hated British. In the mid seventies, however, attitudes were not quite so polarised in South Armagh as they were to become after the hunger strike of 1980–1, and chatting with an engaging fellow like Nairac, whose background was obscure, was not quite such a heinous offence.

As for the Army, while on the one hand it was delighted with Nairac's potential source recruitment, on the other it was becoming increasingly concerned as he extended his activities. There were reports that he had been across the border, singing rebel songs in a bar in Monaghan four miles into the Republic, and there were anxieties in some quarters that he might be getting tired, and perhaps careless. Such was the level of this concern that Philip Sidney, a fellow Grenadier, wrote privately to his Regimental Headquarters alerting them to a possible problem.

H and Robert were good friends. H admired courage above all other virtues, and Nairac fitted his image of a hero. Although he was not on the staff of HQ 3 Brigade, and therefore not H's responsibility, they talked often. Robert sometimes stayed in the Brigade Officers' Mess and on occasions H would invite him home to supper with Sara at Bocombra. Time and again, according to Brigadier Woodford, Nairac assured him that he knew exactly what he was doing and that he was not taking unacceptable risks. Crucially,

Woodford and H were satisfied that Nairac always had adequate Special Forces back-up from Bessbrook Mill, a vast disused linen mill outside Newry.*

If HQ 3 Brigade were becoming concerned about Nairac, so were others. One local SAS commander observed:

> It's not possible to combine undercover work in South Armagh with an overt role. Nairac had done a brilliant job in the intelligence set-up in Belfast but he was trying to do the same thing in South Armagh, which is different. But the myth of his invincibility was well established by now and, although I mentioned my concerns to several people, including Robert himself, and tried to get him redeployed, the powers that be wouldn't have it.[5]

At 2125 hours on Saturday 14 May 1977 – incidentally H's thirty-seventh birthday – Robert left Bessbrook Mill in an unmarked civilian car, heading for the Three Steps Inn at Drumintee, one of South Armagh's popular meeting spots, where two hundred or more Republicans, young and old, would assemble on Saturday nights for a bit of craic. Drumintee is seven miles east of Crossmaglen and about five minutes' drive from the Republic. It was a potential recruiting ground where Robert, with his authentic Irish accent, his long hair and his familiarity with Republican attitudes, would not normally have seemed out of place.

Before he left Bessbrook, he drew his pistol from the armoury, took a personal radio – call sign 48 Oscar – and notified the operations room where he was going, what car he was driving and when he would be back. All this was routine. He was working on his own, thus no one had to authorise his precise mission, although Special Forces back-up would be triggered either by a codeword, or by a missed scheduled radio call.

---

*Requisitioned by the Army in the early seventies and still in use.

At around 2200 hours he reached the Three Steps and, having radioed in to Bessbrook Mill, went inside. What follows is partly conjecture. The pub was packed, and he would have had to struggle to get to the bar and order a drink, before joining in the singing and banter. Whether he was due to meet someone, or was there for a chance encounter, is not known.

It subsequently emerged that a visiting Republican was present that night who recognised Nairac as the same man who used to frequent the Republican clubs in North Belfast. He did not know who Nairac was, but remembered some rumour that he was associated with the security forces. He mentioned this to a local man who, with all the suspicious instincts of insecure South Armagh Republicans, alerted two friends at the bar. By this time – it was now 2315 – Robert is remembered as being in the thick of it, singing 'The Broad Black Brimmer', and then leading his party piece, 'The Boys of the Old Brigade'.

When challenged he claimed to be a Danny McErlean from Belfast, which seemed for a while to satisfy his interlocutors. But shortly thereafter he was enticed, or hustled, out of the bar and into the car park, where he got into a fight. Why he did not radio for back-up, or even use his pistol, can only be surmised. Perhaps he thought that would only draw more attention to himself, and that he would be better off bluffing it out – after all, scuffles outside Ireland's pubs are commonplace – and Robert had all the charm and the luck of the Irish. But not that night.

He was overpowered, bundled into a Ford Cortina and driven across the border. At some stage they were joined by another Republican, Liam Townson, who was what the security forces refer to as 'pond-life'– a fringe terrorist with little skill or status. By now Robert's abductors would have found his weapon and radio, and there could be no doubt of the significance of their capture. Townson, perhaps imbued with Dutch courage, decided to handle matters himself. He and nine others started brutally but incompetently to interrogate Robert, who resolutely gave nothing away.

Release of unimportant snippets of information might have gained him time for the search to get under way, but selectively to divulge information under torture is to descend a slippery slope. Furthermore, Robert's sense of honour and duty – strong articles of his faith – ensured that he protected the secrets of his Service to the very end. At some stage in the early hours of Sunday morning – perhaps in sheer anger and frustration at Nairac's failure to provide him with any information with which to ingratiate himself with the IRA leadership – Townson shot him dead through the head. Later he said of his captive: 'He never told us anything. He was a great soldier.'[6]

Back in Bessbrook, the 'operator overdue' machinery was already turning. Nairac had said he would be back at around 2330, but a short leeway would be allowed – those on duty appreciated that casual contact meetings cannot be timed precisely. However, when he missed the mandatory midnight radio check, the balloon went up.

The Commanding Officer was alerted at 0005, and at 0100 Robert's car was located in the Three Steps car park during a covert drive-past. This posed problems in itself: was the car booby-trapped? Was an ambush lying in wait? Could Robert, just possibly, have gone off in another car to follow up a contact? All this had to be considered, but in the absence of any satisfactory explanation, or further news, the decision was taken at 0545 hours formally to alert HQ 3 Brigade and the RUC. Having done so, the Special Forces slipped back into the shadows and let the uniformed units, with all their resources of manpower and helicopters, take over.

H then became the chief executive leading the search for Nairac. He was awakened by telephone at home, and on his way in to the Headquarters decided to alert Martin Edwards. H's consideration for his staff at such a time was remarkable. Martin recalls:

I remember the morning very well. I was a neighbour of H's and, very unusually, as Bocombra was guarded, I awoke to somebody throwing stones at my window. It was H. Thoughtfully, he didn't want to ring and wake up our young children.

He said, 'Martin, Robert has gone missing. I'm going in.' I immediately said, 'OK, I'll come in with you.' He was delighted because it meant he could leave someone in the HQ whilst he was on the ground trying to organise things down in South Armagh. In fact, practically every resource in Northern Ireland was mobilised to do the search. H was very upset about it all.[7]

Even Rupert Jones, then aged eight, remembers the incident. One evening, whilst the search was on, 'H came to say good night and unusually – it had never happened before – he asked me "to pray for Robert who is missing". Then he kissed me good night and left.'

H spent the next four days co-ordinating the operation, mainly from Bessbrook, at one stage even taking Robert's massive Newfoundland, Bundler, to assist in the search for his master. After forty-eight hours without sleep, H was exhausted and the strain was showing. Not only was he grieving deeply, he was blaming himself for not intervening earlier and insisting that Robert be rested. H's staff noticed that he was not himself for several days, and his inner turmoil showed.

Brigadier Woodford recalls: 'I went into my HQ early and spoke to the key people in HQNI and the RUC. I then drove down to Newcastle . . . to play golf at the Royal County Down – my first such outing in months. I was kept in constant touch throughout, with H impressively holding all the threads in his hand at the centre of the web. Everything was being done that could be done.[8] The search continued until, on the fourth day, a senior RUC officer was invited to the Republic by a friend and colleague in the Garda Siochana,* who had reliable evidence of Robert's murder. No body had been found – or ever would be† – but the massive search north and south of the border was so counter-productive for the Provisional IRA that they turned in Liam Townson and the others.

---

*The Irish police.
†Nairac's body was never found. It is believed to have been disposed of in the meat processing plant at the Anglo-Irish Meat Company in Ravensdale, Co. Louth.

PIRA were not pleased with this freelance operation. First, they had lost the opportunity to interrogate Nairac themselves and extract the information that they now knew he had possessed. Secondly, they had lost a valuable propaganda coup that they could have manipulated for weeks. Thirdly, they sensed a wave of sympathy, even among their own supporters, for this charismatic, brave Irishman. PIRA like to depict British Army officers as insensitive thugs, and the romantic, idealistic Nairac did not fit this image.

Two very contrasting events ensued. In December 1978, at the Special Criminal Court in Dublin, Townson was convicted of the murder of Robert Nairac and sentenced to penal servitude for life. He was released in August 1990. In February 1979 Nairac was posthumously awarded the George Cross, Britain's highest civilian recognition for gallantry.

Although the incident was never forgotten, events moved on as fresh issues arose. New officers had joined the Headquarters; one of them, replacing Philip Sidney, was another Grenadier captain, Charles Woodrow,* who was widely experienced and already had a gallantry award for service in the Province. His recollection of H was typical of the views of most of the Brigade HQ's staff:

He looked fit and in good shape; there were no bulges and flab on H. He was passionate about the Army and he always wanted to know what was going on so that he could do something positive about it. He was the keenest soldier I ever met – highly professional and very competitive. But he was great fun to be with – things mattered to him – he had genuine enthusiasm and the will to take things forward. In this context, he wanted the best for his people. He was the epitome of the word 'service'.

He took those that were like-minded under his wing, but he couldn't be doing with those who were not pulling their weight. He expected people to give their all and if they did he was fine. But he was positively disdainful of those that did not; also he

_____

*Later Lieutenant Colonel A J C Woodrow OBE MC QGM.

could be sharply and publicly critical of those with whom he disagreed.

Although warm and kind to newcomers, like myself, this was not inevitable. I did notice later that he had little time for the odd buffoon that was around. As the tour progressed, and especially after the murder of Nairac, he became increasingly competitive and outspoken; and perhaps he was over-partisan on occasions. However, I would have followed him to the ends of the earth. There was something about him which was very special indeed.[9]

From above, Brigadier Woodford was equally positive. He found H thoroughly companionable and they often shared confidences – one particularly stuck in Woodford's mind. They were discussing the bi-annual honours and awards when, debating the appropriateness of awards in general, H murmured: 'Well, we all know that the only award worth having is the Victoria Cross!'[10]

Despite his frenetic life in one of the busiest appointments in the Province, H's family and friends remained uppermost in his priorities. In August 1977, during the Queen's Silver Jubilee visit to Northern Ireland, H's lifelong friend Tobin Duke, commanding a company of the Gordon Highlanders, was very seriously wounded by a sniper in the Falls Road, Belfast, and was rushed to the nearby Royal Victoria Hospital. He would probably have died on the street had not an attached Devon and Dorset officer saved him from bleeding to death.*

H, despite all the extra work involving security for the royal visit, dropped everything and sped the thirty-five miles to Belfast, where he was the first to reach his friend's bedside. This was a mark of his loyalty and friendship that Tobin never forgot. The incident seemed to trigger H's sense of mortality. As Duke's life tottered on the brink, he remarked to Bobby Hanscomb, one of the original teenage trio,

---

*Captain Cedric Delves (now Lieutenant-General), with SAS experience, carried six field dressings – rather than the standard issue one – and needed every one to staunch the flow.

who also happened to be serving in the Province: 'Perhaps Tobin will be the first of the "Trio" to go?'[11]

Tim Jones, H's brother, was equally concerned for Duke, but as he was serving at the time on HMY *Britannia*, attending The Queen, he could not get ashore. On a lighter note his signals from the Royal Yacht gave Tobin, who was to make a complete recovery, a certain kudos in the hospital.

By now H was well into the second half of his tour. At this point the career planners plot an officer's next posting. H had not been selected for promotion in the 1978 batch of officers, although King-Fretts, somewhat surprisingly, had. So H would have to do another job as a major. He was appointed to the School of Infantry at Warminster, Wiltshire, where he was to be the team leader on the Combat Team Commander's Course. An informal inter-office memo designed to 'sell' H for the job still exists, giving a rare glimpse into the machinations of those responsible for postings. It begins by extolling his abundant virtues as a staff officer, company commander and tactician, and then, lest perhaps it had over-sold its candidate, concludes: 'Obviously very talented, but arrogant, rides roughshod over others, is deaf to counter-arguments, shows signs of immaturity – but otherwise, a superb choice for the School of Infantry!'

This seems a harsh judgement, even for an internal, tongue-in-cheek memo, following a brilliant tour in a tough job, but its root cause was about to be manifest again. After H had routinely read and initialled his exceptionally good confidential report, it was forwarded to HQ NI. Some time later, H found his Brigade Commander vexed: the rare 'Outstanding' grading Woodford had given him had not been supported up the line. The reason, succinctly set out,* was H's 'tendency to stick to more parochial views longer than is wise if broader interests are to prevail'.

It was the same old problem: H fought like a tiger for his own, be it at platoon, company or brigade level, and, arguably, went well

---

*By the Commander Land Forces HQ NI.

beyond the point of reasonableness on their behalf. For those in his team, it was splendid to have such a strong advocate, but to those who had to contend with conflicting priorities and other loyalties, H came over too strong. Clearly many in HQ NI found it exhausting and time-consuming having to argue with H and HQ 3 Brigade so often, and over so much.

By September 1977 the packing cases were out again and the Joneses were preparing to head back across the Irish Sea. Reflecting on H's time in Portadown, BM of 3 Brigade was perhaps his most satisfying tour of all. He had been right on top of a job he relished; he had been given free rein and plenty of encouragement from his immediate superiors. He was admired and popular with the best of his staff – the others he didn't care about – and he had the great satisfaction of knowing that 3 Brigade's units and soldiers were getting the service they had the right to expect. He knew that his efforts were appreciated where they mattered.

John Waters, promoted to command 3 Brigade in late 1979, confirms this. He remembers being struck two years later by the strength of H's legacy:

> The ghost of H hung over Brigade Headquarters and the ghost was of somebody who had been quite outstanding. He had given his intelligence, his energy, his courage, his everything to being a brigade major and people still spoke of him and remembered him as having been quite exceptional.[12]

Domestically it was a good time. Sara had been happy in Northern Ireland, even though everyone worked ridiculously long hours, including the weekends. Many Northern Ireland families are famously hospitable to friends in the Army, and Sara was often invited out; she also joined a book club and rode locally. A daughter of the New Forest, she bought 'Scrumpy' in Northern Ireland, riding him there and for years afterwards. The boys were well settled at school: David was approaching Common Entrance, and Rupert attended the junior school at Portadown College. There were other children to play with and plenty to do in the holidays. H and Sara had a pleasant quarter, with good neighbours, one of whom, Charles Woodrow's wife, Fiona, remarked: 'H was strongly a family man and Sara was the perfect girl for him. She lived her life through H, whilst maintaining a healthy independence.'[13]

H always knew Warminster was going to be an interlude before moving on to greater things; nevertheless he threw himself into it wholeheartedly. Sara had hoped he would let up a little after the strain and restrictions of Northern Ireland, which often bear more heavily on the wives than the husbands. Furthermore, H had developed the tendency common among many successful men to become so absorbed with their work as their careers take off that they take their wives for granted, and this put some strain on their marriage.

Certainly, some officers at the School of Infantry who had not before heard H *fortissimo* with a couple of drinks inside him, remarked on his chauvinistic attitudes and concluded that Sara had a cross to bear. Typically a heated argument might develop over hunting, which H affected to abhor, whereas Sara enjoyed riding and had hunted enthusiastically in her youth. H enjoyed being provocative just for the sake of it, but those who did not know could be taken aback by the vehemence of his argument, and embarrassed by his bad language. However, old friends recognised this as mostly froth, and never doubted H's inherent devotion to Sara.

At Warminster the Joneses formed a strong friendship with a neighbouring American family, the Seversons, who had children of a similar age to David and Rupert. Major Dan Severson, a Vietnam veteran, who was the US Army Exchange Officer at the School of Infantry, recalls:

H was especially curious about my combat experience in Vietnam. I had spent over a year there as a company commander and provided plenty of combat stories for his consideration.

During my time at Warminster the two of us covered every conceivable combat topic and situation I could recall: tactics, soldiers' morale, care of the wounded, use of air power, artillery, armour, helicopters, equipment, rules of engagement and the treatment of prisoners. Our discussions were always enthusiastic and rewarding. H's desire to visualise the battlefield in a realistic way was intense.

He seemed more willing to accept curious 'Yank' ideas than many of his British counterparts, some of whom felt it was a distracting flaw – the result of his American background. But the fact was that H was always searching for solutions. In the field he was never just running through the motions. Every idea that could favourably impact on the outcome of an engagement was worth considering and worth trying if it showed promise.[14]

H was best remembered at Warminster for his 'war-gaming'. With his love of military history, he was already a devotee of the commercial variety of board games, but Severson introduced him to the US Army's advanced war-gaming, and its application to tactical training. The lure was that it was conclusive. Using dice, and probability tables developed by the US Army, there was always a result – someone won the battle. H embraced the idea with his customary vigour and enthusiasm, and convinced the School of Infantry that the American experience should be pursued. Today, war-gaming, along with battle simulation, still endures in British Army training modules and research, and is viewed as an essential adjunct to training.

In the summer of 1978, the Joneses celebrated three excellent pieces of news. First, David's success at Common Entrance – he had passed into Sherborne and would start there in September. Second, H was most deservedly appointed a Member of the Order of the British Empire (MBE) in the Northern Ireland Honours List, which triggered an avalanche of congratulatory letters. Third, at last he received an 'Outstanding' report and on the strength of it was selected in 1979 for promotion to Lieutenant Colonel.

His prospects could not now be better; but which command he would get, and when, had yet to be resolved.

CHAPTER NINE

Command

When the newly promoted Lieutenant Colonel H Jones MBE reported to Headquarters, United Kingdom Land Forces (HQ UKLF) at Wilton on 28 August 1979, he was wearing the green and tawny stable belt and the cap-badge of the Devon and Dorsets. Appointed General Staff Officer Grade 1, Staff Duties, he was two ranks up, and one floor higher, in the building so familiar from eight years before. Now he had a light, airy corner office just down the corridor from the Commander-in-Chief himself, to whom H was on immediate call if required.

It was that sort of job. Staff Duties (or SD, as it is known) is the most important branch in any headquarters – although not always the most exciting – but with H's appointment even this was to alter. SD is the authorising authority for all resources – manpower, equipment and money – and so, from an organisational point of view, nothing happened in the 218,000-strong* command without the involvement of H's domain. One member of H's branch was a delightful sixty-year-old retired officer (RO) called Bob Flood, who had been commissioned into the Royal Berkshire Regiment before transferring permanently to the Parachute Regiment. Flood had left the Army as a brigadier, having been Assistant Commandant at Sandhurst and Commander of 44 Parachute Brigade, the Territorial Army's airborne formation. His rank and eminence, however, were

---

*156,000 regulars and 62,000 Territorial Army (*Defence Estimates*, 1980).

immaterial in the context of working for H. Like all ROs, Flood provided much-needed continuity on a modest salary but, so the theory ran, in agreeable circumstances. In Bob's case they were just that – he enjoyed being at the centre of things, matching units to tasks, and he worked with capable people. Bob was both amused and intrigued by H. He liked his unconventional and open personality; he was impressed by his energy and sheer ability – and on occasion he was appalled at his bad language.

In Flood H found a depth of knowledge and experience, coupled with a shrewd imperturbability, invaluable in such a vital staff branch. More importantly, he admired and respected him. Bob Flood's most useful influence was to try and exercise some restraint on H's wilder ideas and excesses. 'You really can't *do* that, H!' he would say, which would often elicit: 'Just watch me!', though put in more colourful terms.

Flood recalls how, in light-hearted frustration at some officer's stupidity within the Headquarters, H devised a competition entitled 'Wanker of the Week'. He put up a large wall-chart upon which he scribbled the name of the officer who had most incurred the displeasure of his mighty Staff Duties branch that week. One day Flood noticed that H had scrawled 'C-in-C' on the chart as the week's winner – an indiscretion of some magnitude, even if the great man had perhaps made an unwise decision. Flood urged H to remove it at once. As usual, H disagreed, supporting his argument with chapter and verse of the C-in-C's folly. At that moment General Sir John Archer, the Commander-in-Chief, walked in. This was the same John Archer who had been H's first Company Commander; he was now the Colonel of his Regiment, as well as his C-in-C.

There was no explosion – John Archer was not that kind of man and, anyway, Flood cannot now remember whether Archer even saw the notice. If he had, it was unlikely he would have reacted: this would have been just another 'H-ism', to be allowed to pass. After two years of having him in his company there was not much that H could now do that would shock or surprise him. As it happened,

Archer was about to decide finally on the nomination for command of his Regiment, and the decision was not getting any easier. On one hand, he would have been conscious almost daily of the high quality of H's work, yet on the other he still felt he was probably a bit of a risk and that the other candidate, King-Fretts, would be a safer bet.

On an entirely different plane, the Commander-in-Chief was becoming involved in a politico-military development of international importance. In the autumn of 1979, fourteen years after Rhodesia's Unilateral Declaration of Independence (UDI), the British Government was inching towards an agreement to settle the Rhodesia problem with the support and help of the Commonwealth. At a Lancaster House conference in London, chaired by Lord Carrington, a plan – code-named Operation AGILA – had been drawn up to deploy a Commonwealth Monitoring Force to interpose between the parties in this long-standing and bloody internal conflict. Following a monitored ceasefire between the Rhodesian security forces and the allied armies of the Zimbabwe African National Union (Patriotic Front), the guerrilla forces would gather at collection points before moving to assembly places, where they would hand in their weapons. After this, a binding election would be held, supervised by Commonwealth monitors and international observers.

The conflicting parties were Ian Smith's 'illegal' white Rhodesia regime established on UDI; Robert Mugabe's ZANLA;* and Joshua Nkomo's ZIPRA.† Each had its own regular or irregular armed forces, and although the UK Government's proposed plan was backed by the Commonwealth, and had the consent of those on the ground, there was serious risk of renewed confrontation should one or other party feel it had been duped. There was concern, for example, that the guerrillas, who had taken to the bush and been fighting for many years, would not have sufficient confidence in the arrangements to hand in their weapons.

---

*Zimbabwe African National Liberation Army.
†Zimbabwe People's Liberation Army.

Responsibility for setting up this Commonwealth Monitoring Force (CMF) fell upon HQ UKLF and, within it, on H's Staff Duties branch. H was to devise a structure and composition for the Force; and, with that agreed, to mount it as soon as possible. Christmas 1979 was the deadline. Once the CMF reached Rhodesia, HQ UKLF would have to sustain it there until after the elections scheduled for the end of February 1980. Finally, H and his team would be responsible for its eventual recovery.

With 1,250 British servicemen to be assembled, this was an enormous undertaking. A thousand came from the Army, including 120 officers – many of them the best COs, plucked from their units; the RAF contributed 220 of all ranks; and there were thirty naval personnel. Contingents from Canada, Australia, Fiji and Kenya provided the balance. These bald figures conceal the detail, and it was that which took the time and generated the problems, especially as the British Army was required to provide logistics for all the other contingents.

H was in his element. He threw himself wholeheartedly into the myriad of difficulties. Rules of Engagement – that is, the exact circumstances in which British soldiers could use force – had to be cleared with ministers in London; likewise the terms of the Status of Forces Agreement, which defined the important legal position of British servicemen operating in a foreign country. Then came the endless arrangements for commanding, administering and re-supplying the Force, from medical provision to how the mail services would operate – both important factors bearing upon the morale of those serving away from home.

One young major at Wilton remembers H at a top-level planning meeting, chaired by the Commander-in-Chief, taking copious notes, as well as answering with clarity and confidence the detailed questions posed by Major-General John Acland, the designated Commander of the Monitoring Force. Afterwards, H quickly produced a master copy of the final order of battle. With this agreed, his branch was responsible for moving the force to Rhodesia. This was a prodigious task; moving individual servicemen from all over the UK – plus another 250 from the four other participating countries – it was much more complex than just moving a single unit of that size.

But HQ UKLF's contribution did not end there. Perhaps the greatest problem on the ground was that 22,000 guerrillas eventually gathered at the various assembly places, but no one locally would accept responsibility for their administration. An appalling logistical challenge thus confronted staff established only to look after the needs of the 1,500-strong Commonwealth Force. As a result, hundreds of tons of supplies and tentage had to be air-dropped into the assembly places; and when food ran short, eighty tons of beef was flown up from South Africa in order to head off a mutiny among the guerrillas, who had been reduced to eating maize. Further equipment came from America, clothing from Hong Kong and hundreds of other items from the UK. Even female under-clothing and other similar necessities had to be provided for the hundreds of women guerrillas who had, unexpectedly, assembled in the ZANLA camps along with the men.

The work of the logistics staff and the air transport fleet earned the highest praise, with the result described, in an article in the normally staid *British Army Review*, as 'a near miracle'. Major Nick Beard, one of Wilton's able logisticians, remembers H spending much of his time in the basement operations room, 'almost running himself into the ground'. Major Austin Thorpe, who worked directly for H, recalls more critically that H 'had the quickest "flash to bang time" of any officer I knew, but his innovative approach and the way he cir-cumvented problems and political restrictions was impressive'.

The Foreign and Commonwealth Office, for example, would not sanction the use of the SAS on the basis, understandably, that this was a low-profile, essentially passive operation. But H argued, equally reasonably, that nevertheless the risks were high and that properly trained and equipped evacuation teams were needed should the situation turn sour. He lost the argument, but then achieved his desired result by forming, on his own initiative, reserve monitor teams from the well-trained close observation platoons of six battalions. These were not the SAS but they had some comparable skills and comprised an appropriate force to deal with the worse eventuality.

On 4 March the result of the election was announced. Mr Mugabe's victory was proclaimed by his supporters and accepted by his opponents. The work of the CMF was over, and within ten days they had all flown out, leaving behind a small administrative and training team. The *British Army Review* reported that the recovery – which was also H's responsibility – went 'exceptionally well, from all points of view'.

But there had been another more personal matter for H to ponder from the outset of Operation AGILA. He had been notified of his appointment to command 2nd Battalion, The Parachute Regiment, from April 1981, a development which left the way open for Lieutenant Colonel King-Fretts to take over the Devon and Dorsets. This was a blow for an intensely loyal regimental officer such as H.

It may not be easy for those unfamiliar with the bonds forged in family regiments to understand. But this was official notification that his formal link with the Regiment in which he had served and grown up, in which he had so many friends, and which was his military home – in short, the Regiment he loved – was to end.

The process is termed 're-badging', and it happens infrequently. For H it meant becoming an officer of the Parachute Regiment and transferring his allegiance to them in all respects for the remainder of his service. This is a daunting task for any officer transferring regiments, however flexible he and his wife may be – and the process applies to both of them. Some aspects, like having to buy a complete set of new uniforms, were straightforward. The hardest part for H would be demonstrating that he had *mentally* re-badged. There must never be any doubt in the minds of the officers and men of his new unit that he was delighted and honoured at the prospect of becoming a full member of their Regiment, and the opportunity it represented. He now had to commit himself wholeheartedly to them; and Sara had to do the same with the families. Yet, realistically, the Joneses could not just abandon their twenty happy years with the Devon and Dorsets. The process would be a considerable strain initially – one to which all participants were sensitive – and would require fine balance. In the event, H and Sara handled it skilfully.

For the most part H did not have to dissemble or pretend. He already knew the Parachute Regiment from his earlier service with 3 Para; he had a high regard for the soldiers in the Regiment – the 'Toms', as they were termed by their officers. He liked their professionalism and indomitable spirit. He had several good friends, like Rupert Smith and Hew Pike,* among the officers. His new Regiment had a higher public profile than his old, and that appealed to him – a certain frisson of excitement attends most things involving the Paras. Furthermore, he was genuinely honoured to have been selected to fill this gap in the Parachute Regiment's own ranks and was indebted to those friends who had commended him so highly, like Bob Flood and his old Company Commander, Keith Spacie. The latter had been vocal in his support, strongly believing that H would make a better commanding officer of a parachute battalion than a 'line' regiment: 'H was impatient and restless,' Spacie explained, 'and these are just the qualities needed in a Para CO.'

But these positive feelings did not prevent H from being hurt. He did not entirely trust the way in which his selection had been handled. He suspected that General Archer had never quite forgotten his youthful incompetence and wayward behaviour as a young officer, and recalled a sentence in Archer's warm letter congratulating him on his MBE: 'I look back with some amusement to that exercise in North Africa and to days in Cyprus, some of which I would prefer to forget!' H felt that perhaps his sins as a subaltern were being visited upon him as a Lieutenant Colonel, and he sensed that those contributing to the decision might not quite

---

*Hew Pike had been the Intelligence Officer of 3 Para when H arrived. Later he would command 3 Para in the Falklands. He retired from the Army in 2001 as Lieutenant-General Sir Hew Pike KCB DSO MBE.

have their finger on the regimental pulse. In fairness, it was a genuinely difficult choice for General Archer. King-Fretts' outstanding reports from the SAS, where he had commanded a squadron during the Dhofar campaign in Oman, weighed in his favour, but even that was not clear-cut.

King-Fretts himself had misgivings about the decision. Having earned glowing reports on operations, and been promoted to lieutenant colonel at the earliest possible age, he believed, in his own words, 'that 22 SAS were making a strong bid for me. When the Command List* appeared I was absolutely flabbergasted and, for a while, quite disturbed at the decision.'[1] King-Fretts had not served with the Devon and Dorsets for more than ten years. He knew fewer than half the officers, and virtually none of the soldiers. As he explains: 'I knew that H was a legend in the Battalion; he had commanded a Company well and had been a successful brigade major in Northern Ireland.'

That was to be the Devon and Dorsets' next posting, and Paddy was conscious that he lacked any command experience in Northern Ireland. Furthermore, his wife Thelma was not enthusiastic about spending two years in the Province. 'Finally, whilst I was very comfortable with the strange ways and freedom of command in the SAS, life at the top of a regular battalion was going to be unfamiliar to me.'[2] Neither man aired these very human concerns publicly – they were too circumspect for that. But nonetheless they existed.

To make matters worse, H realised that many old Devon and Dorset friends of all ranks regretted him not taking over his own Battalion; indeed, many simply could not understand the decision. So widespread was this feeling that he felt the need to write to the RSM of the Devon and Dorsets explaining his re-badging. He was concerned that the Warrant Officers' and Sergeants' Mess especially might imagine, erroneously, that somehow he had sought out another command.

---

*The Command List denotes those appointed to command major units in the following year.

What no one knew at the time was how quickly General Archer's seemingly perverse decision over this command appointment was to have such profound repercussions.

H's tour at Wilton still had a year to run. As often happens in the Army, no sooner had one operation ended and life resumed some normality than another unexpectedly occurred. In this case it was the threat of a fire services' strike, which emerged during one of the early showdowns of the Thatcher administration. The Army was duly deployed, and once again arrangements became the responsibility of H's branch at Wilton – principally the provision of emergency cover and the issue and manning of the Army's ageing Green Goddess fire tenders. This was a much more straightforward operation than AGILA and it did not tax H or his team, but nevertheless the Ops Room effectively became his office once again.

It was there, in that basement, that H physically re-badged to the Parachute Regiment in an informal but stylish ceremony. Nick Beard recalls Brigadier Bob Flood arriving in the Ops Room before lunch on the appointed date with a silver tray. On it was a bottle of pink champagne, as well as a Parachute Regiment stable belt and beret, and new shoulder flashes. H duly removed his Devon and Dorset insignia and donned the distinctive accoutrements of the Parachute Regiment. Brigadier Flood made a short, light-hearted speech welcoming H to his Regiment – this time properly, and for good – and proposed a toast to 'H and 2 Para', to which H responded with equal style and warmth. H had re-badged and his transfer was now complete.

Later, over a glass of champagne, someone asked H whether the process had posed any difficulties so far. Beard was struck by his reply. 'Only for the children,' he said. 'They don't really understand what re-badging means and they're worried about it.' In fact, Beard felt it was rather more a case of H being concerned on their behalf, which spoke volumes for his intense sense of responsibility for his sons.

H took fatherhood extremely seriously. He would play with the boys for hours on end, and treated them as small adults, answering their questions with full explanations. A mark of their unusually grown-up relationship was indicated by David and Rupert always calling their father 'H', although initially this was just a baby attempt at a name which stuck, rather than a conscious decision. Although H was a model father in many ways, Sara sometimes felt he was over-indulgent and showered too many presents on the children for their own good. These mostly involved trains, Scalextric and other games which she suspected were given, at least in part, so that H could have fun playing with them himself.

Another feature of H's relationship with his boys was the strict keeping of promises. No one let his sons down with impunity. One of the biggest rows H and his brother Tim had as adults occurred when Tim promised to take David and Rupert sailing on *Romanel.* For some innocent reason he forgot the time, missed a critical tide and had to abandon the trip. H was furious: to him this was a breach of the trust the young should have in grown-ups, as well as a missed opportunity to implant knowledge in eager young minds.

Early in 1981, H's tour at Wilton drew to a close. He received another outstanding confidential report, and in the New Year Honours List his contribution to Operation AGILA was formally acknowledged by his elevation to an Officer of the Order of the British Empire. H was now Lieutenant Colonel H Jones OBE, The Parachute Regiment. The renowned General Frank Kitson, the British Army's foremost exponent of the theory and practice of Low Intensity Operations, who was then Deputy Commander-in-Chief, wrote to him: 'My own view is that you have done more to hold this place together than most people and that you probably deserve more than one medal for doing so.' This was praise indeed from a senior officer not given to platitudes or wasting words. On this high note, H assumed command of 2 Para on 3 April 1981.

Like all incoming commanding officers, H found assuming command to be an exhilarating yet awesome moment. For the first time in his service he was in sole charge of a major unit with no one to tell him what to do next. This is the joy and the essence of regimental command. COs receive broad directives on what is to be

COMMAND

achieved, but implementation is up to them, within agreed limits.

It is often said that command is lonely; and so it can be, having to make a far-reaching and unpopular decision. It is lonely, certainly, when all eyes turn on a CO for inspiration or action at critical moments. And standing at a soldier's graveside as a consequence of some botched operation is the loneliest place on earth. But for the most part, command of a battalion, or any other major unit, gives an immense sense of purpose and satisfaction. It should be, and usually is, a pleasure every bit as great as the honour and privilege of holding the appointment.

The British Army understands the importance of its commanding officers, and invests heavily in them. Their preparation is thorough, their authority considerable – in some respects it is absolute – and their status high. A CO arguably has more instant and effective power than the holder of any other appointment. Of course, generals may command more men and carry wider responsibility but none has, at his immediate disposal, almost 800 men, known personally, at the end of a direct and responsive chain of command. Moreover, every single subordinate acknowledges the need and desire to be well led; indeed, the tougher the situation, the more amenable soldiers are to strong leadership. Their instinctive wish is to satisfy their commanding officer and help him achieve the unit's aim. So it would be hard to find any organisation potentially as responsive to the direction of one man, whether the matter be great or trivial.

One new CO illustrated the point by recalling how on his first day in command the Quartermaster and the Regimental Sergeant Major were showing him round the barracks. Passing the vehicle sheds, he was incautious enough to remark, as an aside: 'What a horrid colour those doors are!' When next he walked that way he found, to his horror, men feverishly repainting them. It was a lesson well learnt as to the consequences of a loose word or a casual opinion.

The job of a commanding officer, fundamentally unchanged from the Duke of Wellington's decree, is 'so to train the private men under his command that they may without question defeat any enemy opposed to them in the field'. Historically, regiments were often named after their commanders – Skinner's Horse, for example – and even today, a CO's character and style rubs off on his command. The Commanding Officer is the personification of his Regiment and vice versa. As Major-General Jeremy Moore was to say of H after the Falklands campaign: 'When battalions go into battle they take the character of their CO – 2 Para was H's Battalion and he gave it a real driving force.'[3]

Moreover, in principle, and invariably in practice too, loyalty to the office holder is absolute. A CO may assume the inherent loyalty of his subordinates, irrespective of their personal feelings about him, at least until such time – if that should ever occur – that he be unwise enough to forfeit their good will or trust.

Thus, far from being isolated and lonely, a good CO is pivotal to the lives of a community that can number 1,500, including families. Official business reaches him up a formal chain of command, through his company commanders and the adjutant. A good RSM with his finger on the pulse of the battalion is another invaluable source of official and unofficial information. But of greatest importance is the commanding officer's own eyes and ears, and the 'feel' he gets from contact – on duty and off – with his soldiers and their families. Moreover, the commanding officer's wife can also play a significant role in the life and well-being of a unit, her positive influence contributing to its success and confidence – while the reverse equally applies.

Two other considerations affected H as a new 'imported' CO. First, it is arguably more difficult to command a battalion as an 'outsider'. A home-grown commanding officer knows, and is known by, his command. On taking up his appointment, there will be few new names to learn, no unfamiliar regimental history or legends to absorb, no new customs or traditions to recognise. His previous knowledge and experience will see him through – at least initially. But for a CO from outside everything is new. Most of his officers and all his men will be unknown to him; he is thrown into the deep end with no familiar face or trusted friend on hand for counsel or moral support. Aware that first impressions count and take swift root, he must make a positive initial impact. However, the argument is not entirely one-sided. A new incumbent can enjoy the distinct advantages of a fresh start, for he carries no previous baggage, and is not constrained by myths or prejudices stemming from his earlier service with the Regiment.

The second factor was the understandable element of regret – even resentment – on the part of H's new Regiment that an internal candidate had not been selected for command. Inevitably, the question was asked: 'Why couldn't one of *our* officers have commanded; surely we had people good enough?' Accentuating the point, Paras tend to label dismissively as 'crap hats' those of other regiments. Although this tag could not accurately be stuck on H, who had already served with 3 Para, he was well aware of the perception, undeniably held in some quarters, that 2 Para were regrettably getting an outsider as CO. This made for a less easy start for him, and for Sara, than if he had taken command of the Devon and Dorsets.

Whatever the genesis, that was history. Now all that mattered was how well H did the job, and that, in part, was determined by a legacy. It was widely agreed that 2 Para, having been in Northern Ireland for almost two years, was not in good shape. Since mid 1979, they had been stationed in pleasant surroundings at Ballykinler in County Down, with easy access to the beach and spectacular views of the Mountains of Mourne. But professionally, this was the least stimulating of all the postings in Northern Ireland. There was no role for the Ballykinler Battalion as a whole – their rifle companies were 'rented out' piecemeal to other units, who worked them hard – and their own CO had little opportunity to exercise command of his soldiers. By the end of their time in Ballykinler, 2 Para lacked cohesion, and were stale and tired.

To make matters worse, their tour had been marred by two tragedies. The first was a major terrorist-initiated incident at Warrenpoint in which eighteen soldiers were ambushed and killed;

and the second was the terminal illness of their Commanding Officer, Colin Thomson. This fine man was bravely fighting cancer through the latter part of his tour, and the loss of his leadership over several months had had a detrimental effect on 2 Para. He died shortly after handing over command to H.

The Warrenpoint ambush occurred on 27 August 1979 – the same day that Lord Mountbatten, two members of his family and a young boatman were blown up in a fishing boat off County Sligo, in the Republic. On the opposite coast, Warrenpoint lies on the northern shore of what is locally termed the 'Narrow Water', a finger of Carlingford Lough running up from the sea to the port and town of Newry. The southern shore of the Lough at this point is in the Republic of Ireland, and it was from here, safely in the south, that the terrorists activated the ambush by remote control. As a three-vehicle Army convoy drove routinely towards Newry from 2 Para's base in Ballykinler, the IRA detonated a bomb in a hay trailer parked in an adjacent lay-by. The last truck took the full force of the explosion. Six paratroopers were killed instantly, one died later and two others were severely wounded.

In the aftermath of any such incident there is a speedy follow-up. In this case medical teams and reinforcements arrived by road from Newry, and from Bessbrook Mill by helicopter. These reinforcements rendezvoused unwittingly close to a second device concealed in a stone pillar beside the road. Observing through binoculars from the Republic, the terrorists detonated their second bomb, killing eleven more men, including Lieutenant Colonel David Blair of the Queen's Own Highlanders, one of the most popular and respected commanding officers of his generation, and Major Peter Furzeman of A Company, 2 Para. He, like Blair, was another exceptionally able and talented officer, and the gap he left as a company commander was later to be keenly felt by H. Warrenpoint constituted at the time the highest number of casualties sustained by a single battalion in Ulster and it severely affected the unit.

Shaking off the dust of Northern Ireland, 2 Para returned to Aldershot in March 1981. This was the Parachute Regiment's traditional home, and they quickly settled into Bruneval Barracks, where H joined them. They were pleased to be back in England, even though the barracks was one of those modern flat-roofed monstrosities, built by the disgraced developer Poulson. In terms of regimental history and battle honours, Bruneval Barracks seemed particularly appropriate in view of the famous raid of that name in 1942, where the original 2 Para distinguished itself in the first airborne operation of the war. The omens for rejuvenation seemed propitious.

H's first task was to get to know his Battalion, and convert them back into an 'in-role'* parachute unit. Once their essential airborne re-training was completed, H devised a demanding hostage rescue exercise on Salisbury Plain to test their mettle and get the measure of his new command. This involved a battalion parachute drop, a long night march across the Plain leading to a dawn attack, and the rescue of the hostages. Captain David Benest, then H's Regimental Signals Officer, recalls:

> It was exactly what the Battalion needed. We were re-acquainted with airborne operations and injected with fresh ideas and dynamism. It was great; and I was very impressed with our new CO. But it is fair to say that I also saw the down side of H's impatience with his command team. He didn't take prisoners when it came to telling people what he thought – and he made some pretty sharp comments. But certainly, he was exactly the right man in terms of getting the Battalion back into fighting shape.[4]

By now myths were growing about H. They attend all commanding officers, in every unit, so this was not unusual; yet the intensity of those relating to H reflected his strong personality. So different was

---

*Two of the three parachute battalions were trained and equipped for airborne tasks at any one time. This was termed being 'in-role'.

he from most COs that anecdotes about him tended to be more embroidered and colourful.

Soldiers soon recognise their new commanding officer and may be presumed to 'know' him, but despite the fact that daily they are affected by his decisions, few get close. Yet soldiers are remarkably shrewd – their very lives may depend on judging whether a comrade is phoney or genuine. So, although most might not be familiar with their commander, their overall perceptions – positive or negative – tend to be remarkably prescient. Furthermore, once an opinion – or hunch – takes root, for good or ill, it cannot easily be changed.

In H's case, the majority – but not all – of 2 Para were enthusiastic about their new CO. 'He was a really tremendous guy,' said Rob Powell, who had recently rejoined the Battalion as a Colour Sergeant. However, he continued:

> He wasn't liked by everyone – no CO is – but he was extremely straight and very, very concentrated. He was utterly determined on what he wanted. You could walk past him, throw up a salute and he wouldn't even acknowledge you, not because he couldn't be bothered but because he didn't notice; he was away somewhere deep in thought. He was very, very focused like that. He'd get a problem and he wouldn't stop until he'd worked it out.'[5]

To maintain the impetus of their training, H arranged a series of challenges in preparation for a major NATO autumn exercise in Denmark. This was to be followed by Exercise Strident Call in Kenya, before Christmas.

When a unit arrives in a new location, it is placed under an appropriate operational command, termed a 'formation'. This is a brigadier's – or one-star – level of command. In Aldershot, 2 Para now came under a new formation, 6 Field Force, with its headquarters in the adjoining barracks. It is seldom conducive to easy relationships to be stationed next door to one's superior HQ, and this was no exception. The Commander 6 Field Force, and

COMMAND

H's immediate boss, was Brigadier Edwin Beckett, a heavily built man with strong opinions, who liked to make himself felt. But he had some powerful personalities among his commanding officers and this caused conflict. Several noticed that H and Brigadier Beckett often did not see eye to eye and had formidable arguments.

Lieutenant Colonel Tony Holt, commanding 4 Field Regiment, Royal Artillery, supported with his guns all the major units of 6 Field Force and so had good access to each unit. He kept his ear to the ground and knew exactly what was going on. For example, he was present in Denmark on a major NATO exercise* – always something of a showpiece – when Brigadier Beckett ordered 2 Para to move forward in helicopters to seize a feature. H, realising that this would place him outside the range of his own supporting artillery, demurred. The Brigadier explained that there were not enough helicopters to move the guns forward as well, and told H to get on with it. But H refused to move without them, thus threatening to bring the whole exercise to a halt. After much argument, and a direct order, H reluctantly agreed to fly 2 Para forward without artillery cover. But he re-stated his view that the order was operationally unsound. He would do it, but only for the sake of NATO solidarity with the Danes, who had put so much effort into hosting the exercise.

Tony Holt tells the story not primarily to show how argumentative H was, but rather to illustrate how very conscious he was of the importance of artillery support, something that would be of great significance later, in the Falklands. It is a view echoed by H's Battery Commander (BC), Major John Patrick, who supported 2 Para throughout H's first year as CO.

The relationship between a CO and his BC is vital and, if it is to work effectively, must be close and based on mutual confidence.

*This was one of a series of the United Kingdom Mobile Force exercises in BALTAP (Baltic Approaches), held at that time every other year.

181

Battery commanders are often disappointed to find themselves attached to commanding officers on exercises who pay only lip service to fire support. But John Patrick was lucky:

I was fortunate to be H's Battery Commander for most of 1981. We got on splendidly from the outset. Our relationship was close but based almost entirely on our professional responsibilities . . . Of all the COs I have supported as a BC – about twelve – H had the best understanding of the importance and use of indirect fire. This stemmed from his previous experience as a mortar officer. I never had to push the artillery dimension. It always seemed a perspective with which he was completely comfortable and eager to consider.

H was a true professional soldier and commander in every respect. Every exercise was taken seriously, as though it were an operation. For example, in the assault I had to keep a good distance away from H to minimise the risk of enemy fire – the danger of an incoming shell hitting us both. He would bollock me vehemently if I got too close.[6]

As a general rule, the larger the exercise, the smaller is its value for the soldiers taking part. Nevertheless, big NATO exercises are important in demonstrating the resolve of the members of the alliance to work together, to commit resources to training and to test their command, control, communications and intelligence-handling procedures. Furthermore, the logisticians always get a good workout. But for infantrymen or tank crews at the front there is much hanging around, and even when the action does come, it is invariably constrained by artificiality.

Not so exercises in Kenya. Exercise Strident Call, on which H took 2 Para from October to December 1981 was a commanding officer's dream. His Battalion relished the prospect of two months there. Those on their first visit were struck by the majesty of the country and by the sights, the sounds and the smells of Africa. Old hands – and H was one – knew what a marvellous opportunity this was, and how realistic and tough the training could be, with Kenya's extremes of terrain and climate.

The normal procedure on such exercises was for units to rotate through a series of camps or activities. Accordingly, H ordered work-up training at platoon and company level, followed by a demanding battalion test-exercise. Soldiers also had opportunities to experience the vast emptiness of the plains and the abundant wildlife, to explore the forests of the Central Highlands, including ascents of Mount Kenya, and to take some R & R* down on the coast.

One of the military attractions of Kenya was – and still is – getting away from the distractions of soldiering in the UK. The predictable cycle of guards, routine duties, visits, courses and administration in barracks gives way to concentrated, realistic training. Furthermore, a commanding officer away on his own is better able to imprint his personality on his command and shape it to his will, in a way not possible on a score of NATO exercises or months on Salisbury Plain. So H set about this rare opportunity with his customary infectious enthusiasm.

His influence was soon felt in every corner of the Battalion. On live firing exercises, in particular, he would be found one moment in a trench beside a machine gunner; next back on the 'mortar line'; and then at a company or rifle platoon commander's elbow as the man was giving his orders. Some found his drive and energy stimulating. Others, especially those he loudly castigated for ineptitude, felt his presence was a distraction and his public criticism humiliating. One young platoon commander, Mark Coe, of A Company, remembers a live firing company exercise on which 'Colonel Jones rode my Company Commander† very hard in front of his Company.'[7]

Others, like David Benest, the Signals Officer, were more circumspect, recalling how, in his enthusiasm, H pushed realism to the limits, and perhaps beyond:

---

*Rest and recuperation.
†Major Dair Farrar-Hockley

On the live-firing phase of the exercise there was the CO and his Tac right out in front for all to see, and it did cause adverse comment . . . He was pushing against all the rules of live firing. We were running risks there that we would never have got away with had we had someone accidentally killed or wounded; but he was determined to do it. I take my hat off to that sort of style and attitude, of saying: 'Sod the rules.'[8]

H's Mortar Officer was Captain Mal Worsley-Tonks. In many ways his position could have been unenviable, as H himself knew so much about mortars. But Mal knew his business too and had the self-confidence to be as direct with his Commanding Officer as H was with others. He recalls:

Colonel Jones had extremely high standards which he expected people to achieve and if they failed to achieve them he was certainly not happy. Furthermore, being a very outspoken person – not without justification sometimes – he would tell people where their failings lay. So I would not hide from the fact that there were people who he did not get on with particularly well. But in the main he was a popular man, and certainly from my perspective I got on with him famously and felt very privileged being his Mortar Officer from the moment we left Northern Ireland until he was killed.[9]

Good Army padres are greatly valued, and in David Cooper, 2 Para had such a man. Not only did he possess the strength of character and faith to fulfil his pastoral obligations superbly, he was also an expert on small arms, and a Bisley shot. With easy access to all ranks, and a confidant of many, Cooper had his finger on 2 Para's pulse and hence a good feel for the CO's relationships with his officers and men. As he put it:

If you were *interested*, Colonel H would go to any lengths to support you. But if you weren't, he wasn't interested in you. If he did have a weakness it was the ability to close out anybody who wasn't with him; and not to be with him was not to share his enthusiasm for soldiering or not to try your best. In short, if *you* weren't with him, he'd rather have someone who was![10]

As David Cooper manifestly fell into the fully committed and enthusiastic category, he got on splendidly with H. He understood and put into context another facet of his CO's personality – his excitability:

> Yes, H would blow a fuse, but he never blew it irrationally. If frustration got to him he'd get it off his chest and then solve the problem. At no time in my experience of him 'blowing up' did he ever follow it by any decision or attitude that showed anything other than absolute calmness and grip of the circumstances. He'd just let it rip; and then he'd get back to thinking clearly and rationally.[11]

All are agreed that H was driven by a single-minded determination to make 2 Para the best-trained unit in the Army, and he knew Kenya presented the finest opportunity in years to do so. He felt the Battalion had not yet shaken their Northern Ireland experience out of their system. They were not working as effectively as they should and he had identified some weak links in his team. He himself was attracting admiration and criticism in about equal measure, but this was not unusual – any new, innovative CO worth his salt does so, at least until everyone adjusts to the new regime.

In Kenya, perhaps more than anywhere else where the Army trains abroad, perceptions of a unit and its officers abound. There is a strong and knowledgeable expatriate community there descended from the early British settlers: those who had emigrated after the Great War, those who had farmed there for decades, and those who had been in the Colonial Service. Almost all of them were embodied in some official capacity during the Mau-Mau insurgency of the fifties, and their links with, and interest in, the British Army remain strong. Some, like the renowned Major Digby Tatham-Warter, living in Nanyuki, had distinguished themselves in the war. An airborne officer himself, Tatham-Warter had been on the bridge at Arnhem – depicted in the famous film *A Bridge Too Far* carrying an umbrella – and could recognise a well-led battalion when he saw one. Another was Rogue Barkas who, together with his wife Peggy, had guided and befriended the British Army for years. Such people kept a discreet eye on battalions passing through; they were generous hosts and introduced soldiers to the many wonders of Kenya.

Halfway through the exercise, H and some of his officers took time off to watch game at the Ark in the Aberdare Forest. This is a massive wooden viewing platform resembling an enormous Noah's Ark, overlooking a large clearing with a floodlit water hole and salt lick. In this magical place, throughout the night animals leave the forest and make for the water hole. Disregarding the illumination and the hundred or so onlookers safely 'embarked', they come almost within touching distance.

The senior 'hunter' and host on duty the night of H's stay was Ian Hardy, who had been warden of the Ark for the past twenty-two years. Formerly a Lancashire Fusilier, and later in 4th Battalion, The King's African Rifles, during the Mau-Mau emergency, Ian took the 2 Para party under his wing. It was a good night for viewing and Ian entranced his guests with his knowledge of the animals and their magnificence and variety – forty-six buffalo, sixteen elephants, three rhinos, thirty-four giant forest hogs and seventeen hyena were recorded in the Ark's log of 26 November 1981, along with many other species seen on the track leading to it. Hardy, a quiet, shrewd man, talked with H late into the night. He had met thousands of British officers but remembers being particularly struck by this one.

There was something about H which made him stand out as a man apart. I remember him clearly – right there at the bar as if it were yesterday – thinking he's not just another CO. The only other officer who had made a similar impression on me was Frank Kitson, with whom I had worked in intelligence during the

Emergency. Both had something unusual about them – a sort of aura and reserve – that was not evident in others.[12]

On another occasion, Sam Weller, a round, Pickwickian character, one of Kenya's foremost wildlife experts, and a particularly good friend of the Army, remembered a dinner 2 Para gave in their Officers' Mess at the well-known Nanyuki Show Ground. A local ranch manager was invited, to thank him for the use of his land for live field firing. The man could be an awkward fellow, and he failed to arrive at the appointed time. A phone call was made, eliciting that he knew of the invitation, had changed and was on his way. H told the Mess Sergeant to delay serving dinner, and the officers and their other guests continued patiently chatting in the anteroom. After an hour the man had still not turned up, so H ordered dinner to be served. As everyone settled at the table, the missing guest arrived – drunk.

The Mess was about to have a problem on its hands more serious than a delayed dinner and an inebriated guest. The ranch manager, sitting one away from H and now drinking copiously, began loudly and roundly to condemn the Parachute Regiment in general, and 2 Para in particular, citing the Regiment's youth, lack of tradition, and alleged poor record of behaviour and bad field discipline when camped on his ranch. This was fighting talk, touching, as it did, on sensitive areas. It was no comfort to the officers present that he had abused the hospitality of other regiments in similar terms over the years.

H affected to hear none of this. He would have been perfectly justified in having the man ejected, but Sam Weller recounts that instead he 'exercised a remarkable restraining influence on his officers, who understandably were getting somewhat upset by this abuse of their hospitality'. The sequel is recorded in H's official post-exercise report, dated 20 January 1982. Dealing first with more important military issues, he then wrote of his unworthy guest:

His behaviour that night became worse and worse; the other

guests left at approx 0200, but Mr X did not leave until 0400, at which time he was escorted from the Mess by me. His behaviour ... can only be described as intolerable. Unfortunately he continued to drink elsewhere in Nanyuki, and telephoned me at about 1000 hours to continue his threats and abuse. At this point Major (Retd) Tatham-Warter (an ex member of 2 Para) intervened, and as a result Mr X calmed down, and apologised verbally, and later in writing.

Kenya is a cradle of gossip, and by dawn the bones of this story were doing the rounds of the local ex-pat community. Later, with more enticing flesh upon them, they became the talk of the Muthaiga Club and other social watering holes in Nairobi. Interestingly, the surprise was not at how outrageous the guest's behaviour had been – that was predictable – but at the constraint of the officers of 2 Para and the diplomacy with which their Commanding Officer had handled an awkward situation.

Undeniably H stamped his mark on his Battalion in Kenya. Many testify to the importance of that long and searching exercise in getting the basic drills and skills of infantry procedures and tactics right. Mastery of such fundamentals as moving under fire from one position to another across open ground, and closing with and assaulting enemy positions was to pay dividends five months later in the Falklands. H's leadership and drive imbued in 2 Para a high level of determination and spirit that were later to be battle-winning ingredients. But it came at a price. He had to get rid of a couple of officers, he set some teeth on edge and other animosities were aroused. He earned a reputation in some quarters as a hard taskmaster: arrogant, dismissive and possessed of an excitable nature.

Reflecting on this years afterwards, one senior officer in another parachute battalion observed that there were those in 2 Para who perceived H to be 'too spicy, too rich, too extrovert and too unconventional'. Some, he added, felt uncomfortable with H's unorthodox style and language and what they considered to be his high-handed attitude. Nevertheless, even his critics accepted that his commitment to the Battalion was total and that his striving for the best was selfless, and very much in their overall interests.

By mid December, 2 Para were back in Aldershot in time to take well-earned Christmas leave. The Joneses spent theirs in Leipzig House, their Army quarter outside Aldershot. H's mother Dia, widowed for twenty-seven years and showing her age, had a thoroughly happy Christmas with the family. Dia and H were close and she had followed his career with pride. She also took a keen interest in her grandchildren, and was generous with their Christmas presents. David had had another good term at Sherborne and Rupert, at St Peter's, was approaching his Common Entrance exam.

H kept copies of all his confidential reports and showed Dia his latest. Although he and his Formation Commander may have had their differences, Brigadier Beckett had written well of him, describing him as 'an outstanding tactician'. True, Beckett had expressed some reservations about the administration of 2 Para, mentioning a series of disciplinary problems with which H had had to deal. But ending on a high note, he graded H 'Excellent' and recommended him for command of a brigade. He concluded: 'Lt. Col. Jones is an officer of much potential who merits consideration for early promotion.'

H never saw the key part of the report. This was the assessment (in the second part of the document), written by Beckett's immediate superior, designed to give a wider perspective and introduce broader, more experienced judgements than a brigade commander could. These remarks are only shown to the officer being assessed if they are markedly less favourable than those he has already read.* It was here that the General Officer Commanding South East District† commented of H: 'His Battalion Headquarters

---

*This was before the advent of rights of access to personal records, which has changed the arrangements.

†Lieutenant-General Sir Paul Travers.

team is unexceptional but despite this the imprint of his authority
. . . is becoming steadily more impressive. In terms of tactical grasp
and flair he is easily the best CO in the Field Force.'

Finally, in the reporting chain, it was the turn of the
Commander-in-Chief, or his deputy. The latter was Lieutenant-
General Sir Frank Kitson – the same officer with whom Ian Hardy
had bracketed H that night at the Ark. In his opinion, 'Lt. Col.
Jones has had to run his Battalion with rather a weak team – only
one psc* officer besides himself – which makes the tactical handling
of the Battalion very difficult . . . he may well merit an outstanding
grading next time.'

That Christmas it snowed heavily, and Sara remembers having a
row with H over driving Dia back to Devon at the end of the break.
Sara thought it was folly to make an unnecessary journey in those
conditions, but H saw it as a challenge, and 'good fun too!' So he
took Dia home. It was to be the last time he saw her.

When the Battalion re-assembled in the New Year, it found itself
grouped in a new brigade but in the same barracks. This was a
consequence of one of the Army's reorganisations – in this case,
forming larger field force HQs with a wider (and theoretically
cheaper) span of command. This, however, had been proved to be
unworkable, and brigade headquarters had now been re-instituted.
In this way 2 Para became part of 5 Infantry Brigade, under Brigadier
Tony Wilson. Unfortunately, H's relations with the new team were
to be no more harmonious than they had been with its predecessor.

On a brigade exercise in February at Thetford, in Norfolk, 2 Para
pitted its wits against 3 Para, and the element of competitive edge
between the two battalions was very evident. By now H had a new
second-in-command, Major Chris Keeble, and the bonds of trust
had quickly been established both ways. Such trust was a *sine qua
non* of forming fruitful relationships with H, and he confided in
Keeble that he was still not happy with some of his subordinate
commanders, and battalion headquarters staff. By the end of the

---

*Passed Staff College.

exercise, Keeble's more objective assessment had confirmed H's intuitive opinion.

Back in Aldershot, after the exercise, 2 Para's focus now turned to Belize and their forthcoming six months' unaccompanied tour there. It was a prospect that H did not relish: he had unhappy memories of his previous time in Belize and felt three previous tours in that part of the world were enough. The process of briefing, packing and getting ready to go was drawn-out. The tour was to start in mid April; however, the Battalion's heavy equipment and baggage had to sail in March.

In February H went on a short reconnaissance to Belize. Meanwhile 2 Para occupied themselves with various study days, courses, unit administration and sports fixtures. When the bulk of the Battalion started their embarkation-cum-Easter leave, it was time for H to take a break too. But one precaution came first: he double-checked that the Battalion's recall arrangements from leave were in place, so that 2 Para could be re-assembled quickly should the need arise. Not that there was any suggestion that it might; it was just part of H's far-sightedness, coupled with the traditional attention that good units afford to operational readiness.

H took the family skiing. Their fortnight in Meribel suited his ideal of a holiday admirably and it was a great success. On Sunday 4 April they began their return, via Calais, and would in the normal course of events have got home, unpacked and driven down to The Grange for the forthcoming Easter weekend. As described earlier, however, H learnt on the way home that momentous events were unfolding in the South Atlantic. By the time the family reached Aldershot late on Sunday night, he had been able to confirm, using telephone kiosks en route, that the Falklands had been invaded; that the Prime Minister had pledged to recover them; that a task force was already being assembled – and that 2 Para was not involved.

Next morning H went into barracks to get himself properly briefed. Most officers were still on leave, but he was assured, although the exact sequence of events is now hazy, that 2 Para's imminent Belize tour stood. H promptly and with single-minded determination set about changing this and getting his Battalion included in the Task Force. Probably not one of the other fifty infantry commanding officers would have attempted this. Although most would have wanted to be where action was in prospect, almost all would have accepted the virtual impossibility of changing existing arrangements at that late stage. H, probably uniquely, had two advantages. First, he understood how the complicated tasking process worked – after all, until the previous year, this had been his job at Wilton. Therefore, he knew it was feasible to unscramble the Belize plot. Second, he knew personally all the key officers involved in the decision-making process. (Hence, his first call en route from France had been to Bob Flood.) Even so, possessing background knowledge and having easy access do not on their own enable one to overturn established decisions. That requires convincing arguments, leading to a better alternative. H was to provide both.

The logical decision to base the land component of the Task Force on 3 Commando Brigade (3 Cdo Bde) had already been taken. The Brigade, commanded by Brigadier Julian Thompson, consisted of three Royal Marine commando units, each the size of a battalion. Sensibly, in view of the potential task, 3 Cdo Bde was to be reinforced by two Army units: 3rd Battalion, The Parachute Regiment (3 Para), who were the Spearhead Battalion – at a higher state of readiness than any other – and 1st Battalion, Queen's Own Highlanders. The thrust of H's counter-proposal was that it would be a better-balanced force if two airborne battalions were included, rather than one airborne and one infantry battalion. His reasoning was that both para battalions were identically equipped and similarly trained; furthermore, they worked to the same procedures and were virtually interchangeable. Hence his proposal was inherently more flexible and advantageous.

The case against committing both para battalions to the Task Force was that once they had sailed there would be no airborne capability left in Britain (1 Para was in Northern Ireland and therefore could not be touched). H immediately countered that there would be no such capability anyway once 2 Para left for Belize, and 3 Para had sailed south. This was undeniable, and in no time the Belize plan was changed and a battalion of the Royal Anglian Regiment was substituted for 2 Para.

H's Battalion was now unencumbered. Meanwhile, the planners were facing a deteriorating situation as Argentina poured more and more men into the Falklands. It soon became obvious that even a reinforced brigade might not have sufficient strength; and therefore a second brigade should be assembled. This was to be 5 Infantry Brigade, the formation that 2 Para was now in. But they would take some time to deploy, being newly formed and only just notified, whereas 2 Para was ready to go almost at once. This argument, coupled with H's earlier logic about grouping 2 Para with 3 Para, tipped the scales, and 2 Para were released to join 3 Cdo Bde. However, it was emphasised that they should expect to revert to 5 Inf Bde once the situation clarified on arrival in the Falklands. That was a distant condition H was happy to accept.

Thus the composition of the Task Force was altered to include 2 Para within 3 Cdo Bde, but sailing separately. Undeniably H's hand contributed to the evolution of the decision-making, although his fingerprints were not evident. The executive decision anyway was taken far above his head, and it is possible that the planners themselves would have reached the same conclusion independently. Shedding 2 Para's Belize commitment was the key that opened the door to H's involvement in the Falklands. Why did he turn it?

First, he believed it was the correct military solution. Second, he knew that he was reflecting the abilities and wishes of his entire Battalion: 2 Para were fired up and longing for action. Indeed, the thought of 3 Para heading south with the Royal Marines whilst 2 Para flew off to the Belizean jungle on some second-order task did not bear contemplation.

Third, H was temperamentally proactive. It was simply not in his nature to wait and let events unfold. Whilst outcomes were not yet determined, he would agitate to influence them, however exasperating this might be for more conventional colleagues.

Lastly, and almost certainly, H would have felt his whole service had been in preparation for this historic moment – that he, personally, had a destiny to fulfil. This incorrigible military romantic had dreamt in a thousand dreams of leading a charge against the Queen's enemies in some foreign land. He could not know where his destiny lay, but assuredly, he sensed that it was now calling, and he must follow it.

CHAPTER TEN

Going to War

Before British soldiers are committed to operations, they are briefed and prepared assiduously. The process began for 2 Para when H received official notification by signal, at 1330 hours on Thursday 15 April 1982, that his Battalion was to be at seventy-two hours' 'Notice to Move', with effect from midnight.

The signal also opened the floodgates of Army largesse. It was as if 2 Para had instantly acquired a diplomatic passport – peacetime restrictions were lifted and routine bureaucracy fell away. When the balloon goes up, as has been shown before, no organisation is better motivated or quicker to respond than the British Armed Forces. The Battalion was inundated with requests from airborne soldiers serving elsewhere to rejoin, and there was a tangible buzz and a powerful sense of purpose throughout the ranks.

Personnel and briefing teams, stores and ammunition flooded into the barracks – for example, the latest Clansman radios (previously allocated only to units in BAOR and Northern Ireland) were issued, and extra general-purpose machine guns (GPMGs) delivered. This was due to the Second-in-Command's insistence on doubling the number of these powerful weapons in each platoon – a fine piece of tactical anticipation that was to prove inspired.

Before 2 April, few soldiers in 2 Para could have found the Falkland Islands in an atlas, and there were certainly no military maps available. Yet over the following days and weeks, H's officers and men were briefed extensively on everything relevant to the crisis.

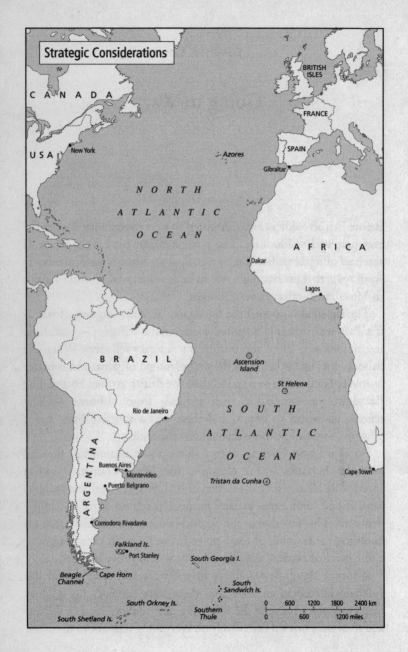

Strategic Considerations

(*Above*) H as Adjutant of the Devon and Dorsets on exercise in Germany.

(*Left*) At a parade in Portadown in 1977, Major Jones receives the Queen's Jubilee Medal from Sir Norman Strong (formerly Speaker at Stormont) who was later murdered by the IRA.

(*Above*) H, as BM 3 Inf Bde, briefs Roy Mason (with pipe) then Secretary of State for Northern Ireland.

(*Right*) Captain Robert Nairac dressed for undercover work.

(*Left*) Major H Jones on Remembrance Day in Belize.

(*Below*) Lt Col H Jones, CO 2 PARA, on exercise in Norfolk, early 1982.

(*Right*) 2 Para embarking on an LCU whilst practising landing drills at Ascension on the way south to the Falklands.

(*Left*) H's cabin on board *Canberra*.

(*Right*) On alert. GPMG and gun team on *Canberra*.

(*Above*) San Carlos Bay, looking NW from 2 Para's defensive position on Mount Sussex, soon after the landings.

(*Right*) The Type 22 frigate HMS *Broadsword* turns towards *Norland* in order to fire the landing orders across by gunline.

(*Below*) 2 Para preparing their defensive position on Mount Sussex.

(*Left*) H's sangar on Mount Sussex.

(*Below*) Another position on Mount Sussex. The flag is a recognition panel.

(*Bottom*) 2 Para moving off Mount Sussex en route for Camilla Creek House.

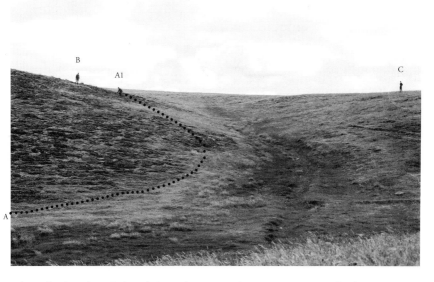

(*Above*) The photo shows the line of H's assault (A) against the position at B. He was shot from a trench at C when he reached A1.

(*Below*) H's brother, Commander Tim Jones RN, pays his respects during a visit to the Falklands in October 1982.

(*Above*) H's grave at San Carlos Military Cemetery. The wreath in the foreground is from All Ranks of The Devonshire and Dorset Regiment, H's first regiment.

(*Below*) Sara with H's VC in the Quadrangle of Buckingham Palace flanked by Rupert (left) and David on 4 November 1982, after the Investiture.

They learnt that the Falklands – two main islands and some 700 smaller ones – were set deep in the South Atlantic, 8,000 miles from Great Britain, yet only 350 miles from Argentina. They heard that the islands were British dependencies with a population of around 1,800, whose combined land mass was similar in size to Wales, and in appearance to the Western Isles of Scotland, with whose inhabitants the islanders shared a similar outlook and rugged independence. There was no direct air link between the Falklands and 'home', as the islanders referred to Britain. Until 1971, when a service commenced via Argentina, a monthly passenger and cargo vessel operated between Stanley and Montevideo in Uruguay. Here, islanders and visitors transferred either to one of the Royal Mail vessels for the long passage to Britain, or latterly caught connecting international flights. Although the Falkland Islands Company ran a direct cargo service once every three months, it did not carry passengers. The remoteness of the islands meant that isolation and insecurity were endemic.

Despite their CO's passion for military history, it is unlikely that many of H's Battalion spent long absorbing the Falklands' historical complexity. Nevertheless, their briefings would have mentioned that the renowned Florentine navigator Amerigo Vespucci was thought to have first sighted the islands in about 1502, although it was not until 1592 that the British captain, John Davies, in his ship *Desire*, landed and staked his claim on behalf of the Crown.

The first undisputed landing was made by Captain John Strong RN in 1690. It was he who named, after the First Lord of the Admiralty, the narrow stretch of water between the two main islands 'Falkland Sound' – which was to become for a fortnight nearly three centuries later the most hotly contested spot on the globe.

In the eighteenth century, intense international trade rivalry developed between Britain, France and Spain. Spain's control of her territories in the Americas, which included what are now Argentina and the Falkland Islands, was established in the Treaty of Utrecht of 1713. It was the provisions of that treaty that lay at the root of all subsequent ambiguity over Argentina's rights to the Falkland Islands.

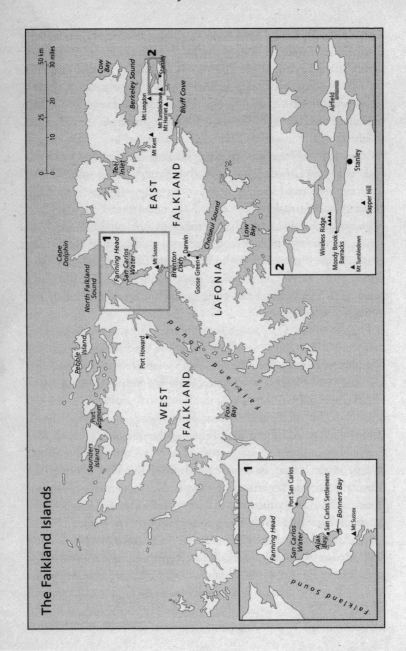

The Falkland Islands

The next claim to the islands was in the name of Louis XV, through de Bougainville's French expedition of 1764, which established a settlement on East Falkland at Port Louis, where Port Stanley now stands. Meanwhile, 'Foulweather Jack' Byron, a commodore under the orders of the British Admiralty, developed a settlement at Port Egmont north of the other main island, West Falkland.

The next few years were spent in evictions, re-settlements, claims and counter-claims. Following a period of renewed British construction and development at Port Egmont, a Lieutenant Clayton laid formal claim to all the islands on 20 May 1774 by engraving, on a lead sheet then attached to a blockhouse:

Be it known to all Nations that Falkland Islands* with this Fort, the storehouse, Wharfs and Harbours, Bays and Creeks thereupon belonging are of the Sole Right and Property of His Most Sacred Majesty, George the Third, King of Great Britain, France and Ireland. Defender of the Faith, etc. In witness whereof this plate is set up and His Britannic Majesty's Colours left flying as a mark of possession.

By, W.S. Clayton, Commanding Officer at Falkland Islands. AD 1774.

Whereupon he sailed away; but the islands were not left unoccupied for long.

A year later a Spanish settlement was established, but stirrings of independence had begun, and in 1810 the local authorities in Buenos Aires laid claim to the islands and ejected the Spanish settlers. Between 1826 and 1831 Argentina established a colony at Port Soledad (previously de Bougainville's Port Louis, and now Port Stanley), with its own governor, who in an excess of zeal ordered the arrest of three visiting United States sealing schooners, for alleged

---

*Some versions are recorded in the singular – Falkland Island – thereby undermining this claim.

poaching. Retribution followed swiftly. The USS corvette *Lexington*, under Captain Silas Duncan, was sent to destroy the whole settlement, which he did with vigour, declaring the islands 'free of all government'.

Two years after that, in 1833, Charles Darwin, aboard the famous *Beagle*, called in on the unoccupied Falklands, and a continuous British presence has been maintained on the islands ever since, despite his recording in his log: 'An undulating land, with a desolate and wretched aspect, is everywhere covered by a peaty soil and wiry grass of monotonous brown colour.'[1]

The most important point emerging from this history, which struck a particularly responsive chord with H's soldiers, was simply that the Falkland Islanders, whatever their origins, had for 150 years been fiercely and proudly British. They had consistently rejected any claim by Argentina to their islands. All suggestions and encouragement – even, at times, coercion – by successive British governments to be realistic and recognise the economic benefits and practical advantages of closer links with Argentina, including better trade and communications, had cut no ice at all. In terms of self-determination – a vital principle enshrined under Article 1 of the United Nations Charter – they had regularly, consistently and unanimously expressed their wish to remain British. They were British citizens, on Great Britain's sovereign territory. On that point no compromise was possible, although few imagined at the outset that Britain would have to go to war over it.

Further information on the more immediate causes of the impasse was gleaned from the media. The salient facts were presented starkly in the newspapers and on TV and radio: there had been a failure of intelligence, a failure of diplomacy and a failure of British defence policy. The general drift of most opinion was that, as usual, it would now be up to brave British servicemen to rectify the mistakes of incompetent politicians and diplomats.

The reality, of course, was far more complex, springing from a series of interconnecting, although separate, circumstances and decisions. In Argentina a three-man military Junta, led by General

Leopoldo Galtieri, had assumed power in December 1981. Inheriting chronic domestic problems, the regime believed that the recovery of the 'Islas Malvinas', as they termed the Falkland Islands, was one of two popular measures behind which the nation could unite, during what was going to be a period of severe economic austerity. (The other was the recovery of three islands in the Beagle Channel claimed by Chile.) These were not just cynical diversions. Mr Costa Mendes, the Foreign Minister, was genuinely affronted that no progress had been made in resolving the issue peacefully in the fifteen years since he had last held that office. He was convinced, for all the talk and studies, including the Communication Agreement of 1972 and Lord Shackleton's 1974 report, that Britain had been deliberately dragging her feet. He doubted anything could now be resolved without vigorous unilateral action by his country.

Furthermore, the Junta correctly appreciated that the United States favoured a pro-Western regime in Argentina, its interest being to show support for one of the few anti-Communist powers then in South America. As evidence of this, Galtieri himself had been warmly welcomed on an early official visit to Washington.

Moreover, when the Junta turned their attention on Britain, they noted a series of recent policy decisions that seemed to indicate a lessening of British commitment to the Falklands. First was the publicly announced intention to withdraw the Antarctic patrol ship, HMS *Endurance,* to save £2m a year. They noted, too, that the British Antarctic Survey base in South Georgia was scheduled to close. Then, in the summer of 1981, the British Nationality Bill had passed through Parliament withdrawing the right of full British citizenship from, *inter alia,* the Falkland Islanders. (In fact, the measure was primarily intended to prevent three million Hong Kong citizens applying for right of automatic entry to Britain, but that subtlety was lost on Buenos Aires.) Finally, there was Defence Secretary John Nott's 1981 White Paper, which postulated major reductions in the Royal Navy's capability to operate alone in the world's farthest oceans. The Navy was to dispose of two aircraft carriers – HMS *Hermes* and HMS *Invincible** – and both its assault ships, *Fearless* and *Intrepid*, essential for amphibious operations. In future the Fleet, enhanced by more modern ships and systems, would concentrate on strengthening the anti-submarine capability of NATO in the North Atlantic. It was hardly surprising, therefore, that early in 1982 the Junta concluded that Britain's interest in the Falklands and her ability to preserve the status quo there were on the wane.

So confident were the Junta that within weeks of returning to power, their navy's original invasion plan was reconsidered, and revised. They concluded that the invasion should take place, without warning, in the latter half of 1982, calculating that by this time their latest delivery of Exocet missiles from France would be in service; that *Endurance* would have been withdrawn; and that the other cuts in the Royal Navy envisaged in the Defence Review would have begun to bite. These assumptions were essentially correct – which makes it ironic that, on all sides, miscalculation was then to be heaped on miscalculation.

Two earlier events had a conditioning effect in both Buenos Aires and London. Late in 1976, Southern Thule, one of the islands in the Sandwich Group and another British dependency, was illegally occupied by Argentinians. Then, a year later, the fuel supply to Stanley, one of the 'confidence building' measures enshrined in a painfully negotiated earlier agreement, was cut off.

There had been a swift British response to that, but not to the Southern Thule incident, news of which was slow in reaching London. The then Prime Minister, James Callaghan, ordered a submarine† to the Falklands, and two frigates to position themselves in the South Atlantic, but before they were evident, fuel was restored. However, as the British response had not been made public, it was unclear whether Her Majesty's Government's prompt reaction had resolved the matter, or whether the fuel supply would

---

*HMS *Hermes* was to be scrapped and *Invincible* sold to Australia.
†The nuclear submarine *Dreadnought* was dispatched.

have been restored anyway. Neither side could, for certain, link cause and effect. Nevertheless, an impression persisted that the intelligence assessors in London had overreacted to the threat and that the islanders had cried wolf too loudly. A suspicion also took root that this was just another case of Argentine huffing and puffing. Furthermore, the rapidity of the Royal Navy's response had been inconvenient and costly for the Ministry of Defence. Thus the seeds were sown from which fresh miscalculation would sprout.

In February 1982 the Anglo-Argentinian talks at the UN in New York – delayed a few months until the Junta had settled in – resumed. This was the latest in a series of meetings under UN auspices, supposedly to resolve the conflicting claims of sovereignty. Britain was represented by a newly appointed* FCO minister, Richard Luce,† who was warned before the talks began of Argentinian bellicosity. At the meeting, he was confronted with three fresh demands, the last being an end-of-the-year deadline for resolution of the sovereignty issue. With diplomatic skill, he agreed to nothing other than to keep talking – and more frequently. A joint communiqué was prepared and agreed in New York, to be issued simultaneously in both capitals. The UN Secretary General, Perez de Cuellar, even endorsed this positive development personally.

However, back in Buenos Aires, trouble was brewing. Costa Mendes refused to issue the agreed communiqué and declared publicly that Argentina had already been negotiating, in good faith, for quite long enough. He decreed that unless Britain ceded sovereignty in the near future, Argentina reserved the right to employ 'other means' to regain the islands.

One would have imagined this would have set alarm bells tolling up and down Westminster and Whitehall. But it did not. It was interpreted, particularly in view of the Argentine media manipulation, as just another puff of hot air from Buenos Aires, largely for domestic consumption. Nevertheless, as a precaution,

---

*A Conservative Government had been elected in May 1979.
†Now the Lord Chamberlain.

warning cones were hoisted and the intelligence community alerted to any subsequent follow-up action. Graduated responses, such as cutting off fuel and disrupting air traffic, are the billboards of diplomacy, and they would have indicated that there was substance behind the latest protestations. But no such indications emerged, until on 19 March, as outlined in the Introduction, Constantino Davidoff and his team of scrap-metal contractors landed at Leith on South Georgia, some 800 miles east-south-east of the Falklands, and raised the Argentine flag.

Even this, however, was by no means seen as conclusive. Davidoff had been contracted months before to clear up the old whaling station at Leith, and had obtained permission from the British Embassy in Buenos Aires to do so. Arguably, he had merely failed to observe the correct protocol. In fact, it appears with hindsight that the Junta were genuinely ignorant of the timing and extent of his action. Indeed, their national interest would best have been served if nothing at all had occurred around the Malvinas to jeopardise their secret plans for invasion later that year. For them, the scrap-metal incident and the reaction to it had come six months too early.

Unaware of the Junta's true intentions, London ordered that the extent of the South Georgia incursion be investigated. It did not appear to be sufficiently grave to dispatch even a submarine unnecessarily, at least until the situation was clarified. So HMS *Endurance,* with a detachment of locally embarked Royal Marines, was sent to investigate and report back. Davidoff was ordered to obey the terms of his licence and leave. He did so, but not all his men followed. In the meantime, frenetic diplomatic activity began.

At times like this, diplomacy most resembles a game of chess. Because *Endurance* had been deployed and might evict Argentinians from disputed territory – action that would inflame home opinion – the Junta felt compelled to respond. They sent the *Bahia Paraiso*, their equivalent of *Endurance*, to protect the scrap merchants by putting ashore an armed party under the internationally notorious

Captain Astiz.* On both sides these moves were accompanied by de-escalatory diplomatic noises behind the scenes. Britain did not want conflict over an insignificant incursion; conversely, the Junta, although determined to seize the Falklands, did not want to provoke a fight – yet.

But, as in chess, a move, or even the absence of a particular counter-move, can be misinterpreted. Although London had not dispatched a submarine or any other external reinforcement to deal with the incursion, the Junta assumed that it had done so, or would do so shortly. Therefore they felt they should move first, and quickly in the light of a deteriorating domestic situation at home – rioting had begun in the capital and press hostility was becoming uncomfortable. Thus, in secret session on or around 25 March – Argentina's National Day – the Junta decided to advance their intended seizure of the Falklands.

Under cover of annual naval manoeuvres with Uruguay, an amphibious exercise was put in motion. All exercises are set within imaginary but realistic scenarios, and this one could equally have been connected with a notional seizure of the disputed islands in the Beagle Channel as with the Malvinas. So those, such as the British naval attaché in Buenos Aires, who declared it as evidence of something more sinister were held in London to be alarmist.

Nevertheless, there was disquiet in informed circles. Reports and intelligence indicators were pieced together over the next three days, and when Captain Astiz and his commandos did not leave South Georgia, as earlier pledged, action could no longer be postponed. On 29 March the Cabinet decided to repeat Callaghan's earlier unannounced dispatch of a nuclear submarine to the South Atlantic. Accordingly, HMS *Spartan* was armed and made ready in Gibraltar, sailing two days later. She was to be followed by *Splendid* and *Conqueror* from Faslane.

Admiral Sir Henry Leach, First Sea Lord and professional head of

---

*Captain Astiz was implicated in the interrogation and 'disappearance' of many who had previously opposed the Junta.

the Royal Navy, was concerned, notwithstanding the lack of firm evidence, that three submarines might not be enough to cope if the situation deteriorated. So he ordered certain additional precautionary measures. As it happened, this suited his purpose well, because Sir Henry was in a virtual state of unarmed conflict with his political master, John Nott.

The Defence Secretary had recently published a significant White Paper entitled *The Way Forward*, which postulated a substantial reduction in the Royal Navy. This had already occasioned the resignation of the Navy Minister, Keith Speed, and Admiral Leach had considered resigning himself.[2] Indeed, two of his predecessors had suggested he should go. He considered, however, that the issue was not a matter of honour – had it been so, he would have resigned at once – hence he determined to stay on and fight the Navy's corner. Experience had taught him that high-level resignations over matters of policy rarely get that policy changed, although they do find favour lower down the Service as evidence that someone at the top cares sufficiently to make a personal sacrifice. But in this case, no one could doubt Henry Leach's own commitment.

Leach's father had been in command of the battleship HMS *Prince of Wales* when, on 10 December 1941, in company with the battle cruiser HMS *Repulse,* she was attacked by Japanese aircraft in the South China Sea. Without air cover both ships were sunk quickly, with devastating loss of life, including that of Captain Leach himself. It so happened that young Henry, then a midshipman serving in another ship in Singapore, saw his father the night before the *Prince of Wales* sailed.

It was no surprise, therefore, many years later when Leach became First Sea Lord he should passionately advocate Britain retaining a strong, balanced Fleet. A policy that relied solely on an ally, or another Service, to provide essential air cover, or maritime support, was to him unwise, if not downright heresy. He was equally convinced that the Navy's most likely future task would entail responding to the unexpected. How right, and how soon, this was proved to be.

At the very pinnacle of the British Armed Forces is the Chief of Defence Staff (CDS). He and the three professional heads of each Service,* constitute the Chiefs of Staff. As chairman, CDS is *primus inter pares* and represents their collective view to the Defence Secretary. Each Chief has right of direct access to the Prime Minister, but at that time CDS could formally offer his own opinion only if there was a divergence of view among his colleagues.†

When the three submarines were given their orders on 29 March, CDS, Admiral of the Fleet Sir Terence Lewin, was on an official tour in New Zealand. Although kept in touch, he was not recalled because the sense of impending crisis would have been accentuated by publicly foreshortening his visit. British diplomatic effort was still directed at trying to buy time by defusing the situation. Hence the statement by Richard Luce to an anxious House of Commons the next day was crafted to that end, with specifically no mention being made of the submarine deployments. However, either by leaks or inspired guesses, the British evening news bulletins and morning papers carried the conjecture. These stories were flashed instantly to Buenos Aires where, coincidentally, rioting against recent austerity measures was escalating. The Junta, therefore, found it both expedient and easy to order the recovery of the Malvinas – forthwith.

In London the next evening – Wednesday 31 March – Mrs Thatcher called a meeting, in the Prime Minister's office at the House of Commons, of her key ministers and advisers. In preparation for this crucial gathering, John Nott had been briefed in the Ministry of Defence, forming in the process a pessimistic view of the feasibility and likely effectiveness of any of the emergent military options. Accordingly, as he outlined these to the Prime Minister, a sense of gloom enveloped the meeting. At some point

---

*First Sea Lord and Chief of the Naval Staff (CNS); Chief of the General Staff (CGS); and Chief of the Air Staff (CAS).

†The arrangement has now changed, and CDS has his own policy and implementation staff.

news was received that the First Sea Lord was in the Lobby – he had come to see his Secretary of State. The PM invited him to join them, although it would not have been lost on the Defence Secretary, or on some of the others present, that Leach was neither CDS, nor even Acting CDS.

The First Sea Lord's entrance made a tremendous impact. Resplendent in uniform with five inches of gold braid down each sleeve, Admiral Leach looked just the part. His open face, firm jaw and piercing blue eyes under bushy eyebrows exuded confidence and determination. The meeting was discussing how best to brief President Reagan and Britain's key ambassadors, and debating what instructions to give the Islands' Governor. Leach stirred in irritation at some of the limp suggestions. When invited to speak, it was apparent that he was more up to date, better briefed and considerably more convincing than was his political master. Firmly he corrected the Prime Minister's misconception that the Falklands were three days' steaming away and that therefore reinforcements could soon be there – the islands were three *weeks* away.

His bravura performance offered his Prime Minister, for the first time, both hope and a practical way forward. He insisted that a substantial and balanced task force – ships with integral air cover, anti-submarine protection and logistic support – could be assembled, and should be dispatched, at the earliest opportunity. Such a task force would be ready to sail within two days. But he needed the authority to proceed.

He got it. Here was a man prepared to deliver, and Margaret Thatcher must have felt like hugging him. John Nott, on the other hand, could probably have throttled the Admiral for exposing, so starkly in front of his colleagues, the false assumptions of his recent Defence Review.

Over the next forty-eight hours, frantic activity took place at every level. Diplomatic traffic flowed continuously to and from Washington, where Sir Nicholas Henderson was Her Majesty's Ambassador; and similarly to Sir Anthony Parsons, Ambassador to the United Nations in New York. The Prime Minister spoke to

President Reagan, who in turn tried contacting General Galtieri, but without success – until it was too late.

Meanwhile, sailors and dockyard workers toiled round the clock to get armed ships and merchant vessels ready for sea. Intelligence analysts scoured the airwaves for Argentine naval radio traffic – there was no satellite photographic coverage of that part of the world then. Meanwhile, in Plymouth and elsewhere, key Royal Marines, just alerted, besieged reference libraries for every available scrap of information on the strength and capability of Argentina's armed forces.

At dawn on Friday 2 April, Argentine commandos landed near Stanley and headed for the harbour and the barracks at Moody Brook, where they hoped to catch unawares the two detachments of Royal Marines stationed there. (By coincidence, both forty-strong incoming and outgoing detachments were on or near the Island, in the process of hand-over.) Some had already deployed to South Georgia with *Endurance* and the rest were protecting Government House and other key points. The previous day's frenzied headlines and broadcasts from Buenos Aires, predicting imminent invasion, had compromised any surprise Argentina may have planned. By 0830 Falklands time – four hours behind Greenwich Mean Time – the Argentine navy was in the harbour, and unloading. After initial resistance, in which two enemy had been killed, the Governor ordered his Royal Marines to lay down their arms.

The remoteness of the Falklands and Britain's un-preparedness to defend them was well illustrated by the fact that, with all direct communication cut, the first confirmation that the islands had been seized did not reach London until four o'clock that afternoon. Even more extraordinary, this only came about through a ham radio operator in Wales making contact with a fellow enthusiast on the islands.

Two hours later, Lord Carrington and John Nott held a press conference to confirm what Buenos Aires had been exulting in all day. Both appeared tired and shocked as they announced that diplomatic relations with Argentina had been broken off; that a large task force was ready to sail (in fact, it was *not* yet ready); and that the House of Commons would meet the next day. Carrington had already resolved to resign* as a matter of honour.

In their book *The Battle for the Falklands*, the distinguished journalists Max Hastings and Simon Jenkins described the scene in the Commons the following day:

To some, the debate in the Commons on Saturday 3 April represented British Democracy at its best. The House rose almost as one voice to speak the collective shame of the nation and did so in terms that no government could ignore. Yet to others, the debate was a depressing re-run of the negative qualities which for years had prevented any sensible resolution of the Falklands dispute.

Mrs Thatcher made the best of an impossible task in her opening remarks. Clearly tired and in a speech which bore the traces of many hands – most of them the Foreign Office – she pointed out that 'It would have been absurd to dispatch the fleet every time there was bellicose talk in Buenos Aires.' As for keeping a permanent deterrent force on station, 'The cost would be enormous . . . no government could have done that.' Stepping painfully across the no-man's land between past failure and future restitution, she announced only that 'A large task force will sail as soon as preparations are complete.'

As she sat down, contempt rolled like thunder from the benches round her. It was the culmination of a dozen Falklands question times over the past decade, a demonstration of disgust not just of the Foreign Office but of executive government in general. Those excluded from the joys of office could at last take their revenge on the placemen of power. MPs seemed to revel in the self-righteousness of their rhetoric . . . As in Buenos Aires so in London, the hour seemed to call for emotion rather than clear heads.

---

*He saw the debate through and resigned over the weekend; Richard Luce followed him.

Never was the absence of the Foreign Secretary from the Commons more painful. While Carrington was presenting a careful apologia to a respectful audience in the Lords, John Nott had to face the final firestorm in the lower house. His speech, which he later admitted could 'only have been a disaster', received scant attention for its content. No amount of government bellicosity would appease his audience. His plea for support for the armed forces as they set sail was brushed aside amid uproar and cries of 'Resign!' MPs left the Commons blinking into the sunlight of Parliament Square, to find it packed with tourists eager to witness the bizarre spectacle of the wounded British lion sending its fleet to war.[3]

Confirmation of the Argentinian invasion accelerated decision-making in London. The Navy's prudent anticipation, the Prime Minister's resolution, the mood of Parliament and the genuine affront felt by millions of Britons who, until now, had scarcely heard of the Falkland Islands gave the impetus – and justification – for a military response. Its speed and scale were awesome, the more so because it was spectacular.

Within seventy-two hours of the PM's statement to the Commons, live TV coverage of the departure of HMS *Invincible* and HMS *Hermes*, with their escorts, was being beamed round the world. They left Portsmouth on the evening tide of Monday 5 April to scenes of great emotion, with thousands of spectators and the families of those embarked lining vantage points along the Solent. There were bands and banners – one prominently proclaiming 'Good Luck – Give 'em 'ell'; and there were emotional farewells. The more tears there were, the greater seemed the determination of cameramen to capture them. Ships' companies lined the decks, salutes were fired and ensigns dipped at the appropriate moments. The last nautical exodus on this scale must have been on the eve of D-Day in June 1944. But that was shrouded in secrecy. This was the opposite; and it was not to be the last such spectacle.

Five days later, on Good Friday, P & O's flagship *Canberra*, having been hastily converted from its role of luxury cruise liner to troopship, left Southampton with 3 Commando Brigade, including 3 Para, embarked. Their departure was attended by similar displays of emotion and patriotism. Those on the dockside who were already wondering where all this might lead kept their thoughts to themselves.

H's own departure was quite different. Having succeeded in getting 2 Para included in the Task Force, his Battalion would now have to catch up the main body, already on its way to Ascension Island. This was a British-owned extinct volcanic island lying two-thirds of the way down, and 2,000 miles off, the west coast of Africa. With an unusually long runway, its airfield (Wide-Awake) was leased to the United States as a communication station and an alternative landing site for space shuttles.

To get 2 Para there, the North Sea Hull to Rotterdam ferry MV *Norland* and the *Europic* were requisitioned. These were two of scores of civilian ships used under an established emergency procedure called STUFT: Shipping Taken Up From Trade. The *Norland* was to sail from Portsmouth with 2 Para aboard, under H's Second-in-Command, Chris Keeble, on an unspecified date – unspecified because there was no certainty at that stage that those in the proposed 'second wave' would be needed. (The *Europic*, carrying their vehicles and equipment, loaded in the rush in any order, had already sailed.) Some felt that Argentina might be persuaded by the show of force and sense of purpose already displayed to withdraw behind a face-saving formula. More realistically, others believed that a solution acceptable to both sides could be finessed through the massive diplomatic activity now under way. But military men plan for the worst whilst hoping for the best, and thus there was no let-up in preparation and training.

On 17 April, Admiral Sir John Fieldhouse, who as C-in-C Fleet had been appointed 'Joint Commander',* held a conference in HMS *Hermes* off Ascension Island for all his subordinate

---

*The overall four-star commander of the whole operation.

commanders. Its purpose was to co-ordinate operational planning, and to examine the various options open to the Task Force. Among those present were Rear Admiral Sandy Woodward, Flag Officer 1st Flotilla; Commodore Michael Clapp, Commander Amphibious Warfare; and Brigadier Julian Thompson, Commander 3 Commando Brigade. These officers were to feature prominently in H's immediate future.

At this conference, Julian Thompson was told of the recent decision to put 2 Para under his command. He was delighted, as he had known H in South Armagh as Brigade Major 3 Infantry Brigade,* when he himself had been commanding 40 Commando. They had established a rapport, and Brigadier Thompson now authorised H to fly out to Ascension ahead of the main body of 2 Para for briefing, before returning to the UK to update his soldiers prior to their embarkation.

So when H and Sara said goodbye on 22 April, Sara was expecting to have H home again in a couple of days. It has been said that as H left, Sara had a premonition that she would never see him again. This was not so. She recalls: 'H was definitely coming back so there were no tender loving farewells. He said, "I've got to fly out for this planning session and then I'll return because I must travel down south with the Battalion." His departure therefore was very matter-of-fact.'

H had earlier put in a call to America to give Dan Severson his news.† Sara continues:

Then the staff car came and collected him at the back door and I, more or less, just gave him a peck on the cheek. I remember saying afterwards that in a way it was probably the best way to say goodbye. The last thing you need is a traumatic farewell. Ours

*3 Infantry Brigade should not be confused with 3 Commando Brigade, of which H and 2 Para were now part.
†Severson, H's friend from Warminster, was now back in USA serving with 101st Airborne Division.

was so simple I even remember what I gave him for supper. He had come back and said: 'Right, I'm off in a few hours and I've got to pack quickly.' I remember sitting on the edge of his bath while he bathed and then I gave him spare ribs, and pretty nasty they were too! Then off he went – with indigestion, I should think.

Later it became clear that it was more important to stay there [at Ascension]. One meeting wasn't enough – plans were always changing – and he felt his input was needed. So he stayed on a bit. Time went by and it became obvious that he would not be able to get back before *Norland* was called forward. So we never did say goodbye. And then his letters started arriving.

H wrote daily – sometimes several times a day – giving an insight into his mood and attitude as war became more likely, and then inevitable. His letters provide a chronicle of going to war in a converted luxury liner; of floating off Ascension for days on end, whilst the Royal Navy steamed south to evict trespass from the 200-mile total exclusion zone (which Britain had by then declared round the Falklands); and of the final preparations for the assault landing.

SS *CANBERRA*
Off Ascension Island
24 April 1982

Darling Sara,

Our flight was late leaving, of course, but once airborne it was OK. Apart from me and five other passengers, the VC10 was absolutely jammed solid with ammunition, beer and soft drinks! We stopped at Dakar to refuel, but weren't allowed off the aircraft, and got here about 11.30 yesterday morning.

I was flown [by helicopter] out to HMS *Fearless* for lunch. After that we had the usual briefings. I met the Brigade Commander, Julian Thompson, who looked very tired, and the Commodore who commands the ships here.

We then flew on to *Canberra* at about teatime. I've got a small cabin to myself, with a bath and loo, and the whole thing is air-conditioned, with piped music and BBC World Service available in the cabin! So I'm quite comfortable, apart from the noise of soldiers running round the deck overhead, and the sound of a medical training film next door!

It's been decided that since communications between the various ships is not good, that I should stay on *Canberra* until *Norland* arrives here. So I feel a bit of a spare wheel at present . . . I do hope *Norland* gets away on time – I'd hate just to be a spectator!

Mind you, I haven't really learned anything more than I heard in England, and what I said then still applies, so don't get in a worry about it! I think that my main problem is going to be boredom.

I was woken this morning at 6.30 by a charming young lady called Chris, who brought me a cup of tea! I'm not sure what else she does, apart from clean my cabin; she doesn't seem to make the bed (I did that myself), and there doesn't seem to be any laundry, so I washed the shirt, trousers and socks I travelled in. It's all now dripping into the bath. I'll try to iron it all later, I hope I remember how! [H only had enough clothes for his originally planned thirty-six-hour stay – his kit would follow on the *Norland*.]

Time for lunch now. Love to Jimmy [H's black Labrador].

All my love.

H.*

Joining an established group of fellow commanding officers who had been together since sailing from Southampton three weeks earlier was not easy. It was like arriving late at a party: friends had already been made and relationships established. Furthermore, H had nothing to do, until his Battalion caught up the main body. His cabin was next to that of his old friend Hew Pike, commanding 3

---

*First in a series of forty-four letters from H to Sara.

Para, a charming and able officer with an impeccable military background. H was delighted to find someone on board on the same wavelength. Nevertheless, their temperaments were different – Hew was more measured and well established – and, although they did not indulge in it personally, inevitably there was an underlying rivalry between them and their battalions.

Hew Pike recalls:

H arrived on *Canberra* having flown to Ascension ahead of his Battalion, and we had talked while he settled into his cabin. An old, battered copy of Creasy's *Decisive Battles* was placed prominently on a shelf. There were no other books. Always immensely likeable, he was now more energetic and argumentative than I had ever remembered before, and that was saying something.

I had the impression, even then, that he saw the unfolding events in a very personal light and that his destiny was bound up with it. Having been left behind at the start, he was pounding alongside the rest of us in a fast outside lane at a pace which made me at times feel distinctly pedestrian in comparison. He was in overdrive.[4]

This did not always endear him to the other commanding officers. Yet Pike recalls his professionalism shining through. At one of the daily meetings on board, COs were told that the usual infantry-artillery affiliations of gunner battery commanders (BCs) and forward observation officers (FOOs), who direct the guns on to the target, were being changed. Hew recalls:

H was back as an instructor at the School of Infantry, and launched on a brilliant justification for permanent affiliation of BC and FOO parties, regardless of which guns were supporting a particular battalion at a particular time. The incident was typical of his style, and his arguments rightly won the day. Plans for re-affiliation were dropped.[5]

H's next letter to Sara shows that he had settled into life on board, but he was finding it frustrating.

25 April 1982

Darling Sara,

I went for a run yesterday evening – ten times round the Promenade Deck, which equals two and a half miles. It is quite humid so I was sweating like a pig by the time I had finished. I had a quick shower, and then the 3 Para officers had a surprise birthday party for Hew (only 39!) after which I had dinner with Hew and a *Daily Mirror* reporter called Alaistair something, and a bloke called Max Hastings who writes for the *Evening Standard*.

I had a quick drink after dinner and went to bed about ten. Drink is incredibly cheap here – I bought a round last night of three whiskies, one port, one brandy, and one vodka, and it cost 91p! I couldn't believe my ears. I'm not sleeping terribly well, so far, but no doubt I'll get used to it soon.

Everything seems to change here every time the clock strikes, so I have no idea what's going on or when we are going to sail . . . I read a few signals in 3 Para's Orderly Room, but apart from that I haven't done a thing, and I'm getting pretty bored.

I had a long talk the day I arrived with Michael Rose* about Woodward . . . I've been keeping quiet about Tim, although I did tell Michael.

H's reference to keeping quiet about his brother Tim, referred to an occurrence a few weeks earlier. Tim, in command of a Leander Class frigate, had suffered a serious setback to his career while serving in Rear Admiral Sandy Woodward's flotilla. Although there was nothing dishonourable in the circumstances, this was a severe blow for a promising officer, who had already earned a Commander-in-Chief's Commendation in Germany for gallantly saving a drowning

---

*Lieutenant Colonel Michael Rose was commanding 22 SAS in the Falklands. He and H had been at Staff College together.

man. But to H it was an affront, given his intense family loyalty and pride.

Whatever Rose said about Woodward on *Canberra*, mere mention of the Admiral's name evoked a passionate and unflattering response from H, who considered him, rightly or wrongly, to be the architect of his brother's misfortune. Moreover, these strong feelings endured, even to the extent that he alluded to them on the eve of battle.

But next day, other matters were preoccupying him. His letter of 26 April stated that he had sustained an injury which was to inconvenience and worry him for the next three weeks, and which would still be troubling him on landing:

I was trying to find the loo through the darkened cinema when I bumped into a chair and did something to my knee. I could hardly walk last night, but it's a bit better this morning, although going up and down stairs is pretty painful. If it doesn't get better I suppose I'll have to go and see the doctor, although it just seems to be a bruise, just above the kneecap. Very irritating.

We sailed during the night because there was a submarine scare – I gather they are now flapping about Argentinian frogmen! An Argentinian freighter was seen yesterday, and chased off by our attendant frigate. We expect to be back at anchor off Ascension tonight, though, and there should then be about four days of helicopter training, although we are at six hours' notice to sail.

The capture of South Georgia seems to have gone off very smoothly: I wonder if the Argentinians on Falkland will surrender as easily – I think they might well.

Although H could not know it, the South Georgia operation had gone far from smoothly. A small group of ships, helicopters and Special Forces, led boldly by HMS *Antrim*, had forced the beaching of the Argentinian submarine *Santa Fe* and the surrender of the 140 Argentinian marines, including Captain Astiz's party, at Leith. In the process two Wessex helicopters crashed on to a glacier in a blizzard, and a party of the Boat Troop (SAS) were swept away in hurricane winds, yet miraculously no British lives were lost. South Georgia would anyway have fallen when the Falklands were recaptured, and so militarily it was of low priority. However, three weeks after the loss of the Falklands as sovereign territory, it was considered to be politically essential to demonstrate continuing British resolve. This was manifestly accomplished, prompting the Prime Minister, outside No. 10 Downing Street, to exhort the nation to 'Rejoice, just rejoice!' at the news. In fact, hers was probably more an expression of relief from deliverance than the jingoism of which she was accused – because she knew what the media did not: that it had been an incredibly close-run thing.

As *Canberra* continued to ride the swell off Ascension day after day, with very little to do on board except train, certain themes were apparent from H's letters. First was the lack of information on operational plans or diplomatic progress, accentuated by H's immediate superiors being either in *Fearless* or *Hermes*. Thus the BBC World Service news broadcasts became his principal sources of information, as his next letter home indicated:

> I've just heard on the radio that the US has given up mediation, and have imposed sanctions on the Argentine. I wonder why; no doubt there's a good reason, though. Poor darling, I expect you're feeling depressed about that. I don't think you need to, though. None of the journalists think Maggie can risk any serious casualties, and I very much doubt whether anything will happen until the Fleet Air Arm have flattened the place. Certainly at the moment the idea seems to be to have a very heavy bombardment before anyone lands.

H assessed Sara's mood correctly: she *was* feeling depressed. She had not said goodbye to him properly; the *Norland* had now sailed, and she had gone dutifully down to Portsmouth to see 2 Para off. It was certain now that H would not be flying back as planned. She had just taken the boys back to school, and she was now alone in her rather soulless Army quarter. As ever, rumours were rife, yet no one was around to quash them authoritatively. She realised that the wives of the Battalion, meeting at coffee mornings, looked to her for reassurance, but it was difficult to give it convincingly. Sara now admits to feeling extremely upset, although typically she did not show it at the time.

Meanwhile, on *Canberra*, H struck up a friendship with Max Hastings and Robert Fox, of the BBC, usually to be found with the other reporters and senior officers in the ship's Crow's Nest Bar. Fox, who was to accompany 2 Para at Darwin and Goose Green, records of H:

> Of all the officers he was the most outstanding that I met in the entire campaign. He seemed to understand the diplomatic and international setting in which the crisis was unfolding better than almost any other officer with the landing force except Julian Thompson . . .
>
> He was something of an oddity, and aboard *Canberra* he seemed to stand apart from the others. He was clearly a soldier for the love of it, for he had considerable wealth inherited from his American father . . . Though possessed of a great deal of charm, he was shy and never found small talk easy. I learnt later that he far preferred the company of children to the tedium of the social round of adults, and at dinner parties he would remain almost tongue-tied. Soldiering was his life and military history his hobby. I saw him at his most animated locked in argument with Max Hastings and Hew Pike about the latest assessments of the Earl Haig as a commander. The conversation became heated and ranged far and wide.[6]

Another habitué of the Crow's Nest Bar recalled how, one evening, H declared that the Pope's forthcoming State Visit to the United Kingdom should be banned on the basis that Britain was at war with a leading Catholic country. (In fact, war had not been – and never was – formally declared against Argentina.) Most of those listening thought H's notion absurd, but that did not deter him: the more outrageous his proposition, the more he enjoyed defending it. Perhaps it was after such an exasperating occasion that Hew Pike wrote in his diary: 'H is still here. I shall be quite glad to see the back of him; we get on well but he does try to be so damned clever and pushy the whole time – not my style these days.'

Meanwhile, H's knee was still troublesome, causing him to tell Sara: 'I've decided not to run this evening and if it is still bad tomorrow I'll go and see the doctor again. It really is rather boring. I did it some six days ago now and it really ought to be getting better.'

Always prominently in his mind was the arrival of his Battalion. On 1 May he wrote:

> *Norland* is due to get here on 4 May. We will fly out to meet her, and stay aboard after that, and the next day we will do helicopter and landing craft training. And then on 6 May, I think, we all head south. For goodness' sake keep that to yourself though . . .
>
> I went ashore today in an LCU [Landing Craft Utility, which takes about 150 men] with C Coy 3 Para, and a couple of Scorpions from the Blues and Royals. We zeroed our SMGs [9mm Sterling machine gun, H's personal weapon], and then got a lift to the American base, where we had a couple of cold beers and a hamburger and chips for lunch . . .

Unbeknown to H, a momentous event was in progress on another part of the airfield. An RAF Vulcan bomber, armed with twenty-one 1,000-lb bombs, was staging through Ascension on its way to drop them on Stanley airfield. To accomplish the 8,000-mile round trip, the Vulcan had to be refuelled in flight seventeen times, from Victor tankers pre-positioned rather like petrol stations along the route. This remarkable operation resulted in a direct hit on the airfield but, even so, it did not prevent Argentine short landing and take-off transport aircraft from using the airfield throughout the conflict.

H paid generous tribute to the work of both sister Services in his next letter to Sara:

The RAF Vulcan crew who bombed Port Stanley were all getting drunk on Wide-Awake, I gather! I must say they did bloody well. The Navy seems to be doing very well down there, too. Needless to say, all we hear is what comes over the BBC World Service.

The pace of events was intensifying. On 2 May the ancient Argentine cruiser *Belgrano* (as the USS *Phoenix*, it had been at Pearl Harbor on 8 December 1941, when the Japanese attacked) was torpedoed and sunk by HMS *Conqueror*, with the loss of 368 lives. Retaliation was swift. Two days later HMS *Sheffield* was hit by an Exocet missile fired from an Argentine Super Etendard aircraft. Although the missile may not have exploded, its velocity caused extensive damage and ignited the frigate's fuel tanks, causing massive fires. *Sheffield* had to be abandoned, and subsequently she sank. Television coverage of the incident – particularly the shots of *Sheffield*'s captain, Sam Salt, being recovered to *Hermes* in distress, and with his hands in plastic bags – brought home to viewers in the UK, perhaps for the first time, that British servicemen were not immune from the horrors of war.

H seemed to acknowledge this in his next letter to Sara:

I hope you're not worrying too much, poor darling. I still don't know what the actual plan is, but you can be sure that we will all be very careful. I certainly only intend to attack with very heavy fire support from artillery, mortars and machine guns, and I don't honestly believe that we will have to do anything more than occupy the Argentinians' positions since their artillery will have been wiped out by air strikes. So please don't worry. I shall take very good care of myself and make sure I come home to you. (And to Jimmy!)

This was intended to be – and no doubt was – reassuring. But H went on to confess what Sara already realised: that he was where he most wanted to be:

I still find it incredible that we're all here; particularly, that of the 50 battalions in the Army, it should be 2 and 3 Para who were chosen. I would be going mad with frustration if we were still in the UK, watching it all going on. I almost feel like saying: 'And gentlemen in England now abed' but not quite, not yet!

His feelings showed in other ways, too. Heading towards a war zone tends to make men, who might not otherwise naturally be so, reflective in quiet moments. H must have found one on 3 May:

I have just realised from the radio that it's a Bank Holiday today! I wonder what you are doing and where you are. I shall feel a lot happier once I start getting letters from you . . . I feel very jealous when I see Hew's pile of mail! The trouble is that I'm besotted about you – one doesn't realise normally, or to be more accurate, *I* don't normally, how much I love you and need you. All sorts of silly little things affect me and how I feel, and although I know I love you all the time, I still feel irritated at times. And it's not until a time like this, when I haven't got you near, and don't know when I'll see you again, that I realise how very much I love you.

And later:

It makes me realise again how lucky I am to have you; it's awful to think that we either might never have met, or that you might have married someone else. And don't tell me I would have found someone else, because, although I probably would have, I couldn't have loved her as much as I love you, or been as happy as I am with you. When I'm away from you it really brings home to me what a fantastic wife you are. It's not just that our sex life is good . . . or any one single thing, it's the fact that the whole of our life together is so complete, and that even after 18 years of marriage we still go to sleep cuddled up together.

Time for a shower and a drink!

All my love, always.

H.

His next letter, with a certain amount of exasperation, revealed the semblance of a plan forming:

> It's all changed again! The latest plan is that *Norland* should arrive here on 6 May, as before, with us flying out to meet her in the morning, but that *Canberra* will leave here also on 6 May. We will do some helicopter and/or landing craft training on the morning of 7 May, and then will sail, with *Fearless* planning to catch *Canberra* up on our way south. I hope all that works out.

On 6 May, with his Battalion approaching Ascension, H wrote three times to Sara, and to the boys.

> Bad news this morning; I've just heard that *Norland* doesn't get here till 0600 tomorrow morning. Doom and gloom! *Canberra* will have gone by then, so they will either fly us off to join *Norland* before dark tonight, if she's in range, or we'll be cross-decked (i.e. moved to *Intrepid* to spend a night there).
>
> The radio is a bit more hopeful this morning, though whether Maggie will agree to the UN cease-fire plan I don't know. I don't want a war, but it would be nice to land after all this build-up.
>
> I've just heard the one o'clock news; Nott has said we won't negotiate unless there is a complete Argentinian withdrawal. I would be surprised if the Argentinians would agree to that, but you never know. No doubt we will know the form later today. This on-off, on-off business is very unsettling indeed. Luckily, it won't have affected 2 Para much yet.
>
> I've just heard that we're leaving for *Intrepid* by LCU at 2.45, so I had better finish this off, and post it. Not long now till *Norland* arrives, and I get some mail (I hope) and my photographs of you all.
>
> If this is my last letter, darling, please don't worry. I will take very good care of myself. And in case anything does happen, thank you for the happiest 18 years of marriage anyone could possibly have had.

I love you with all my heart. Take care of yourself.
All my love always.
H.

That afternoon, after thirteen days kicking his heels in *Canberra*, H was flown off to spend the night in *Intrepid* before — at last — rejoining 2 Para in the *Norland* at dawn the next day (7 May). The previous day, Hew Pike had made a diary entry:

H rejoins 2 Para tomorrow; we have looked after him pretty well but I am afraid his approach to command is rather different from mine, albeit very similar in so many ways, and therefore a little goes a long way.

H was of course delighted to be back with his Battalion again, and to receive some mail from home. He told Sara that 'everyone seems to be in good heart, although there had been one or two problems on the way', and continued:

It's very strange working again. I've been a bit ratty, I'm afraid; they have done a tremendous amount on the way down, but there is still an awful lot to do — nobody had thought about stretcher bearers for example, and I'm trying to sort that out now.

H's admission of being 'a bit ratty' was a massive understatement, as seen by those closest to him in Battalion Headquarters. On *Norland*, they viewed his attitude as 'verging on the impossible'. Nothing seemed to satisfy him, and he gave the impression that he felt insufficient had been done on the way down to prepare his soldiers properly for the harsh realities ahead. This is the 'returning chief's syndrome': the egotistical view — seen in all professions — that without the boss permanently present and chasing people, nothing gets done. H well knew this was unfair, as indeed his letter to Sara acknowledges, so perhaps the root cause of his behaviour was a feeling of insecurity at a vulnerable time, and nagging doubts about his fitness. According to one officer present: 'he saw the need to re-exert himself and was anxious to be taken seriously as the Commanding Officer'.

Whatever the reasons, the Army has a well-tried, informal way of coping with such difficulties. Chris Keeble, his Second-in-Command, took him to one side. He recalls that 'I spent one evening in H's cabin over several glasses of whisky tactfully urging him to modify his critical attitude, which was in danger of weakening confidence in his ability to remain objective, balanced and wise.' Done discreetly and without posing a personal challenge, Keeble's quiet remonstration had the desired effect. H calmed down somewhat and threw his weight around less. Indeed, some good work was in progress, which he acknowledged. For example, the Regimental Medical Officer (RMO), appreciating the crucial need for good battlefield first aid, taught soldiers how to insert quickly a saline drip – rectally if necessary – into the wounded. Several men were to owe their lives to this. H himself was equally insistent on the proper treatment and handling of prisoners of war – an aspect of training rarely exercised in the British Army.

The departure of the amphibious Task Force from Ascension was a turning point, after which attitudes hardened. Blood had now been spilt on both sides and, despite the tireless diplomatic activity, especially by the US Secretary of State Alexander Haig, neither adversary felt the need to sue for peace on the terms available.

On 8 May H wrote to Sara describing his new surroundings and routine. There was much less room than on *Canberra*, and in particular it was difficult to keep fit. His knee, on which he'd had physiotherapy, and applied ice packs, was a little better.

I've taken the bandage off but it's still very weak. I hope to goodness it holds up once we are ashore.

The whole ship is blacked out so we can't see out – very irritating! In fact, it's rather a dull day, and the wind is getting up to 20 knots, with quite a long swell. We're doing 15 knots, and are quite comfortable at present, though she does vibrate rather a lot.

On Sunday 9 May he wrote:

> We had a good church service on the flight deck, and I went to communion afterwards. Quite a lot of soldiers turned up – a sure sign that the full seriousness of the situation is dawning on people – and all the hymns were chosen by the soldiers: 'He who would valiant be'; 'I vow to thee my Country'; 'Eternal Father' etc.
>
> We had had emergency drills earlier in the morning, which were not good, so I read the riot act to all of them, and I hope they'll be better next time. Frankly, the sooner we get ashore, where our destiny is in our own hands, the better.

Sara felt exactly the same. She commented later: 'I was never very happy about the whole thing, but I felt that once they had landed at least they would be safer in their own environment.'

H's next letter was full of news:

> MV *Norland*
> At Sea
> 12 May 1982
>
> My darling Sara,
> A lot seems to have happened since I wrote last. We have continued to head south, and the weather has been good.
>
> A Hercules flew over and dropped mail this morning and I got three letters and a birthday card from you, so morale is high! The latest letter had only been posted three days before, which I thought was a good effort.
>
> Yesterday, a couple of Russian Bear long range reconnaissance aircraft flew over, so presumably they and the Argentinians know where we are.
>
> On Monday I went over to *Fearless* for an O Group* and briefing. The plan gets more and more boring every day! [H meant that 2 Para had been given the least exciting role: forming

---

*An 'Orders Group' at which formal orders were given.

a reserve.] I had rather a nerve-racking return flight, as it was raining and the Sea King couldn't find *Norland*! After 40 minutes it found *Intrepid* and landed to ask where to go! All was well in the end.

The Brigade Commander's O Group – final one that is – is tomorrow afternoon. So we should then know finally what is going on. We still have quite a long way to go, and we have to cross-deck quite a lot of people before we land, so a landing isn't imminent yet, but I should think we'll go ashore in the next 10–14 days, although diplomatic activity could change all that. The main worry at the moment is the Argentinian Air Force, since it very sensibly has so far mainly stayed in the background. We should be OK but we are all a bit worried about what happens to *Canberra* and *Norland*, which may be a bit vulnerable during daylight.

My knee is still a bit stiff and painful, but I think it should be OK.

H was correct. The planning was complete and about to be divulged. Nothing had been straightforward. Not only had it been difficult to get agreement to the plans, the process had been hindered by the lack of a single, taut chain of command. This led to an absence of clear direction and the usual pockets of inter-service and inter-branch rivalries that historically have bedevilled the Armed Forces when thrust together at short notice for a common operational purpose.

While the Royal Navy yields to no one in its admiration of the Royal Marines – they are part of the Navy, after all, although engaged almost entirely in military activities – the Navy invariably satisfies its own nautical needs before meeting those of the 'Royals', as it affectionately terms them. Consequently, the Royal Marines often perceive themselves to be the poor relations. Certainly the requirements of amphibious operations come low in the Navy's list of priorities. As the Commander Amphibious Warfare himself put it: '[Amphibiosity] raised little excitement with the Royal Navy as a whole who expected the role to be subject to the next series of cuts and who were more interested in purely naval tasks such as submarine or anti-submarine warfare.'[7]

Furthermore, few senior naval officers have risen to the top on the basis of their amphibious skills or interests, with the possible exceptions of Lord Mountbatten and Admiral Ramsey, the architect of D-Day. If this were not burden enough for the Royals to shoulder, the Army has its own perception of them: that Royal Marines are splendid at getting ashore and establishing a beachhead, but not good at developing operations thereafter. This is no reflection on the quality of the officers and men themselves, but rather a view of their limited 'all arms' experience on the wider battlefield. These perceptions were to affect planning and subsequent operations in the Falklands, which in turn would affect H directly.

As far as military planning was concerned, it centred on selecting what the Navy termed the 'amphibious objective area': put more simply, where best to land. There was an important precondition for the success of any such landing: that Rear Admiral Woodward's Carrier Battle Group, which had proceeded ahead, had first established 'sea control' of the area, and preferably air superiority too. But, although the former had been achieved with the sinking of the *Belgrano*, and the consequent withdrawal of the Argentinian navy to port, the latter had not yet been accomplished. The Argentinian air force was a potent foe and would continue to be so throughout the campaign.

It was the job of Commodore Michael Clapp to propose a suitable site for the landings, in conjunction with Brigadier Julian Thompson. Luckily these two senior officers, co-located throughout in HMS *Fearless*, worked in harmony. They had many factors to consider. Among the more critical were that the proposed site was clear of enemy; that it afforded a safe and secure landing, even in adverse weather; that the approaches were free of mines and other obstructions; and that the site was within reasonable striking distance of the eventual objective of Stanley. (It was this last factor that precluded a landing at Low Bay in Lafonia, on the south coast of East Falklands, strongly advocated, late in the day, by Rear Admiral Woodward).[8] Finally, and most importantly, the site had to be defensible during the dangerous period of, and after, the initial landings before all remaining troops, ammunition and stores had arrived ashore.

According to Commodore Clapp,[9] the planners considered nineteen potential sites and whittled them down to three: San Carlos; the exposed Cow Bay, on the north-east tip of East Falklands; and Berkeley Sound, a large protected inlet about five miles north of Stanley, which, however, was probably in enemy hands.

The critical factor, as in all military operations, was the aim. An aim should be crystal clear and preclude any doubt as to what is required of those tasked to achieve it. Unfortunately, this was not the case here. On 10 April Commodore Clapp and Brigadier Thompson were given, as their initial aim, 'To plan to land on the Falklands with a view to repossessing them.' A month later, on 12 May, they were ordered by the Joint Commander, Admiral Fieldhouse, 'To repossess the Falkland Islands as quickly as possible.' But what was meant by 'repossess'? Were the whole of the Falklands to be 'repossessed' by Thompson's relatively small force? Or just part of them? Should 3 Commando Brigade wait for 5 Infantry Brigade to arrive, or 'crack on' on their own?

The answers seemed to lie in a parallel directive received on the same day by Brigadier Thompson. It came from the Commander Land Forces,* Major-General Jeremy Moore, who had been appointed to take charge of a strengthened force of divisional size.† and would shortly join the *QE 2* on passage to the South Atlantic,

---

*Admiral Fieldhouse, the Joint Commander, had a Land Deputy and an Air Deputy. Major-General Jeremy Moore, a Royal Marine, was initially appointed the former. When the decision was made to send a second brigade he became the Commander Land Forces and moved down to the Falklands.

†Normally at least two brigades with some armoured reconnaissance, supporting artillery, engineers and logistics.

with 5 Infantry Brigade already embarked, becoming Thompson's immediate superior on landing. Moore's directive ordered Thompson:

> To secure a bridgehead on East Falkland, into which reinforcements can be landed, in which an airstrip can be established, and from which operations to repossess the Falkland Islands can be achieved.
>
> You are to push forward from the bridgehead area, so far as the maintenance of its security allows, to gain information, to establish moral and physical domination over the enemy, and to forward the ultimate objective of repossession.

Next, he told Thompson to retain operational control of all forces landed until he (Moore) had established his headquarters, probably aboard *Fearless* 'approximately on D + 7' (that is, a week after the landings). He finished: 'It is then my intention to land 5 Infantry Brigade into the beachhead and to develop operations for the complete repossession of the Falkland Islands.'

As Michael Clapp wrote later:

> Julian and I felt this directive while helpful was too vague, omitting as it did any reference to a strategy for a subsequent land battle ... What was clear was that Julian should not move his Brigade from San Carlos until after the arrival of Jeremy Moore, although we were drawing up plans for any such move.[10]

The fourteenth of May 1982 was H's forty-second birthday, and on it he wrote to Sara:

> I thought it would be nice to have my first (and last?) real O Group for war on my 42nd birthday! But I'm not allowed to brief the soldiers yet, however I can brief my full O Group, which I am doing this afternoon.
>
> My letters have got rather factual again, I'm afraid, mainly

because I'm busy, and having to write in our briefing room, with other members of Battalion HQ working around me. I would like to be able to tell you what the plan is, because I think it would reassure you. All I think I can say is that we are not expecting any enemy to be around when we land. So there really is no need to worry – all we'll be doing is watching the air battle above us! Shades of the Battle of Britain!

Must stop, they are starting to get the room ready for my O Group. What a strange birthday! All my love darling, I'll write again before we land.

In fact, he wrote again as soon as he finished giving out his orders.

> MV *Norland*
> At Sea
> 14 May 1982

My darling,

My O Group went off OK; but ten minutes after it ended the Brigadier arrived to say that D-Day [the day of landing] had been put back by 24 hours and H-Hour [the time the first landing craft was to drop its ramp on the beach] by four hours. D-Day has been changed on Maggie's orders because of the UN negotiation, which is fair enough; and H-Hour because the Navy want to have more of the run-in [to Falkland Sound] in the dark, which is also quite a good idea, but does mean a bit of a change of plan.

They've decided to close the mail in 30 minutes, so I won't have time to write much! It has been rather a strange birthday! I'm glad I had my O Group on it; it gives me something to remember it by. Apart from that, it's been a bit of a non-event – I was pleased to get all the birthday cards through (especially yours!); none from the kids, though, yet.

Must post . . . I love you; take care.

Remembering that Sara was shortly due to go to Colchester for the Presentation of New Colours to the Devon and Dorsets,* he wrote again the next day, providing an interesting reflection on where he would rather be:

> I suspect we may be ashore by the date of the Presentation of New Colours, in which case you should be able to bask in some reflected glory! That's always assuming 1 D and D† have heard of the Falklands! Thank goodness I got command of 2 Para; how dreadful it would be to be doing a ceremonial parade in UK while battalions were fighting in the South Atlantic.

By 16 May, the weather was worsening, and tension grew.

> Darling Sara,
> The weather was appalling during the night – Force 10! The only reasonable place to be was on one's bunk. Most of the other ships lost contact during the night, so we had to slow right down for them.
> We are pretty close to the Falklands now (800 miles or so) and we are just stooging along waiting for Maggie to give the word. I think she will probably make up her mind tomorrow, unless she thinks some more sabre-rattling would help. Until then I imagine they will keep us out of range of the Argentinian strike aircraft.
> I'm still feeling rather fluey, and I got Stephen Hughes [2 Para's RMO] to look at my knee. He told me to keep off running, but to do leg exercises – he thinks I tore a ligament, which would explain why it's taking so long to get better.
> Must stop, it's nearly lunch time . . .
> LATER

---

*New Colours are presented about every twenty years, so this event on 22 May 1982 was a major regimental occasion which H would have attended if he had been in UK. He had been on parade at the previous Colours Presentation.
†The abbreviation for his old Battalion in his first Regiment.

We have just joined up with all the LSLs [Landing Ship Logistics] and their RN escort (*Antrim*, *Broadsword*, *Brilliant*, *Yarmouth* and one other) and are continuing south, but only at about seven knots. The wind has gone right down, but there is still quite a large swell.

Throughout their passage south, the Task Force had been kept under hostile surveillance. At Ascension, H had mentioned the Russian Bear aircraft and the 'spy' trawler; also, an Argentinian submarine was thought to be shadowing them. Now H became aware of yet another threat:

I went to bed early last night, just as well, as we went to Action Stations at first light. We think an Argentinian Boeing 707 was picked up on radar; no sooner had we stood down than we stood to again! *Hermes* has now joined us, and one of her Harriers went zooming off [to intercept the Boeing, and if necessary to shoot it down],* but we didn't see anything. The sea is now covered in ships from horizon to horizon – most impressive!

Despite the pressures he was under, he wrote again the next day:

MV *Norland*
At Sea
18 May 1982

My dearest Sara,
We are now (it's evening) under 400 miles from the Falklands. I've just heard the News say that *Canberra* had joined *Hermes* and the rest of the Task Force, but no mention of *Norland*, as they don't want the Argentinians to know we've arrived.

I've pretty well finished packing now, my Sterling magazines are filled, and it's just a matter of waiting for D-Day.

---

*According to Commodore Clapp, authority had been given by London to do so, once certain checks had been completed.

From now on we will be sleeping fully dressed except for boots, in case there is a submarine attack, and we are all standing to before first light. It's been very calm all day, but there is an extraordinary grey light all the time. We expect bad weather fairly soon, which should help to stop Argentine air attacks.

He wrote at greater length the next day, imagining that it would be his last letter at least until the postal arrangements* were working from shore.

I had an early bed last night, and we were woken at 0615 by 'Rule Britannia', from Last Night of the Proms, played over the loudspeakers! We're having 'Land of Hope and Glory' tomorrow!

We still don't know when D-Day is, but it looks as if it may be Friday (21 May) since the UN have said Thursday is a key day. We are now on the edge of the Total Exclusion Zone, WNW of the Falklands. Mail closes in 30 minutes, so I had better hurry up and finish . . .

By the time you get this I expect the whole thing will all be over; we will certainly be ashore, and I expect there will have been some sort of settlement. Most important of all, you'll know whether I'm OK or not.

I don't suppose there's any chance of anything happening to me, but just in case I want to tell you how very much I love you, and thank you for being such a super wife for the last 18 years. I know we have had our ups and downs, but despite all that it's been a wonderful time, and you have made me very happy. I certainly wouldn't want to change any of it. Marrying you was the best thing that ever happened to me, and thanks to you I can look back on a life that has been pretty good so far. I've been very lucky – let's hope my luck holds!

---

*Incoming mail was air-dropped to the Task Force at sea in a Lyndholm container. Outgoing mail was taken by helicopter to ships returning to Ascension Island. Once established ashore, a regular mail service (by air and sea) to and from Ascension was set up.

I've written last notes to David and Rupert, and to Dia, which will go off in this mail, too . . . Must stop or I'll be too late.

Look after yourself, darling; give Jimmy and Scrumpy [Sara's horse] my love.

All my love darling, always.

H.

But it was not the last opportunity. He wrote once again from *Norland*, on the eve of the landings.

My darling Sara,

We are now well inside the Total Exclusion Zone, about 100 miles from the Falklands. We think tomorrow is D-Day, but we still don't know. All the ships are closed right up, about a half-mile apart, with frigates and destroyers all round us, and *Invincible* has just turned up too.

It's a filthy day, blowing Force 7 and low cloud and fog – ideal weather. It is a bit unsettling not knowing whether we are going in early tomorrow morning or not. I suppose Maggie is still discussing it with the Cabinet.

I've just heard the radio newsreel on the World Service, which says the Government has rejected the latest Argentine proposals, and that invasion is inevitable. We still have no news, though, and it's now 4 p.m. your time. The fleet is still heading for a RV about 100 miles or so north of the Falklands; we have to be there by 9.30 p.m. your time, and we need a decision by then.

It's an amazing sight outside; I don't suppose many of us will ever see anything like it again. Whatever happens, I feel incredibly fortunate and privileged to have been here. I do feel sorry for poor old 5 Brigade; I'm sure they'll be delighted just to be coming, but there won't be many more moments like this.

I gather the Press are talking about tonight as 'The longest night'! By the time you get this I expect you'll know all about it from the Press, but just in case you don't hear, we are going in first, at H-Hour, followed ten minutes later by 40 Commando, with 3 Para and 45 Commando three hours later. They are all occupying high ground around the anchorage, while we march about four miles to a blocking position [on Sussex Mountain] and wait for Argentine reaction. We should just be in position by first light, but it's going to be touch and go, and we expect air attacks once it's light.

LATER

The Navy have struck again; we have been trying to find out all afternoon what is happening, and at last light *Broadsword* fired a signal to us by line. It was the decision that D-Day is tomorrow and we go in tonight, and it had been sent seven and a half hours earlier but had not got to us. The Navy really are almost totally incompetent.

H was justifiably angry. The encrypted signal to all commanding officers had been sent from *Fearless*, but *Norland*'s decoder had broken down, leaving 2 Para in limbo for more than seven hours. The loss of precious time at such a crucial stage did not instil confidence. Remarkably, in the circumstances, H still found time coolly to finish his letter.

Thank goodness the weather has been too foul for any air attacks on us today; by midday tomorrow our own Army air defence will be in position. It is now just after 9 p.m. your time; we go through the narrows between East and West Falkland at 3 a.m. your time, get in landing craft at 4.45 a.m. your time and land at 7.30 a.m. your time. I hope you're awake and thinking of us then!

We don't expect to meet any enemy during the night, although the SAS and SBS are doing diversionary raids . . .

I'd be lying if I didn't admit that we're all frightened, but I hope and pray we'll manage to do what we have to do. Thank God for Dair [Major Farrar-Hockley, commanding A Company] and John [Major Crosland, commanding B Company], I don't know what I'd do without them.

Even now it doesn't seem very real; I almost keep thinking it's just a bluff – unfortunately, my bergen doesn't feel as if it's bluffing!

It's quite cold out, but not more than a bad winter's night on Dartmoor! I expect I'll be too cold when I'm in the landing craft, and too hot when I'm marching!! You can't win.

My knee doesn't feel too bad; I think there's a reasonable chance it will hold up. If not, they'll just have to carry me!

I suppose I must stop. Who would have thought six weeks ago as we drove up the AutoRoute that I would be leading the first battalion to land to retake the Falklands!

Enough of all that. Time for a meal, and we are then having a final church service. Let's just pray that God is with us all tonight, and with all of you at home.

I love you so much, my darling, take care, and give my love to David, Rupert, Jimmy and Scrumpy.

All my love, always.

H.

H's attention now turned exclusively to the task in hand. As *Norland* closed the coast and then sailed into Falkland Sound, H and Chris Keeble stood on the flying bridge watching HMS *Antrim*'s 4.5-inch guns in action. They were engaging an enemy position on Fanning Head, a promontory overlooking them, to be eliminated by the SBS before the beach assault and landings began. H was very calm and thoughtful, as if his fretting was over and he had finally come to terms with the burden of operational command which, for the very first time, he was about to exercise. For H the war was about to begin.

CHAPTER ELEVEN

Action

The bravest are surely those who have the clearest vision of what is before them, and yet, notwithstanding, go forth to meet it.
Pericles (*c.* 429 BC)

Command . . . turns on the recognition that those who are asked to die must not be left to feel that they die alone.
John Keegan, *The Mask of Command*

Participation in an amphibious assault landing is the least favoured of all operations an infantryman may be called upon to perform. He has no control over the method of getting ashore, which is conducted by the Navy, and there is the uncertainty of what he may find when he gets there. Packed like a sardine into a landing craft, he feels literally and metaphorically out of his depth until he is dumped unceremoniously on some hostile beach. Then, with his equipment, and the lower half of his body probably soaked, he must re-orientate himself and re-form quickly into a proper fighting unit.

For an officer of H's temperament, instinctively liking to be in charge of events, it was particularly frustrating when changes and mishaps occurred outside his control, which was what now happened. The plan was straightforward enough: 2 Para were to be put ashore in the first wave on Bonner's Bay, near San Carlos Settlement (designated Blue Beach Two), to clear the immediate vicinity, and then to establish themselves on Sussex Mountain by dawn.

But the four Landing Craft Utilities (LCUs) sent from HMS *Intrepid* to pick them up from the MV *Norland* arrived late and the whole process of loading took far longer than planned. Each LCU carried a company of infantry. Transferring them from a civilian ferry, not designed for speedy disembarkation, into the small LCUs, took time. As 2 Para had had opportunity for only one rehearsal at Ascension, it was unlikely to run smoothly anyway. To confuse matters further, the loading sequence went awry, with the company earmarked to land first put on an LCU due ashore in the second wave. Also, one soldier fell between the *Norland* and a heaving LCU and was nearly crushed.

Once loaded, the LCUs circled *Norland* like ducklings round their mother until all were ready to head for the shore. Luckily the sea was calm and the night very clear. Those waiting huddled in the boats who looked up to the heavens observed a magnificent sight: a million stars twinkled in the firmament with a brilliance rarely seen in the polluted Northern Hemisphere. Meanwhile, the din of Fanning Head being pounded by HMS *Antrim*'s guns intruded upon a moment when mankind's place on earth otherwise seemed infinitesimally small and unimportant.

Eventually 2 Para were ready, and escorted by HMS *Plymouth*, they set off for Blue Beach approximately sixty-five minutes late, which put the whole landing plan behind schedule. As they approached the beach, all eyes eagerly sought the green flashing torches of the SBS showing that it was safe to land. None was evident. At this tense moment, with the crucial element of surprise uncertain, a couple of weapons were fired negligently as safety catches were released. Then, an echo-sounder alarm activated in one of the LCUs – it should have been switched off – as it entered shallow water. This was the last straw for H. The accumulation of mishaps and other people's blunders over the past six hours, starting with the failure even to receive the notification of H-Hour on time, caused him to explode. 'This is a bloody shambles, David,' he roared at his unfortunate Royal Marine liaison officer.

In fact, the absence of shore signals was not significant – the SBS reception party had secured Blue Beach Two, but as they had not been notified of the various changes of plan, they were not expecting 2 Para. Moreover, neither the beach nor the approaches had been mined. So the landings were unopposed, although Argentinian soldiers fleeing from Fanning Head reported them.

Safely ashore, H's immediate task was to re-assemble his Battalion in the proper order and get them off the beach and on to Sussex Mountain as quickly as possible. Sussex Mountain, an 800-foot craggy ridge towering five miles to the south-west, was 3 Commando Brigade's 'vital ground' – that is, a position to be denied to the enemy at all costs lest the British foothold at San Carlos be jeopardised.

It was a mark of Brigadier Thompson's esteem for H and for 2 Para that he had put them ashore first and entrusted them with this crucial task. The anticipated threat came from the Argentine forces at Goose Green, twenty miles away. Even though it had been softened up during the night as part of the diversion plan, it was thought that Brigadier-General Mario Menendez's* strategic reserve might still be intact at or near Goose Green. If this reserve could reach Sussex Mountain, perhaps by using helicopters, and launch a counter-attack before the bridgehead was properly established, it would be serious. Luckily they made no such attempt, and by midday on 21 May 2 Para had secured the position.

Nevertheless, getting there had been gruelling. H's soldiers were grossly overloaded for their trek up a mountain, initially in darkness. Each man carried an enormous bergen containing all his kit, his immediate rations, his personal weapon – in many cases a heavy GPMG – and his share of at least two rounds or missiles for the various weapon systems.† All this might weigh over 110 pounds,

---

* The Military Governor and Commander-in-Chief of Argentine Forces on the Falklands.
† The Milan anti-armour weapon, the Blowpipe air defence system and 81-mm mortar bombs.

especially if the bergens became soaked, as most had. Everyone's feet had been immersed on landing, of course, and would mostly stay wet throughout the campaign. The Army's standard boot at the time readily let water in through the lace eyelets, but could not drain through its rubber sole. To make matters worse, the going was very rough, with clumps of tussock grass, boulders and peat-bog outcrops. A few soldiers collapsed on the way up, and all were exhausted by the time they reached their defensive locations, in which they then had to dig their trenches.

The clear sky that morning afforded the Argentine pilots a perfect opportunity to find and attack British ships and positions. There is no better incentive to digging-in than threat of imminent attack, but the topography of Sussex Mountain impeded that. Even one foot down, a trench filled with water, so H's soldiers had to build upwards, constructing sangars of peat and stone not only for protection from air and ground attack but also to shield them from the cutting wind which never seemed to ease.

H's Battalion was to stay on Sussex Mountain for the next six days, during which the ships in Falkland Sound were being off-loaded. It was a depressing, static period as the soldiers, from their grandstand position, watched the Argentine air force launch wave after wave of attacks against warships, and strafe some of their own positions.

By the end of D-Day, all but two of Commodore Clapp's frigates had been hit by a variety of air-delivered munitions – bombs, missiles and cannon – with differing results. HMS *Ardent* was hit on the morning of 21 May and abandoned that evening – she blew up and sank during the night – and on 23 May a massive explosion and fire illuminated HMS *Antelope* grotesquely against the night sky. She foundered the next day.

Some Argentinian pilots, particularly from 5th Fighter Group, pressed home their attacks with great verve and skill, approaching at almost wave-top height to escape radar detection. At such low levels their bombs often did not have time to arm, rendering them inert on impact – a critical piece of information apparently reported on the BBC. Other pilots, less brave or perhaps less experienced, released their loads early and fled.

Many incoming and outgoing aircraft were intercepted by combat air patrols, sustained by Sea Harriers of the Fleet Air Arm, lurking over West Falkland, although news of this seldom reached those on land. Furthermore, these operations were frequently hampered by bad weather, which restricted flying off HMS *Hermes* and HMS *Invincible*, on station well to the east.

H spent much of his time in observation posts (OPs) looking south towards Goose Green. He also visited positions, observing what was going on, and talked to his soldiers. Colour Sergeant Rob Powell, who had met H back in Aldershot when he gave the CO formal notice that he intended to leave the Army at the end of his present contract, recalls:

> I saw him on Sussex Mountain. He remembered I was going to join the police and said: 'Hello, Colour, how's it going?'
>
> 'Not too bad, sir,' I replied.
>
> 'It could be worse – you could be at some football match coping with drunken hooligans!'
>
> 'But I still think I'd rather be there at this minute,' I answered, and he laughed.
>
> Oh my God, yes. He was a great guy really. Not liked by everybody – but extremely straight and very determined on what he wanted.[1]

However, some felt that H was out and about too much. The retired Major-General John Frost, who wrote with inside help *2 Para Falklands* soon after the war, formed that impression:

> At this stage the functioning of the Battalion Command Post left much to be desired. The CO's enthusiasm led him to want to see everything for himself, and thus spend many long hours in forward OPs when all and sundry needed answers to problems which could only be given from the HQ . . .

Of course, a commanding officer must balance the allocation of his time. However, most soldiers in action, as Colour Sergeant Powell implied, would prefer to find their Colonel among them up front discovering for himself what was going on. Answering questions further back is primarily a staff function, properly left to others.

With the remarkable Forces Postal Service operating again, H wrote his forty-fourth letter to Sara:

SAN CARLOS
24 May 1982

My darling love,
You will know we got ashore OK – first! And took our objective with no casualties. So far so good!

It's very wet and cold, but I'm fine. Lots of air attacks, but none really bad on us – mainly on the Navy. *Ardent* and *Antelope* have been sunk. We shot down two Mirage today with our machine-guns, which was good.

Tonight, 2 Para break out of the bridgehead, and we hope in 48 hours' time to have captured Darwin and Goose Green.

We're walking, because the choppers say it's too dangerous!

I've just given Robert Fox an interview. It's going to be a very long walk, but only the enemy air force is any good.

Don't worry about me, I'm fine, if cold and wet – and my knee is still rather dodgy.

My love to the boys. I got their birthday cards and two letters from you (plus chocs) last night, which was nice.

All my love.
H.

This crossed with a letter that Sara had written on the same day – the Monday after the landings. It was subsequently returned to her, unopened, after H's death. One extract reads:

I hope you are not too uncomfortable – you must be. I just can't imagine your conditions. You must be so cold and wet! I worry about you so much but I have to keep going – there is no good thinking about it too much! I long to have you home safe.

PS Pamela [H's sister-in-law] says Tim is tired and upset by the Navy's hammering and is wishing he was there with you all.

By now, media video footage and radio tapes were reaching the UK. They made compulsive viewing and listening. Even twenty years later, the slow, melancholy, almost haunting voice of Ian MacDonald, the MOD's chief spokesman, reporting that another ship had been lost sends shivers down many spines – and not only of those personally involved. For many, like Sara, watching and listening to every broadcast, it was a chilling daily ordeal.

On 26 May, having perhaps listened to another such bulletin, she wrote:

My dearest darling,
What a sad day, two ships gone. This is one of my down days. The poor Navy are taking a hammering, when really they are supporting you – for that I am grateful!

How do you always manage to be in the right place (or wrong place depending on how you look at it) at the right time? It is typical that you should be there in front during this do. Why on earth did I marry you? I must have been mad. I suppose I love you, silly me!!

That letter, too, never reached H.

The move to which H had referred in his last letter had been in prospect for several days. In keeping with his directive to maintain pressure on the enemy, Julian Thompson intended 2 Para to conduct a raid on Darwin and Goose Green, twin settlements – the second largest outside Stanley itself – some fifteen miles to their south. A raid, a favoured Marine operation, essentially entails attacking a key enemy installation from the sea, with the benefit of surprise, and withdrawing just as quickly.

H, delighted at the prospect of getting his Battalion off their miserable mountain and taking the fight to the enemy, drew up a plan, cleared it with Brigade Headquarters and briefed D Company. They were to move forward by night to secure a position at Camilla Creek House, so that three 105-mm light guns and their ammunition could be inserted by helicopter before dawn to support the raid by the rest of 2 Para. It was straightforward and would probably have worked well, but that night the weather deteriorated. As Julian Thompson explained:

> The main mission for the helicopters that night was to get D Squadron [of 22 SAS] on to Mount Kent as part of the prelims for the move of the Brigade forward to the primary objective, Port Stanley. As the weather closed in it was important to carry out this move first, so the move of the guns to support 2 Para was scrubbed.[2]

H was experienced enough to understand the problems of adverse flying weather, and although naturally expressing his disappointment, according to Thompson he accepted the decision loyally and without demur. However, of the many accounts of the incident since, most offer a story of H allegedly remarking: 'I have waited twenty years to go into action and I am not having some fucking Marine preventing me now.'

The story implies that H displayed a rather gung-ho, childish and even irresponsible attitude at this juncture. Although harmless enough, and more amusing and colourful than the probable dull truth, it portrays the inner man falsely. He may well have lightly voiced something of the sort – he was given to over-exaggeration, and anyway he knew his Paras would have relished any dig at the Marines, for their rivalry is traditionally strong. But the Brigade Commander is adamant that no such remark was uttered to him. On the contrary, Thompson says he learned later from his Brigade Major, John Chester, how well H had accepted the decision. This was another occasion when H's sayings and doings were distorted, and by public repetition myths have developed. There were to be many other examples over the next few days.

Back in Britain, relief at the successful landings was soon being replaced by concern at the lack of subsequent progress. From eight thousand miles away it looked as if nothing much was happening ashore. The cancellation of 2 Para's raid on Darwin and Goose Green confirmed these suspicions. Moreover, the loss of *Ardent* and *Antelope* accentuated public anxiety. The Prime Minister and War Cabinet represented strongly that some positive ground action should begin. Admiral Fieldhouse, the overall Joint Commander, agreed that something had to be done. But what?

Unfortunately, the man best able to provide the answers was incommunicado, on *QE2*. This was Major-General Jeremy Moore, the designated Commander Land Forces, who would be Brigadier Thompson's immediate superior on landing. *QE2* was steaming at best speed to the South Atlantic with Moore and 5 Infantry Brigade on board, but she was still several days away from the Falklands. The fact that the key commander was inaccessible at the critical moment probably constituted the greatest single mismanagement of the whole campaign. It nearly proved disastrous.

The vital secure satellite communications terminal* on *QE2*, which had just been fitted at a cost of £1 million, had broken down within minutes of Major-General Moore embarking at Ascension Island, and all efforts to repair it were in vain. The inability of *QE2* to communicate securely with the outside world meant that Julian Thompson had no ally† to whom to turn at a particularly difficult time. Similarly, Admiral Fieldhouse was without an experienced senior emissary ashore who could interpret the situation and reassure London that 3 Commando Brigade was not bogged down, nor was the ghost of Gallipoli stalking the beaches of San Carlos.

---

* A terminal of the secure SCOTT British military communication network worldwide.
† Jeremy Moore, also a Royal Marine, was not only a colleague of Thompson's with shared experience but a friend too.

On 25 May, the destroyer HMS *Coventry* (Captain David Hart-Dyke) was hit by three Skyhawk-delivered bombs. Nineteen sailors were killed instantly; the ship capsized and sank within twenty minutes. This was the fourth of Her Majesty's ships to be lost, and gloom in London was intensified further when the massive bulk-freight carrier *Atlantic Conveyor,* carrying vital heavy-lift helicopters, was hit later that evening. (Three Chinook* and six Wessex V helicopters went to the bottom with her.) The news was politically as well as militarily dire. One backbench MP remembers: 'We were getting extremely edgy and were starting to ask awkward questions.'

Around this time General Sir John Stanier, Commander-in-Chief United Kingdom Land Forces, went to see Admiral Fieldhouse at the Joint Headquarters in Northwood, outside London.

Stanier clearly recalls 'an atmosphere of very considerable stress' in the Admiral's underground bunker. His opposite number greeted him sharply with: 'I've put five thousand troops ashore and absolutely nothing has happened! The weather is deteriorating and I'm taking stick. What are *you* going to do?'

General Stanier had no executive authority, having already transferred all requested military assets to the Joint Commander. He knew that five ships had been sunk. But he did not know that communication with *QE2* had been lost, or that she was still several days' steaming from the Falklands.

The situation was indeed grim. In fact, so gloomy was the mood at Northwood that General Stanier:

> . . . formed a firm impression that the Joint Commander simply could not sustain any further loss of ships in the confined waters of the Falkland Sound; and that unless something on land were to happen quickly he would be forced to contemplate lifting 3 Commando Brigade off the beaches.[3]

---

* There were four Chinooks on board but one had flown off just before she was hit.

That prospect was appalling.* It would have meant re-embarking the whole Brigade and their off-loaded equipment over one – perhaps two – nights, and starting again, presumably nearer Port Stanley, at a later date.

The General went into a quiet side room, away from the highly charged atmosphere of the Operations Room, to think and to discuss the options with the senior Army representative at Northwood, Lieutenant-General Sir Richard Trant.†

First, he asked to be briefed on the existing plan. But apart from confirmation that 3 Commando Brigade were continuing to build up their stocks ashore, albeit more slowly now with the civilian shipping being kept outside the range of enemy air attacks, no forward planning for the 'break-out' was evident. That plan was aboard *QE2* presumably in the mind of Major-General Moore. All were agreed, however, that the Falklands could only be recovered militarily by re-taking the capital, which remained the overall intention.

There was some discussion as to whether Brigadier Thompson had to await the arrival of Moore and 5 Brigade. Moore's directive of 12 May implied that he did; and some felt this was the reason for the lack of offensive action so far.

Next turning to intelligence, Stanier heard that a weak Argentine force – ground and air – was still based at Goose Green, forming a small garrison with an active airfield and a reserve. He felt this was militarily unsatisfactory, as it would pose a threat to Thompson's rear and to his lines of communication when the advance on Stanley did begin. He was sure that, at the very least, Goose Green would have to be 'masked' and the airfield made inoperable. Ideally, the threat should be removed at once.

General Stanier now drew up a proposal: that a battalion, provided it was properly supported with artillery and naval gunfire,

---

* Such a possibility has not been disclosed before.
† Trant had just been appointed the Land Deputy to the Joint Commander at Northwood.

should eliminate the threat at Goose Green. Furthermore, the advantages of doing it straight away were overwhelming. Accordingly, this was the recommendation he offered the Joint Commander. The General then left Northwood, as he was not involved in the decision-making, departing with the clear impression that 'if the Brigade Commander remained sitting where he was, Fieldhouse might have to get them all off again'.[4] This would have been catastrophic, leading almost certainly to military failure, to the loss of the Falklands, and to all manner of serious national and international ramifications.

Next day in London, Stanier expressed his concern to General Sir Edwin Bramall, Chief of the General Staff, and told him of his recommendation. Stanier recalls his Chief's only comment: 'I hope you were right to recommend only one battalion!'

Meanwhile at Northwood, the Joint Commander resolved to accept Stanier's advice, and Julian Thompson was summoned across from his Headquarters to the communication centre at Ajax Bay. Over the satellite link, Admiral Fieldhouse ordered him to take speedy action to reconstitute the Goose Green operation 'at first light tomorrow'.* It was now up to Thompson to allocate the resources necessary.

The Brigadier was dismayed, as is anyone who receives seemingly out-of-touch instructions from thousands of miles away. Moreover, he was stung by the insinuation that he and his Brigade had been doing nothing for the past six days, when in fact their efforts had been herculean.

He had assured Northwood earlier that taking Stanley would be his main effort when 5 Brigade arrived. He had explained that the Darwin/Goose Green isthmus was a sideshow, to be safely masked by a company on Sussex Mountain, and insisted it made no military sense to dissipate his already slender resources. With the majority of his helicopters lost in the *Atlantic Conveyor*, he was refocusing his Brigade to move on foot to Stanley – indeed, the

---

* Lieutenant-General Trant heard only the Northwood end of this conversation.

'yomp' was being planned at that moment. It was already clear that he needed to establish forward observation posts on Mount Kent, overlooking Port Stanley, and this would be his immediate priority.

But Admiral Fieldhouse invited no such discussion. What was now needed 'was more action all round'. An immediate and obvious success was required to reassert British dominance; to forestall those in the UN who were using the delay as an opportunity to negotiate on more even terms; and to lift spirits at home. If Thompson could not or would not do it, somebody else would be found who could.*

Such a scene is familiar to most senior military commanders: the wider political imperative conflicting with the immediate operational need. There is nothing unusual or necessarily wrong with this, but at such moments the man closest to the front – invariably the more junior in rank – feels misunderstood, helpless and very alone. In this case Julian Thompson, with Jeremy Moore incommunicado, had no realistic option but to comply. He sent for H.

H was delighted to learn that the operation against Darwin and Goose Green had been resurrected. He was even keener now to get his men off Sussex Mountain, where 2 Para were suffering from cases of exposure and trench foot. However, this time the operation was not to be just a raid, but a proper attack to capture and hold Darwin and Goose Green. Whereas the previous plan had involved dashing in, inflicting maximum destruction and getting out, now they were going to mount a deliberate attack to seize and retain the two settlements, the airfield and the surrounding features. According to Sergeant Pip Hall, H was thoroughly sober and realistic about their impending task: 'The CO came and sat with the Mortar Platoon and then told us what was going on; and that's the sort of guy he was. He told us about the communications from London to the Brigade, and how he got involved.'[5]

---

*Colonel David Seccombe, Deputy Commander 3 Cdo Bde, or Lieutenant Colonel Nick Vaux, CO 42 Cdo, were obvious candidates.

Doubts have been raised that H and his Brigadier might not have been at one about this change of emphasis. But Julian Thompson's valued liaison officer with 2 Para, Major Hector Gullan, was present when H formally told his officers that 2 Para's mission was 'to capture Darwin and Goose Green'. If that had not been correct, Gullan would have intervened on behalf of his Brigade Commander. Nevertheless, there are those who still think that it was H who turned Thompson's intended raid into a formal attack.

What is correct is that H was not provided with, and did not insist on having, the proper resources for the task. A battalion going into battle against an enemy of comparable size requires substantial extra assets. H was only allocated three 105-mm light guns, as opposed to the normal six in a full battery; and in view of their weight, he took only two of his eight mortars and only half his Milan firing posts. Nor was he supported by any light armour, where a troop of tracked armoured reconnaissance vehicles would have been the norm. In addition, there were insufficient helicopters to fly in any more guns with their ammunition,* or mortar rounds and Milan missiles – another reason for reducing the number of mortars and Milan. H, who was meticulous about being properly supported, must have been persuaded to accept that the allocation of HMS *Arrow* during darkness, with her 4.5-inch automatic gun, would compensate for the lack of artillery. The effectiveness of naval gunfire had already been demonstrated convincingly at Fanning Head and on other occasions. The only other explanation for his acceptance of the risk is that H's prime concern was to get his men off Sussex Mountain where casualties from exposure and trench foot had already cost him the equivalent of one platoon out of action.

Julian Thompson's one abiding regret, which still troubles him

---

*Thompson explained that his staff had calculated that with all the other tasks that night they only had enough assets to lift three guns and crews, plus 200 rounds per gun, from San Carlos to Camilla Creek, a round trip of about twenty-five miles. Even this required twenty-four Sea King sorties, i.e. the four Passive Night Vision-fitted Sea Kings flying six sorties each. That would take three hours to complete.

twenty years later, is that he did not send a troop of armoured reconnaissance* with 2 Para, believing that the tracked Scorpions and Scimitars would sink into the peaty bog. (In fact, these vehicles had a remarkable cross-country performance and were immensely useful in subsequent battles.)†

On 2 Para's initial ascent of Sussex Mountain, H had seen the adverse effect of overloading infantrymen. To avoid any such repetition, he decided that the Battalion would move on light scales and be that much fitter to fight at their destination. Thus, adequately equipped but in conventional terms under-supported, 2 Para gathered in the designated assembly area at Camilla Creek House at dawn on Thursday 27 May. D Company had secured overnight this large, derelict white farmhouse-cum-shearing-shed, halfway between Sussex Mountain and Goose Green, at the northern end of the isthmus, out of sight of both settlements.

Here tired Paras, who had been marching most of the night, cooked their breakfasts and got some sleep. Meanwhile, H prepared his orders. This was 'battle procedure': a complex series of con- current activities preceding an operation, so that ideally, when soldiers eventually cross the 'start line',‡ they are well prepared, well rested and thoroughly motivated. It is akin to a football team staying at a nearby hotel the night before an important game and getting themselves into 'match mood'.

Shortly after arrival, the Regimental Signals Officer tuned into the BBC World Service, the prime source of news since leaving UK, and was stunned to hear that a parachute battalion was on the move

---

*Often inaccurately referred to as 'light tanks'.

†It has been said mischievously that the Blues and Royals, who manned these vehicles, had created the impression on *Canberra* that the whole operation was a confounded nuisance and interfered with their forthcoming polo season. So initially neither the Royal Marines nor the Paras took them very seriously. Unsurprisingly, when the action started, they acquitted themselves with distinction and played a critical role in 2 Para's last battle, Wireless Ridge.

‡An obvious physical, or marked, feature at ninety degrees to the objective crossed at H-Hour.

to re-capture Goose Green. Their very lives depended on the maintenance of absolute secrecy – surprise being one of their few
advantages. It had now been stripped away, as by some malign hand.

At such times all eyes turn on the CO. H immediately ordered
everyone to disperse and postponed his orders. Camilla Creek
House was emptied. A man of different temperament perhaps might
have sought to minimise the significance of the broadcast,
suggesting it would be interpreted by the enemy as disinformation
to divert Argentine attention from the real thrust to Stanley. But not
H. Entirely in character, he led the outrage and issued all manner of
threats and vengeance. He would get Sara to sue John Nott, or
Margaret Thatcher, or whoever else might be responsible for such a
devastating breach of security.

Robert Fox arrived shortly afterwards. He recalls Chris Keeble
confronting him, but was able to reassure him that the offending
report had not emanated from him. Many assumed it had come
from the MOD press office, or higher, but that was investigated in
London and denied. Then fingers pointed at a political leak – after
all, the backbenchers were restless and needed reassurance that
something was about to happen. Rumour later had it that a member
of the War Cabinet, lunching at his club, was responsible. However,
no one was ever held to account, and whether the leak did any
practical harm is another matter.

H's opposite number on the isthmus, Lieutenant Colonel Italo
Piaggi, interviewed by the historian Martin Middlebrook after the
war, claimed that 'Contrary to British beliefs . . . no reinforcements
of any kind were sent to Goose Green as a result of the broadcast. I
did not take it too seriously; I thought it was more a psychological
action because it would be crazy for them to announce an actual
move.'[6]

According to Middlebrook, Piaggi was 'a tall officer, whose
shaved head and hearty nature gave him the appearance of the
television detective Kojak'. He commanded 12th Regiment, made
up from three different units, all part of III Brigade, the last
Argentinian formation to be sent to the Falklands. At the start of the

battle, eleven Argentine rifle platoons were ranged against 2 Para's ten. Piaggi's total infantry strength was 554; but overall there were some 1,200 service personnel at Goose Green, including a large air force element with an anti-aircraft detachment. Piaggi's and H's artillery were roughly comparable, although the former had appreciably more ammunition. Against that, Piaggi's men were generally poorly equipped conscripts and, with a thirty-one-kilometre perimeter to defend, they were thinly spread.

So in numerical terms (excluding the Argentinian air force personnel, who were not involved) the two forces were roughly equivalent. However, the conventional military wisdom is that an attacker needs a 3:1 superiority over the defender at the 'point of application'. Realistically 2 Para could never have achieved that.

Regardless of what Lieutenant Colonel Piaggi may have said or believed, some soldiers of 2 Para are adamant that they heard helicopters flying into Goose Green on the afternoon of the broadcast. They remain absolutely certain that the BBC made their job that much harder.

Robert Fox's trained journalist's recollection was that at least part of H's tirade 'was in fun'. Later, when the furore had subsided, H offered the view that in a democracy the media should have freedom to broadcast and publish news that was inconvenient, even at times against the national interest. This surprised Fox somewhat, for in the circumstances he did not imagine H would hold such a belief, and he noted yet another unusual side of the private man.

By now the broadcast had been widely disseminated. In the UK, there was wide conjecture by those following developments in the South Atlantic about how events would unfold. One debate was in Colchester, where the Devon and Dorsets, recently returned from Northern Ireland, had received their New Colours — with Sara present — five days previously.

The officers gathered as usual in the Mess at lunchtime, and discussed the day's news.* One remarked that H must be getting

---

* The author, as CO at the time, was present throughout.

H JONES VC

excited at the prospect of the breakout. Another chuckled: 'He'll be leading it!'

One major who knew H well said jocularly: 'I'll bet H gets a VC at the end of all this,' a notion which evoked no surprise, just supportive laughter. Whereupon, Captain Chris Biles, the brightest and best of the next generation of up-and-coming young officers,* possessing many of H's finer qualities, shook his head:

'If he does, it'll be posthumous!'

There followed one of those momentary, barely perceptible silences which hung in the air before the bustle of mess chat intruded again. These were officers who had known H all his adult life and had much affection for him, but no illusions.

Eight thousand miles away, H was giving out his orders. The process by which orders are issued is one of the Army's rituals. Before every operation, at whatever level, an 'O Group' (or Orders Group) is held at which the commander states his aim, tells his subordinate commanders how it is to be achieved and specifies the tasks of each.

The book *Not Mentioned in Despatches* by Spencer Fitz-Gibbon† criticises severely the rigidity of H's plan and the alleged inflexible grip he exercised over his subordinates, whose initiative thereby was stifled. Others, too, have said his orders were too detailed and too prescriptive; that they contained some inaccurate intelligence; that they were rushed; and that he himself was impatient and irritable throughout the process.

As already explained, there is a mass of conflicting evidence about H – about his relations with other people, and about what actually happened in the battle. Some contradictions are impossible to reconcile; others are honourable differences formed in the confusion

---

*Colonel Biles, as he later became, was killed in the Mull of Kintyre helicopter crash in June 1994. He was the head of Army intelligence in Northern Ireland at the time and destined for high rank.

†Fitz-Gibbon researched and wrote the book in connection with his PhD at Manchester University, where he subsequently taught in the War Studies Department. He was at one time a TA officer in 4th Battalion, The Parachute Regiment.

of impending battle, and the action itself. Others were agenda-driven.

H gave his orders in the prescribed fashion. With eight different units represented among the twenty or so officers present, this standard format was essential. The doctrine of *Auftragstaktik*,* a Bundeswehr concept of giving subordinate commanders the freedom, indeed the duty, to use their own initiative to accomplish what they knew to be their commander's intention (because they were metaphorically in his mind), had not then been adopted in the British Army. Thus criticism more than a decade later that H's orders imposed too much restraint on his company commanders, and that he could with advantage have adopted the German approach, ignores the fact that in 1982 commanding officers abided by the standard British doctrine. Furthermore H, recently an instructor at that doctrinal mecca, Warminster, understandably saw himself as an upholder of the 'School of Infantry way'. To expect otherwise is to misunderstand the influence of the British Army's training schools.

Two unexpected developments, however, did interfere with the smooth progression of H's orders at Camilla Creek House. The first was the capture of an Argentine patrol, giving 2 Para up-to-date information through immediate interrogation.† The second was a muddle over the time for the rearranged O Group. This caused further delay – and justified annoyance to H – so that when the O Group finally began, there were only ninety minutes of daylight remaining. Time, or lack of it, was to dog H from then on. He realised that 'time and space' was to be the single most important factor affecting 2 Para's fortunes. The need for speed, surprise and maintaining the momentum to compensate for the airborne soldier's light scales of weapons, ammunition and firepower were notions H had drummed into his Battalion for the past year.

In this case the timings were doubly crucial. First, the twin

---

*A German military term translated as 'mission tactics'.
†A Spanish-speaking officer was on hand.

settlements had to be taken in daylight – otherwise, the islanders held captive could be accidentally embroiled in the action. Second, H realised that the lie of the land provided excellent daylight observation and fields of fire, which favoured the defender and exposed his men to long-range attrition. The Battalion therefore had to eliminate the enemy in the hours of darkness, and be positioned on the edge of the settlements as dawn broke. But there were only fourteen hours of darkness and the distance on foot from Camilla Creek House – from which they could not advance in daylight without being observed – to Goose Green was fourteen kilometres. Hence, 2 Para must advance at an average of one kilometre an hour, including fighting through the enemy positions. This was certainly feasible for a fit and determined battalion, as 2 Para was, but only if brisk momentum was maintained from the moment they left Camilla Creek House, and if nothing at all went wrong.

One more factor crucially affected H's actions. To a greater or lesser extent, it is equally applicable to all commanders; indeed, it relates to any serious professional endeavour. This is the human factor – the chemistry between one person and another. H held strong views, mostly black or white, on people and he was more inclined to display his feelings than most. Sometimes these views were arrived at fairly, sometimes not, and occasionally his rating of people would change. His appraisal had nothing to do with rank, status or background – he was as openly critical upwards as downwards. If H did not rate someone, he had little or no regard for that person's opinion or judgement. On the other hand, if he did respect someone, he listened attentively to his – or her – opinion.

The rearranged O Group, due to begin at 1500 hours,* started a little late. In Robert Fox's view it was: 'calm and orderly and gently good humoured. We sat in a little bunch beneath a yew hedge as the sun died in the West.'[7] Proceedings commenced with a long

* This and all times henceforth are expressed in local time so that the relationship of events to darkness and light is evident. GMT was four hours ahead of Falklands time; all official records are in GMT.

description of the 'ground', and the current 'situation'. Goose Green and its twin smaller settlement at Darwin, a few houses a mile to the north, were located on a long narrow isthmus connecting East Falkland with Lafonia. Some 120 islanders from these settlements had been held by the Argentinians in the community hall at Goose Green since 1 May.

The next part of the orders dealt with the enemy, and was the genesis of future difficulty. Intelligence from Headquarters 3 Commando Brigade was scarce – maps only arrived as the O Group began and no air photographs were available. Some present later felt that the SAS alleged prediction of an 'easy ride' for 2 Para badly misled them. Others considered that information about the presence of a large number of Argentinian air force personnel in Goose Green – apparently known in London but not passed to 2 Para, because they lacked the necessary security clearance to receive 'intercept intelligence' – was an extraordinary omission. In fact, these men did not fight or affect the outcome in any practical sense: they only magnified the numbers of those who eventually surrendered.

The one significant mistake appears to have been a sin of commission, not omission. A Harrier on a reconnaissance flight had reported an enemy location at a specific grid reference. This was somehow later interpreted erroneously as a company at Coronation Point. That was to have severe consequences.

On completion of the intelligence assessment, H stated his mission: 'To capture Darwin and Goose Green.' Then followed the general outline, or paragraphs on how he intended to conduct the operation.

It was to be a six-phase, night/day, silent/noisy attack. This may sound contradictory to a layman, but to the members of H's O Group, all with years of experience, the concept was plain enough. They would advance to contact in darkness but would assault the settlements in daylight, so that the civilians there could be identified. Silence would be maintained until the first assault, which would of course be noisy. The plan envisaged rolling up the enemy from the north, tackling each position in turn. All officers are familiar with phases – flexible control measures whereby one battle or phase does not begin until the previous one is complete, unless otherwise ordered. Phases may be advanced or delayed, depending on progress. H inserted six distinct phases, faced as he was with a long advance and a series of imponderables: where exactly were the enemy positions and in what strength? How well prepared were they? Had they minefields and, if so, how deep?

A battalion night attack is the most difficult operation of all. It is notoriously hard to control, and disorientation invariably occurs after each action. To make matters worse, the isthmus was five miles long and only a mile and a half wide, with few distinguishing features: no hedgerows, woods or even prominent trees as reference points, only a winding central track to serve as a boundary between companies. The risk of 'blue on blue'* was very real. So H understandably insisted on every possible control measure to co-ordinate the series of company actions in prospect.

The CO then gave each company commander his detailed tasks. First, Major Dair Farrar-Hockley, who had been commanding A Company for about a year. He was considered a high-flyer and, like H, was a Staff College graduate and a former brigade major. His father was Colonel Commandant of the Parachute Regiment and as such kept a close eye on everything pertaining to his Regiment, including his son's progress. Dair was married to the daughter of another general and previous Colonel Commandant, and so his regimental credentials were impeccable. This put him more under the microscope than most officers – for such is the way of things – and he was perceived by officers and soldiers alike to be fiercely ambitious. Dair needed good confidential reports from H (as did all his Company Commanders) if he were to fulfil his potential, and a report earned on active service would carry extra weight. Farrar-Hockley's organisational ability had been useful on the voyage south

* Soldiers firing on their own side. Termed 'blue on blue' because own forces are marked in blue on maps.

ACTION

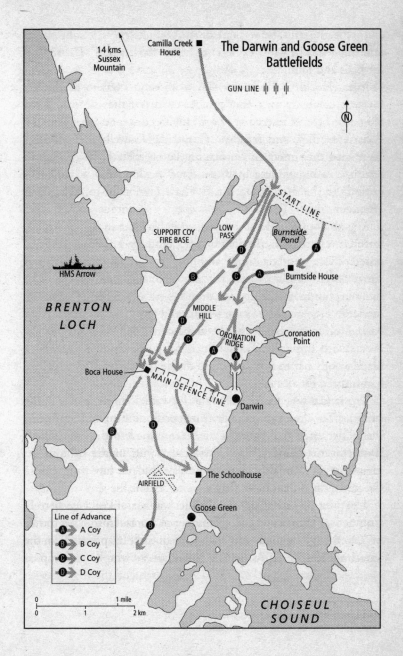

The Darwin and Goose Green Battlefields

261

and, reflecting this, he was one of the two officers to whom H was referring when he wrote to Sara just before the landing: 'Thank God for Dair and John.'

Farrar-Hockley's Company – A Company – was to be the left forward company as 2 Para progressed down the isthmus. They would be held in reserve in Phase One (securing the start line). In Phase Two, they were to capture Burntside House. H ordered them 'to destroy the enemy on Coronation Point in Phase Three'; and to return to a reserve role in Phase Four. A Company was then to exploit* to the edge of Darwin in Phase Five, prior to taking it in Phase Six.

The other officer H had mentioned in his letter to Sara was John, or Johnny, Crosland, commanding B Company. He was a tried and tested officer, greatly admired and popular with all ranks. This was partly on account of his easy, relaxed personality and quick sense of humour, but mainly it derived from his proven expertise on active service in Dhofar. H had great respect and regard for Johnny on that basis, even to the extent that he alone could occasionally flout H's orders with impunity. For instance, he got away with wearing a black woolly hat in action, instead of the steel helmet on which H had insisted for all ranks.

Crosland's was to be the right forward Company down the isthmus. They were to destroy enemy positions south of Low Pass in Phase Two. In Phase Four they were to remove the enemy on the Boca feature† halfway down the western side of the isthmus. In Phase Six B Company were to be involved in capturing Goose Green. In the other phases they were in reserve.

The third rifle company commander was Major Phil Neame of D Company, a man of considerable presence. He had begun his service in the RAF Regiment and had subsequently transferred to the Parachute Regiment. As befits a mountaineer who had attempted

---

*Take every opportunity to advance.
†On which were the ruins of Boca House.

Everest, he was super fit. Chris Keeble described him as 'ubiquitous and brave'. His military background was also impressive. His father had won the Victoria Cross as a Lieutenant in the First World War,* and subsequently became a Lieutenant-General. Neame was to distinguish himself in the battles ahead, and many regret that his own and D Company's contributions were not later formally recognised.

H ordered D Company to follow the two leading companies down the 'centre line',† and then in Phase Three to pass through B Company to destroy the enemy at a specified location. In Phase Four, Phil's D Company were designated: 'Reserve. Boca House if necessary.' Finally, in Phase Six, they were to take Goose Green. In effect, until the finale at Goose Green, H planned to keep D Company up his sleeve.

The Battalion had three more companies – HQ Company, C (Patrols) Company and Support Company – each with an important specialist primary role. H's own Tactical HQ (Tac 1) would follow behind the leading companies in all phases. Tac 1 consisted of a dozen men, among them H's providers of indirect fire:‡ his Battery Commander, Major Tony Rice, Royal Artillery; and his Mortar Officer, Captain Mal Worsley-Tonks. Also in Tac 1 were various signallers and the CO's bodyguard, Sergeant Barry Norman.

After giving out his orders, H had a little time to spare whilst his company commanders were briefing their men. On the eve of battle all human senses are sharpened, as animal instincts intrude – fear, anxiety, irrationality, lack of coherent thought, poor concentration, excessive yawning, and always pressing bodily functions. The whole of a soldier's previous training has been designed to prepare for this very moment: the triumph of self-discipline over instinct for flight.

---

*At the Battle of Neuve Chapelle in 1915. He was in the Royal Engineers and was the only VC also to be an Olympic athlete, competing in the Paris Olympics of 1924.
†A real or notional feature running down the centre of a battalion's advance. In this case a track served the purpose at times.
‡Artillery and mortars.

While H would have experienced these sensations, he was also reflective and pensive amid the small group with him: Chris Keeble, Tony Rice, Hector Gullan and Robert Fox. They remember him saying how shabbily he thought his brother Tim had been treated by Admiral Sandy Woodward. He added that he had written what would probably be his last letter home, asking Fox to deliver it if anything should happen to him. Indeed, he gave the impression that he did not expect to survive the battle.

'I am going to die,' he said calmly to Hector Gullan.

This may sound melancholy and dramatic, but H was given to hyperbole. Moreover, millions of warriors before a thousand battles in history have had premonitions and expressed similar thoughts. Group Captain Leonard Cheshire VC, for one, never believed he would return from any raid. Indeed, the more sensitive the character, the more such thoughts intrude. Such men ask their buddies, or those they trust, to 'take care of things if necessary', and gently request that treasured possessions and affirmations of love be passed on to wives or sweethearts. In H's case, he seemed more withdrawn than anything else, as if he was thinking deeply. Yet by the time they moved out of Camilla Creek House, he was as calm and collected as such an abnormal occasion allowed.

When Tac 1 set off it was a cold and windy black night, which was ideal for 2 Para's purpose. An impressive air strike by Harriers had hit enemy positions at last light and the artillery had been flown in. All was now set. Tac 1 followed behind A Company and was in turn followed by B Company in a 'snake' for the seven kilometres to the start line. No lights shone. The only noise was that of 550 soldiers on the move and the occasional cough, or curse as a man stumbled on the rough track. It was far easier than their earlier move up Sussex Mountain, for this was on light scales: no bergens, few entrenching tools or ancillaries – just the man, his weapon and every round of ammunition he could carry, plus two field dressings and a saline drip.

By 2230 hours 2 Para was in position and A and B Companies were ready to cross the start line. It was even colder and windier, and by now it was raining heavily. At this point unforeseen problems arose, as they always do on operations. First, HMS *Arrow*'s gun jammed just before H-Hour. This delayed things from the very outset, as recalled by Major Rice:

> Various deadlines for completing the repair came and went until finally we gave up waiting. So, instead of the planned simultaneous attack by A and B Companies in Phase Two (one supported by *Arrow* and the other by an artillery troop),* we now had to attack sequentially – A followed by B using the troop of guns only.[8]

The second delay was of less consequence. A Company had planned to cross Burntside Pond on its narrow side, but their Royal Marine guide had only seen the pond in midsummer and did not realise how deep it could get. Hence, they had to skirt around the other, longer side. The net effect of these two delays was that A Company's assault did not begin until 0252 hours, according to the Brigade log sheet, on which all key events were recorded.

On attacking their first objective, A Company poured fire into Burntside House and the adjacent buildings. It appeared to be returned, but it was not – these were ricochets, easily mistaken by the inexperienced for incoming enemy fire. The Argentinians had already gone, leaving behind in the farmhouse where they had been held prisoner the owner, Gerald Morrison, two friends and a dog, Spot. Miraculously, apart from Spot,† the prisoners were unharmed. A Company, recorded on the objective at 0314 hours, seem to have taken rather a long time to reorganise. By the time they were on the move again to their next – Phase Three – objective at Coronation Point, they were eighty minutes behind schedule. H was not pleased.

According to Spencer Fitz-Gibbon, two D Company soldiers

---

*Three 105-mm guns.
†Spot, hit in the mouth by a ricochet, later had to be put down.

claim to have been standing near the CO on the centre line when he was expressing dissatisfaction with A Company's progress. 'Callsign One, get a grip!' he was heard barking over the radio. Their Platoon Sergeant recalled:

> We were just sitting there at the side of the track . . . generally getting wet and colder. The Commanding Officer came up and he called the OC [Neame] over and said to him basically that because A Company was not getting its act together and weren't moving fast enough, he was going to push us through the centre.[9]

D Company were due to push through B Company in any case, and whether or not this was accelerated is unclear. Either way A Company, albeit late, began their move across Coronation Point towards Darwin. As intelligence had warned of an enemy company on Coronation Point, they would naturally have approached cautiously in the darkness. But no enemy were there. Instead, they were on the next feature – Darwin Ridge – a kilometre and a half to the south where just before dawn, Lieutenant Colonel Piaggi had ordered his strongest platoon, commanded by Lieutenant Estevez, to occupy the trenches prepared earlier.

There are two contradictory accounts of H's handling of A Company between leaving Burntside House and dawn breaking at around 0630 hours. The first, in John Frost's *2 Para Falklands*, claims that A Company requested permission to press on but that H ordered them to wait where they were on Coronation Point until he was satisfied of their position. The independent author and military historian Mark Adkin, in his book *Goose Green*, supports this version. Adkin relied on Farrar-Hockley's assertion that H stopped A Company in their tracks, losing a vital forty minutes whilst he found them, only to send them on their way again. Furthermore, Adkin offers a plausible reason for the CO wanting to satisfy himself of their progress. H would not have wanted one company to get ahead of another down the isthmus, thereby exposing an unprotected flank. Until 1995, Adkin's view was accepted as definitive.

That year Spencer Fitz-Gibbon offered another version, supported by no less a compelling body of evidence. He claims that rather than halting A Company, H was snapping at their heels like an angry sheepdog. He cites Tony Rice, the BC, as flatly rejecting the allegation that the CO delayed A Company. Rice said that, as first light began to break, Tac 1 found A Company on the side of higher ground just north of Darwin, hundreds of yards from Darwin Inlet. 'The Company was stationary, they were all sitting down. The Colonel told Major Farrar-Hockley to get a bloody move on. The aim was to try and get into Darwin before the light came up.'[10]

Supporting this version, Fitz-Gibbon was told that when H and Farrar-Hockley met, much of what was said by the CO to OC A Company was in the nature of a reproof.[11] An officer present agrees: 'It was like a one-sided conversation . . . It was very much "Get on with it!" It was not a matter for discussion . . . [The CO said] "What's going on here? Why aren't you moving?" '[12] Fitz-Gibbon, supported by four pages of researched evidence, concludes that 'The sum of these accounts, even allowing for minor discrepancies, seems clearly incompatible with the earlier version that A Company asked permission to press on and were told by the CO to stop and wait.'[13] Indeed, he points out that had H delayed A Company, it would have been grossly inconsistent of him afterwards to rebuke the Company Commander for stopping.

Whatever the truth, at 0520 hours A Company was logged as reporting Coronation Point clear, before moving into their Phase Five task: 'To exploit to the edge of Darwin.' Meanwhile, H took stock. Things did not look good.

HMS *Arrow*'s malfunctioning gun was still not providing the necessary fire support, and anyway the ship would have to sail well before dawn to get safely into open water. (In fact, when her gun was repaired, she bravely stayed on station to support 2 Para until the last possible moment.) The artillery and mortars were not proving effective in the high wind, and ammunition was running low. Moreover, the guns' trails and mortar base plates were sinking into the soft peat every time they fired, affecting accuracy. Ironically, this absorption by the peat had its advantages. At one stage an Argentine 105-mm shell landed close to H. Had it burst on hard ground, the CO, and others in Tac 1, could easily have been wounded or killed. Out at sea, low cloud and early morning fog meant that the pre-requested dawn air strikes on Argentinian positions could not proceed. Yet, maddeningly, enemy aircraft taking off from Argentina were not hampered by the weather, and soon made themselves felt.

Within 2 Para, the situation was patchy. There had already been a number of casualties, as would be expected in any night attack, with one man killed. B Company was making progress down the isthmus and were approaching the Boca feature. When H asked over the radio exactly where they were, Crosland replied, 'Four hundred yards west of the moon for all I know!' – not the sort of remark one makes if one's CO really is a martinet on a short fuse.

Although he did not know it, Crosland was about to bump the enemy. He explained to Fitz-Gibbon that, 'having had the boot very firmly on our foot, and been able to . . . chase Argentinians from pillar to post with our grenading and bayonet tactics',[14] the balance of advantage was about to swing in their favour. As the light improved, the enemy, on the higher ground, had better long-range fields of fire; and with the dawn came the air attacks. It was to be an unpleasant four or five hours for B Company.

Meanwhile, D Company was now in reserve, approaching Middle Hill. C Company, although not a rifle company, was moving forward too.

As H took stock just before dawn, he could not but conclude that his Battalion were badly behind time. They were halfway down the isthmus with four kilometres to go, but without yet having engaged a substantial enemy position. *Were* the enemy ahead? If they had evaporated, all well and good; but if not, 2 Para were not going to reach their objectives as planned.

Yet his assessment was not all bleak. As far as H was concerned, his were the best trained and motivated soldiers in the Army, and they, the 'Toms', were going well. There was nothing that could stop them, given proper leadership and example – and that was reassuring.

Referring to 'The Imperative of Example' in his authoritative work *The Mask of Command*, John Keegan writes that 'The first and greatest imperative of command is to be present in person. Those who impose risk must be seen to share it, and expect that their orders will be obeyed . . .'[15] Discussing 'The Imperative of Action', Keegan explains:

> Sometimes a commander's proper place will be in his HQ and at his map table, where calm and seclusion accord him the opportunity to reflect on the information that intelligence brings him, to ponder possibilities and to order a range of responses in his mind. Other times, when crisis presents itself, his place is at the front where he can see for himself, make direct and immediate judgements, watch them taking effect and reconsider his options as events change under his hand.
>
> The proof of the pudding is in the eating . . .[16]

When H heard that A Company, exploiting as he had directed towards Darwin, had now been engaged by seemingly effective enemy on a ridgeline running into Darwin Hill, he went forward again. He did not need *The Mask of Command*'s endorsement. He would have gone up anyway, because he fell into the first of Keegan's three types of commander, the categories being those placing themselves 'In front – always, sometimes, never?'

H discovered that A Company had been caught in an unfavourable position, in low ground, strung out along the edge of Darwin Inlet. The leading section of Lieutenant Mark Coe's 2 Platoon was almost in a gully. When firing began they ran straight forward into a convenient re-entrant,* where Platoon HQ and

---

* The ground rises on both sides, and towards the end.

another section soon joined them. In the best aggressive tradition, 2 Platoon quickly engaged the closest enemy trenches and developed a left flanking attack up a gorse gully, to try and dislodge the enemy from a troublesome spur. In the process one of Coe's section commanders, Corporal Adams, and his GPMG gunner, Private Steve Tuffin, were shot.

The wounded corporal withdrew his section – less Tuffin, who was too exposed to be recovered without further casualties – into the gorse gully. This provided some protection and would shortly become a firm base for most of A Company, and later Tac 1. Meanwhile, behind 2 Platoon, Sergeant Barrett's 1 Platoon had been advancing. Their left forward section was commanded by Corporal (now Major) Dave Abols. He recalls being caught in the open while crossing a fence as his section ran forward to assist 2 Platoon; eventually they too gained the gully.

By now the gorse was on fire from the burning phosphorus grenades thrown to provide instant covering smoke. Abols says that when the soldiers from 1 Platoon began arriving in the narrow gully they became intermingled in the smoke with those of 2 Platoon:

> By the time the two platoons had taken out the trenches in the gorse area, they'd lost blokes; they'd lost commanders, so there was blokes running round under no control. Those who had made their way south up the gully were returning in dribs and drabs, and the OC and CSM, once they too had arrived, began trying to sort the Company out. It was organised chaos.[17]

Despite another left-flanking attempt by 1 Platoon, a sniper had opened up to account for several more paratroopers – all shot dead through the head. Abols concludes that accurate sniper fire was the main reason A Company was stuck.

Another important factor was the location of 3 Platoon, which had been deployed earlier, before the opening shots were fired, to the northern side of Darwin Inlet, to cover A Company's eventual assault on Darwin. They would have been perfectly positioned had

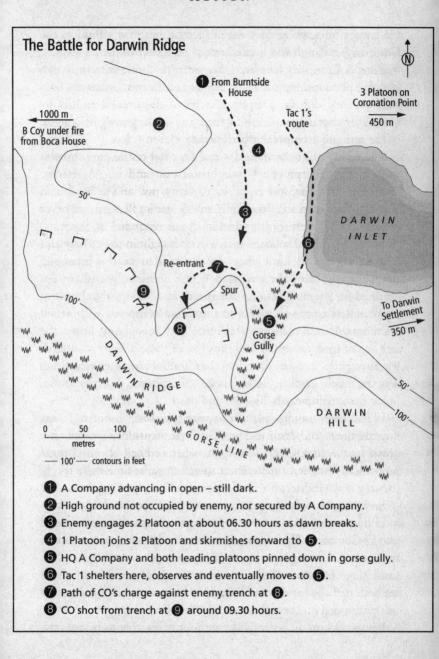

The Battle for Darwin Ridge

① From Burntside House

②

③

④

Tac 1's route

3 Platoon on Coronation Point

→ 450 m

← 1000 m
B Coy under fire from Boca House

50'

DARWIN INLET

Re-entrant

⑦

Spur

⑨

100'

⑧

⑤

⑥

Gorse Gully

To Darwin Settlement
→ 350 m

DARWIN RIDGE

GORSE LINE

DARWIN HILL

50'

100'

0   50   100
metres

— 100' — contours in feet

① A Company advancing in open – still dark.

② High ground not occupied by enemy, nor secured by A Company.

③ Enemy engages 2 Platoon at about 06.30 hours as dawn breaks.

④ 1 Platoon joins 2 Platoon and skirmishes forward to **⑤**.

⑤ HQ A Company and both leading platoons pinned down in gorse gully.

⑥ Tac 1 shelters here, observes and eventually moves to **⑤**.

⑦ Path of CO's charge against enemy trench at **⑧**.

⑧ CO shot from trench at **⑨** around 09.30 hours.

the enemy been where they were expected, but now a third of the Company's strength was located out of position 650 metres away.

Thus A Company had been caught in the open with only two effective platoons, against an enemy, of at least equal strength, who were securely dug in. Despite a series of determined attacks by groups of brave men skirmishing their way up the gorse gully and on to the spur, no progress was being made.

The reality of the battlefield – and for most of the men this was their first experience of it – was brutal and terrifying. As Hector Gullan, with operational experience aplenty, put it: 'The battlefield is a nasty, bloody place.' Its sounds, smells and impressions are never entirely erased. In the biting wind small-arms fire cracked, thumped and whined around soldiers' ears, grenades detonated, artillery and mortars exploded beside them in the sodden peat – incoming rounds mixed with the overhead whine of friendly artillery fire destined for enemy positions just ahead. In addition, the shouts of commanders trying to galvanise their men competed with yelled warnings of fresh danger, while into this cacophony broke the screams of fresh casualties and the cries of those already wounded. Intermittently aircraft screeched overhead. Pervading everything was the smell: cordite, acrid smoke, phosphorus, burning gorse, burnt flesh, damp earth, blood – and death.

H had been monitoring all this with mounting concern. It was now daybreak and Tac 1 had worked their way under sporadic fire down to the edge of Darwin Inlet, where a bank afforded some protection. Tony Rice remembers spending some time there trying to bring down indirect fire in support of A Company, but to no avail – the wind was too strong and his own men were too close.

H now ordered C Company, well to the north, to move up and join D Company. The assumption must be that, despite the lack of space, the CO was preparing to manoeuvre his reserve to help. At some stage he also talked to Johnny Crosland on the radio and realised, perhaps for the first time, how seriously stuck B Company was positioned on the right, tackling the Boca feature.

Being held up on both flanks without being able to by-pass the enemy, and with insufficient space to mount a flanking attack, was intolerable. The enemy would have to be dislodged frontally. To do this, H sensed more dynamism was required, a belief accentuated by receiving at that moment a situation report from A Company to the effect that 'they could go no further: that was it, they'd hit a brick wall and could not go through it.'[18]

Sergeant Norman, closest to his CO, accurately anticipated H's reaction: 'He thought it was a lack of motivation, as opposed to firepower, etc. He felt if it had been handled better they [A Company] wouldn't have been bogged down.'[19] H's response was typically direct: 'Right – I'm not having this. Come on – we're going!'

'Where?' asked Norman.

H pointed to the gorse gully. 'There!'

So, throwing smoke grenades to give them cover from enemy view, Tac 1 bounded over the bank bordering Darwin Inlet and dashed unscathed some hundred metres into the gorse gully, where they found A Company HQ. H did not get much of a welcome. Probably the last person Dair Farrar-Hockley wanted to see, in unfavourable circumstances for the second time in as many hours, was his CO.

H has been criticised for going forward, as if somehow it was tactically unsound and unprofessional. On the contrary, the commander should habitually place himself where he wants to bring about a decision. This is standard military doctrine,[20] and on that basis alone any infantry commander worth his salt would have been well forward. For a man like H, never asking of his men something he would not do himself, influencing events from a distance was unthinkable.

Spencer Fitz-Gibbon records Farrar-Hockley's written account of H's arrival alongside him in the gully:

H arrived and was frustrated to find that we had not got up the gully. I explained the position and what we were doing. Apprehensions that the attack was coming to a halt across the

Battalion front had manifestly shortened his patience. He began to issue orders – first by radio and then to those around him. The BC, Major Rice, caught the rough end of his tongue for his inability to bring the guns to bear effectively – no easy task in the wind conditions: so did we all to one degree or another. He wanted a platoon to try the gorse gully route again. I dissuaded him from this. He ordered the Mortar Officer to move up the gully and I dissuaded him from that. He determined that I should attack a ledge position – and we got on with the task.[21]

The BC's account of H's arrival is somewhat different. He was meant to have caught the rough edge of H's tongue after all – so he ought to remember. He claims that there was a pause after Tac 1 arrived in the gully, 'while we assessed what was going on. Jones did not get immediately stuck into Dair Farrar-Hockley, there is no question of that.'[22]

The Company Commander's explanation of the situation seemed at variance with his earlier report that they had hit a brick wall. He now claimed to be slowly getting on top of the enemy. As time went by, however, H saw little evidence of the claim. Tony Rice's view, strongly supported by others, was that:

A Company were stuck in the gully and going nowhere. But that is sometimes the lot of the leading company . . . and it is for the Battalion Commander to manoeuvre his companies and sort that out. They had already tried to manoeuvre, right at the start . . . and had frankly been driven back into the gully. It required, I think, something other than straight guts at that stage . . . to get them moving again . . . I have always disagreed with Dair that his Company were quietly reducing the position – they weren't.[23]

Sergeant Norman concurred: 'They weren't going anywhere, A Company. They wouldn't have got out of that hollow. Yet once the

ACTION

CO got there and instilled his form of authority on them, things started to happen.'[24]

H began to direct the action. As usual, he made his views forcefully known. Asked what he thought the CO was trying to achieve, Sergeant Norman replied:

> Motivate the blokes . . . it was his opinion that the blokes needed motivating . . . He felt that the morale was on the ebb . . . It was: 'Come on lads . . . one more bit to go . . . we're going over the top . . . don't just lie there, get your kit together!'[25]

The Mortar Officer, Mal Worsley-Tonks, also nearby, amplifies Sergeant Norman's account: 'Out of pure frustration, the Colonel wanted to get forward – and then it became very much a question of: "Come on A Company, let's get moving – get a grip – let's push on."'[26]

Vital time was passing and the improving light was favouring the defenders as more Argentinian weapons were brought to bear. By now, the Battery Commander and Mortar Officer were concerned that their CO was getting too immersed in the tactical battle. They suggested involving D Company, or C perhaps. Possibly Phil Neame could get his men, with support weapons,* into a position to assist; indeed, Neame had offered to help, as previously had others. H, however, peremptorily spurned these suggestions.

Whilst accepting that decisions in battle have to be taken in highly adverse circumstances, some find it inexplicable that H rejected these offers of help. Others, particularly those who knew H best, can understand his reasoning. Temperamentally it was true to form; and, moreover, it was perfectly logical.

First, he almost certainly felt this was a local A Company difficulty and that with a little more effort it could be resolved by them. Furthermore, he was now very conscious that B Company was held up also. Therefore, his reserve should not be launched

---

* Twelve GPMGs and several Milan from Support Company were available.

prematurely but retained intact, lest it be of more use on the right than on the left. Both judgements subsequently proved to be correct.

Second, perhaps H did not value sufficiently the provenance of the offers of help. If he had already decided what he was going to do – make A Company get forward by dint of his determination and personal example – he would not now welcome another view.

Third, there must have been playing on his mind the imminence of an Argentine counter-attack. Under British Army doctrine for the defence, a counter-attack would have been mounted by now; after all, A Company had been probing away at the position for at least an hour and a half. A counter-attack was due any moment – this was the wolf nearest H's sleigh.

Fourth, each fresh incident or development under fire crowds out the last. As on a radar screen 'clutter' is eliminated electronically, so too in moments of stress the brain rejects that which is not immediately essential for survival.

Lastly, although it could have been first, was H's intuition. He would have known that a critical moment had arrived, at which matters of strategic significance could be determined by relatively minor events. Indeed, war-gaming had taught him that a whole campaign may turn on one throw of a dice. There is no way of knowing for sure, but H had probably concluded that such a decisive moment had arrived, and that it was his duty – indeed, his destiny – to grasp it.

It was now about 0830 hours. Tac 1 had been in the gorse gully for over forty-five minutes and what was left of H's patience was evaporating. According to Fitz-Gibbon, there was: 'considerable evidence that Colonel Jones was becoming irritable with OC A Company . . .' He explained that estimates of how serious this was ranged from descriptions of one-sided conversations (similar to that which allegedly took place at Coronation Point) to observations that H effectively ended up running the battle in the gulley.

Getting men on their feet again once they have gone to ground is never easy, but over the next twenty to thirty minutes, determined effort was made to reach the top of the spur. Accounts differ in detail,* but most recall heroic instances, such as Captain David Wood, the Adjutant, urging the Paras 'to remember Arnhem', gathering up small parties of men on their own initiative, and going forward. But there is unanimity that the outcome was always the same: a surge forward, some ground gained, withering incoming fire, more casualties; yet no discernible progress out of the gully and up on to the spur. Tragically, in just such circumstances, Captain Wood, Captain Chris Dent, the Second-in-Command of A Company, and Corporal Hardman were all killed close by H.

Whether H saw his Adjutant, with whom he had forged a special bond, fall is uncertain; whether he felt responsible for their deaths is speculation; and whether they were the catalyst for what now occurred is surmise. But H's actions from this point onwards were, by any normal military yardstick, unconventional.

He had by now assessed from the battlefield evidence – the lack of momentum and energy, the lack of achievement so far – that, as things stood, A Company was not going to take Darwin Ridge. Without Darwin Ridge, 2 Para would fail in their objective. Worse, without Darwin and Goose Green (insignificant features though they might be) the first land battle of the campaign would fail. In the wake of the lost ships and destroyed aircraft, this would be a catastrophic British reverse impacting on the whole endeavour.

One of H's most valuable skills was an intuitive ability to understand something quickly. This, coupled with his nature and personality,† meant that if he could not persuade others to act, he would do it himself. In effect, this is what now happened. He took command of the situation locally and with the resources

---

*Major Rice is certain that there was only one such attempt from the time of Tac 1's arrival in the gully until H's death. Other accounts cited by Fitz-Gibbon and Adkin indicate there was more than one such attempt.

†Keeble assesses that H possessed a classic INTJ personality: People with INTJ characteristics are independent, trust their own perceptions and judgements more than those of others and can be critical of those who do not see their vision quickly; then they become single-minded and unyielding in pursuing it.

immediately available – just the few men around him – deliberately set out to regenerate the lost momentum. He sensed, as intuitive people do, just what had to be done – and how to rejuvenate the assault on the ridge.

His whole life had been in preparation for this moment. He did not tumble into it; it was coolly calculated. He deliberately led an out-flanking movement to set an example, to show the way, to tip the balance at a critical moment and to determine the outcome. This, in the final analysis, is the commander's job.

Thus, after the latest sally – of which H himself had formed part – petered out, Sergeant Norman, who was beside him, recounts that 'The CO decided to go right flanking. All he said was "Follow me, we're going right," and off he went. We dropped down into the lee of the hill [the spur], which then put us in dead ground.'[27] Mark Coe recalls his CO's exact words as he set off: '"Come on A Company, get your skirts off" – which didn't go down very well actually – and at that moment he stood up and was gone . . .'[28]

H's sensations and thoughts can only be imagined: fear, exhilaration, exhaustion, pounding heart, dry mouth, the freezing wind stinging his eyes and irritating his contact lenses. He had an utter determination to achieve, matched by an equal desperation not to fail. Imagine the impact of failure: on Sara; on the boys – on them especially, as they might not understand. On family, on Tim. On friends like Tobin Duke; on Dan Severson, the American with whom he had discussed such tactical eventualities, and whose expectations of him were so high. On both his regiments – what *would* the distant Devon and Dorsets think if he failed? And all those at The Grange? Above all, his own soldiers – looking defiant yet puzzled, stalled against a conscript foe – were waiting for a lead. He *must* do it, and do it well. *Now!*

'He was one hundred per cent aware of what faced him round that corner, and no one can detract from his own personal bravery,' continued Coe.[29]

Of those who followed their CO, Sergeant Norman and Major

Rice recount what happened. H headed into the original re-entrant where Private Tuffin lay wounded* and as he ran past him, he appeared to notice a trench to his left and above him. At this point, according to Rice, H 'ran at it firing his SMG and then rolled down the slope, changed his magazine and then ran back at the trench again'.[30] By now he was coming into the arc of fire of a well-camouflaged slit trench on his right, probably manned by Lieutenant Estevez's platoon, of which he was unaware. Rounds struck the ground behind him, kicking up the turf, but shouted warnings were too late.

A bullet found its mark and H, collapsing, was carried by his own momentum to the very edge of the enemy trench. There he lay – still, mortally wounded.

It was around 0900 hours on Friday 28 May.

Cause and effect are notoriously difficult to connect in action. Some say H's lone charge, witnessed by so few, neither spurred his men on to greater effort nor had any direct effect on the Argentinians. As Middlebrook points out,[31] Estevez's men did not know it was the opposing Commanding Officer himself; he looked like any other soldier. But undeniably H had penetrated the enemy defences deeper than anyone had done so far. Whether it was the sheer determination of the attack, or the diversionary effect of it, or the sound of firing in an area forward of his own men which tipped the balance will never be known. But the balance did perceptibly begin to shift.

When H fell, his radio operator sent out: 'Sunray† is down,' and Major Rice dashed back round the spur to notify Farrar-Hockley. Those in the gorse gully then remember the exemplary action of Corporal Dave Abols, for which he was later to be decorated. Abols modestly recalls that after his CO had disappeared round the corner, several members of the Company got into a position to bring down 'such a mass of fire that the Argentinians just jacked'.[32] Mark Coe describes the decisive moment more fully:

---

*Tuffin had been wounded on the original assault. He had lain there for ninety minutes and survived.
†Radio title for a commander.

I was quite close ... Sergeant Major Price fired a 66* at the nearest trench that we had not taken, and he missed. Corporal Abols then fired one at the same trench and hit. He fired another at the next, and hit that too.

That I think was the last straw that broke the camel's back. At that point they started to come out, having lost probably six trenches by this stage. At last we were on top of the spur, and then all of a sudden the whole thing just collapsed ... people were putting their hands up and coming out of their holes.[33]

Tony Rice, determined to get to H as quickly as possible, added that it was a slow business:

There was a delay from him being shot to me actually getting there. He had been lying alone for about twenty minutes or more, but when we got to him he was still just alive ... He'd gone a sort of waxy colour and was panting weakly ... It had been drummed into us the importance of getting saline into the wounded, so ... we gave him a drip and a half; then he slipped into unconsciousness.[34]

Casualty evacuation was ordered at once and Coe remembers Dair staying beside H for a while. Tragically, as a Scout helicopter flown by Lieutenant Richard Nunn responded and took off from Camilla Creek House, a passing Pucara† destroyed it. With great bravery and determination, another Royal Marine helicopter, flown by Captain Jeff Niblett, eventually got through. But by this time it was far too late. H was dead.

On the other side of the world, the boys of H's old preparatory school were packing up for half-term – thirteen-year-old Rupert Jones among them. The Headmaster was taking the chapel service,

---

*A shoulder-fired high-explosive grenade.
†Argentinian ground attack aircraft.

at which, by extraordinary coincidence, the approved Old Testament reading for the day was from the Apocrypha: 'And thus this man died, leaving his death for an example of a noble courage and a memorial of virtue, not only to young men but to all his nation.' (2 Maccabees, 6: 31.)[35]

In London, the afternoon shift was coming on duty in the Defence Operations Centre in Whitehall. H's death had been reported by Headquarters, 3 Commando Brigade at 1345 hours GMT and relayed to Northwood direct. In Whitehall and Westminster, as the Prime Minister, ministers, senior officers and officials returned from lunch, they were informed that the Commanding Officer of 2 Para had been killed in action at Darwin, where the enemy locally had surrendered. Most sensed at once that this was an event of major significance – shocking and unwelcome, of course, in personal terms, but a crucial turning point nevertheless.

On the isthmus, where Phase Six had not even begun, Hector Gullan made their point more pithily: 'They've killed our CO; they'll have to kill us all to stop us now.'[36]

CHAPTER TWELVE

The Aftermath

The battle on the isthmus did not end when H was killed and the
Argentinians on Darwin Ridge surrendered. On the contrary,
some of the fiercest fighting was yet to come, and it was another
twenty-four hours before the two settlements were taken. Before
that, most of 2 Para had to endure a hard day's fighting followed
by a long cold night of uncertainty. Many remember it as the most
unpleasant of the whole campaign. The first snow of advancing
winter fell.

The waiting amongst the families back in Aldershot was equally
disagreeable. They knew from every broadcast that their menfolk
were now fully engaged in battle. Furthermore, they were aware that
the Army, after its years of experience in Northern Ireland, rightly
refuses to be drawn on the subject of casualties until any possibility
of doubt has been eliminated. Next-of-kin should learn of a fatality
only through official channels – the media tend to co-operate in this
respect – but there were brief reports in some papers that British
casualties were light. Sara remembers David remarking shrewdly on
the need for caution in interpreting that.

The Army adheres to another strict procedure: bad news should
never be broken to next-of-kin in the middle of the night. So it was
not until next morning – Saturday 29 May – that Sara and the boys,
home for half-term, would be notified of H's death.

Back on the battlefield, Chris Keeble was alerted by the radio
message 'Sunray is down', and after making his way forward to assess

the situation he assumed command. With the left flank now unstuck, he focused on the right, where B Company was still held up, and on prising the enemy off the Boca feature.

Major Phil Neame, whose offer of help had been turned down by H, had found a way for D Company to circumvent the Boca enemy by moving along the shore of Brenton Loch and engaging them from the flank. After checking with Johnny Crosland, Keeble sanctioned what should have been a classic hammer-and-anvil operation – B Company providing covering fire, whilst D swept in from seaward. It did not happen quite so neatly, but by midday the enemy had been removed from Boca, due in part to the unorthodox but effective use of Milan missiles against trenches and bunkers. It had taken around six hours to dislodge the Argentinians from their vital ground – which says much for their tenacity. At last 2 Para could close up on Goose Green and Phase Six could begin.

C Company, as yet unbloodied, and reinforced by A Company's unused third platoon, was pushed straight through towards Goose Green. Meanwhile, D Company moved off towards the airfield, following up the fleeing Argentinians, and B Company swung south to approach Goose Green from the sea.

The soldiers of 2 Para had been continuously on the move for about eighteen hours and in contact with the enemy for most of that time. They must have hoped that now they had them on the run, and that this last phase of only a few kilometres would be easy. They were to be disappointed.

Stiff local resistance – anti-aircraft guns* on the airfield, a minefield, and a strong enemy position around the schoolhouse and 'flagstaff' position – still impeded them, and they came under air attack. However, 2 Para, aggressively determined and working well in small teams, slowly forced the enemy back during the afternoon – it was all rather uncoordinated and haphazard, taking its toll in lives, casualties and resources.

One sad occurrence – the 'white flag incident' – still generates

---

*Firing over their sights in a direct ground fire role.

controversy in Argentina. At some stage in the afternoon, Lieutenant Jim Barry, of D Company, following the appearance of Argentinian white flags to his front, sought to effect a local surrender. Barry, and two of his men, went forward with weapons above their heads to signify they were not attacking. Meeting them, Second Lieutenant Gomez Centurion, speaking perfect English, asked for *their* surrender, only to discover that it was his that Barry expected.

Somewhere in the confusion, the Argentines claimed that Lieutenant Colonel Jones' name was used. Whether this was true or not, Centurion firmly refused to surrender, and gave the Paras time to regain their positions. But during the process, and unaware of this local Para initiative, 2 Para's Machine Gun Platoon opened fire on Centurion's men, killing a number of them. Fire was returned at once; Barry and one of those accompanying him fell dead. Twenty years later, some Argentinians apparently still resentfully maintain that it was H Jones, not Lieutenant Barry, who was killed in this – to them – duplicitous incident, and cite it, without a shred of supporting evidence, as one of the ruses by 'perfidious Albion' that dislodged them from the Malvinas.[1]

As dusk approached, Mark Adkin describes how, after nearly twenty-four hours, much of it in actual combat, 'the troops were exhausted, hungry, freezing, short of water, ammunition and digging tools, missing 47 casualties and disadvantageously scattered'. One senior NCO, with that gift of directness possessed by many soldiers, remarked that 'the Battalion was on its chinstrap'.[2]

All day 2 Para had been requesting air support, without success. Then suddenly, just before dusk, three RAF Harrier ground attack aircraft flying off HMS *Hermes* struck Goose Green. Major Rice witnessed the whole thing:

The cluster bombs, dropped short of the settlement, were the most devastating thing I had ever seen; the ground boiled and there was a thunderous roar, then total silence covered the battlefield. The stuffing was completely knocked out of the Argentinians and they never fired another shot.[3]

One British Company Commander remembers: 'They frightened me shitless, never mind the Argentinians.' Chris Keeble claimed too that the Harriers were to be decisive in cracking the enemy's will to resist further.

Shortly after the Harrier strike – and unconnected with it – the Argentinian 'Force Solari' landed five kilometres south of Goose Green in helicopters. B Company was nearest to them, and a platoon commander called for indirect fire, but the helicopters had flown off by the time the shells registered.

The arrival of Force Solari was potentially serious, indicating that the Argentinians might be preparing a counter-attack. At that moment, 2 Para would have been in no condition to resist fresh troops with a determination to dislodge them. Luckily, the enemy displayed no such aggression – their commander had actually missed his helicopter[4] – and Force Solari headed straight towards the settlement to spend the night.

Chris Keeble, well aware of 2 Para's precarious position, called for extra artillery and re-supply, especially of ammunition. The Brigade Commander, now thoroughly alarmed by the unfavourable turn of events to his rear – he and his headquarters were moving up behind the battalions already yomping east to Stanley – sent a reinforcing commando company, and offered his own services.

Keeble, however, was coping very well on his own. On the one hand he was preparing for a massive final assault on the settlements at first light, supported by another Harrier strike; while on the other he was developing an alternative plan. Some have described it as a bluff designed to convince the Argentinian garrison to surrender on the grounds that they were surrounded, that the Harriers would be back, and that it would be folly to resist further. However, according to Keeble himself, a highly ethical officer, it was not a bluff. It came about:

H JONES VC

... partly due to the collapse in the clamour of the battlefield after the Harrier strike and my perception that the enemy's will had cracked. I did not fear a counter-attack. It was also partly due to an extraordinary spiritual experience earlier when I prayed to God for help. From both sources emerged the option to negotiate, a course of action that also sustained the moral legitimacy of our intervention – violence should only be used as a last resort. Our weak tactical position of course helped my negotiating position.[5]

Robert Fox, who understood the vital importance of honour in the Latin temperament, urged Keeble to give the Argentinians the opportunity to surrender with dignity. They had certainly fought well, and further bloodshed could be spared if it was presented properly without any hint of humiliation.

The approach worked perfectly. Two captured Argentine warrant officers were sent into Goose Green at dawn with an ultimatum. After a stressful wait, involving further negotiations* and un-certainty of outcome, the whole Argentine garrison surrendered to four unarmed British officers and two journalists.† No British soldiers were in sight. First the Argentinian air force contingent paraded under their Commandant who, following their national anthem, addressed them in passionate terms before formally surrendering his side-arms to Keeble. Then it was the turn of the army. Lieutenant Colonel Piaggi declared that he and his men had fought honourably and bravely, and that to lay down their arms to prevent unnecessary loss of life was no disgrace.‡

With the surrender unmistakably secured, the relief in 2 Para was palpable. They had been engaged for over thirty-six hours, their

*Over repatriation terms and the exclusion of TV media from the negotiations.
†Majors Keeble, Rice and Gullan; the interpreter Captain Bell; and Robert Fox and David Norris of the *Daily Mail*.
‡After the campaign, Piaggi was charged with neglect, and was forced to resign his commission and retire.

ranks had been significantly depleted – the Commanding Officer and fifteen others had been killed, and thirty were wounded – and they were almost out of ammunition. They were exhausted, and not a little subdued by their experience. The intensity of battle and the cost of what they had achieved were still sinking in, as hundreds upon hundreds of Argentinian servicemen – in all over a thousand – emerged from the settlement. The Battalion's sombre mood turned to elation as the scale of their victory unfolded. H's men had fought with the greatest tenacity and skill. The Battalion that he had led and loved, and of which he had been so proud, had, with the training and aggressive spirit instilled over the previous thirteen months, turned what could so easily have been a disaster into a very significant victory.

In Britain, a gloriously sunny Whitsun Bank Holiday weekend had begun. Saturday's newspapers were full of the victory at Goose Green, although the settlement had not yet fallen. David and Rupert were playing croquet in the garden of Leipzig House when an Army staff car drew up. Sara saw Colonel Graham Farrell, the Regimental Colonel of the Parachute Regiment, walking towards the house. Ever practical and thinking of others, she assumed he was coming to ask her to join him in breaking the news to bereaved next-of-kin, a job everyone dreads. Instead, he broke the news to her. A few minutes later, Sara composed herself and went out into the garden to tell the children.

The Sunday newspapers were full of the story. 'H FOR HERO' was the huge front-page headline in the *Mail on Sunday*. His photograph was splashed across all editions of the other papers. Brigadier Julian Thompson paid tribute 'to the magnificent fighting spirit of 2 Para under Lieutenant Colonel Jones'. A brother officer said that H was 'the sort of man who believed in leading from the front'. Chris Keeble, in a generous tribute considering how much he himself had contributed to the outcome, said: 'The victory is entirely his. It was H's plan that worked.'

More colourfully, in a by-line filed from San Carlos, Max Hastings described H in the *Sunday Telegraph* as 'an enchanting man who made himself one of the most popular officers of the landing force'. Every newspaper carried Prime Minister Margaret Thatcher's deep regret at the loss of 'this valiant and courageous officer, who was loved by his men'.*

The significance of the battle, and the enormous relief that it had been won, was evident everywhere, nowhere more so than in London. There, the mood was captured in a signal sent on 30 May by the Chief of the General Staff (CGS). First it commiserated with 2 Para on their losses and casualties, then it focused on their achievement:

> Not only was the task given the Battalion of vital and urgent importance to our country's interests and future at this time, but also in achieving all its objectives in a ten-hour battle, after losing the CO and capturing over 1,200 prisoners, the Battalion has executed a feat of arms and gallantry probably unsurpassed in the glorious history of the British Army. It will certainly rate with the other great examples of courage by the Parachute Regiment such as the Normandy landings and Arnhem.

Signals, usually short and dry, are the standard form of military communication in the wake of any incident, but this one was unusually fulsome. At the very top, there was no doubting the significance of this action. Confirming it several years later, Field Marshal Lord Bramall, who had been the CGS of the day, and who had himself, in 1944, landed on the Normandy beaches on D+1, explained: 'If Goose Green had been lost, the whole campaign would have been lost and public support would have evaporated. Goose Green therefore was the turning point, certainly as seen from Whitehall and 10 Downing Street.'[6]

Similar feelings were echoed lower down, too. A shrewd

---

* Ken Lukowiak served with 2 Para in the Falklands and later wrote in *A Soldier's Song*: 'We were paratroopers – we loved no one. We had not been taught to love.'

contemporary, sharing the same dangers and difficulties on the battlefield, is probably the best overall judge of a soldier's worth in action. Such a man was Lieutenant Colonel Hew Pike, commanding 3 Para alongside H's Battalion. Hew had been visibly shaken by the news of H's death, which was broken to him at Teal Inlet as 3 Para advanced towards Stanley.* Pike subsequently wrote of H in his journal: 'He was a good man, a man of integrity, of character and clear intellect. He was a soldier of passion, in a generation too full of cynicism and mediocrity.'

More significantly for those still fighting, Pike felt that the successful outcome of Goose Green and the sacrifice of H, and of the other officers and soldiers who died, gave those still fighting a moral ascendancy. That is one of the vital components of 'fighting power'. 'It derived from the success of the battle – the fact that H's Battalion prevailed over a much larger force. That was what gave us the moral ascendancy. Above all, we knew after Goose Green that we could beat them.'[7]

Others, more jingoistic perhaps, felt that the moral ascendancy derived from the fact that no Argentine commanding officer, despite their national obsession with the 'Malvinas', would so unhesitatingly have given his life for them, as H had done.

Certain achievements, much heralded at the time, can lose their significance long after the event. Not in this case. Baroness Thatcher's recollection of the effect on her as Prime Minister of H's action, and the subsequent victory at Darwin and Goose Green, has not been modified one jot by the passage of two decades.

It gave renewed faith to the people on the Falklands and renewed understanding to all of those who doubted whether we would see it through. We *were* going to see it through. Our resolve – our total resolve – to reclaim those islands was demonstrated by that

---

* One of his officers, Major Peter Dennison, had heard the report on the Brigade fire support radio net.

one particular deed. It was heroic leadership. It is part of our history. It was heroism and leadership of a matchless order, really. There are one or two things in history which have been similar. The bravest of the brave were there that day.[8]

Human nature being what it is, such resounding praise from those qualified to offer it was soon contradicted in some quarters and embellished in others. Poor H's reputation began to be buffeted by exposure and extremes. On the one hand he was turned into an instant hero by the popular press, who began speculating within days of the surrender at Goose Green about the possible award of a Victoria Cross.[9] On the other hand, bizarre interpretations of his character and the manner of his death began circulating.

One of the more absurd rumours was that he had been shot by one of his own soldiers, allegedly because they thought he was about to lead them on a suicidal attack.[10] Spencer Fitz-Gibbon claims to have come by this story at the Parachute Regiment Depot in 1984. He holds that it was circulating also in BAOR.* (Indeed, a researcher for this book even heard it stated convincingly by a London taxi driver in 2000!)

'Supporting evidence' – emphatically not the allegation itself – stemmed from Sergeant Norman, who claims to have given H first aid. According to Fitz-Gibbon, Norman noticed that 'the entry wounds were in his buttocks and there were no exit wounds'. As H faced the enemy, his back was, of course, to his own men, thereby giving casual credence to the story. Likewise, H's signaller, Sergeant Blackburn, apparently told Fitz-Gibbon that 'Jones was shot from a trench on his left, hit about waist height, almost in the rump, and that he saw H hit twice'.[11]

On the contrary, H was shot only once, in the base of the neck, and from the right. The evidence comes from the then Surgeon Commander Rick Jolly, Senior Medical Officer of 3 Commando

---

*Fitz-Gibbon does not personally claim to have believed any of it.

Brigade and the Commander of the Field Hospital at Ajax Bay, to where H's body and all other casualties were taken direct from the battlefield. (Remarkably, every single British casualty who reached there alive survived.) Jolly,* a robust and jovial character of deep conviction, had served in Belfast during the 1970s as the RMO of a Royal Marine commando. During emergencies he had, on occasion, assisted pathologists in the mortuary at Laganbank. That experience had taught him to be meticulous in his examination of the dead, and the recording of the related evidence. He recalls that after the battle:

We carefully and reverently examined all the bodies in the bitterly cold air, confirming each identity and recording injuries on a Field Death Certificate. H was the last – he had the same shy, quizzical half-smile on his face that I knew in life.

I had not received any detailed information about the circumstances of his death, except that 2 Para had called for a casevac helicopter during the action – and I knew that my friend Lieutenant Richard Nunn had given his life in an attempt to recover H.

When his bloodstained clothing had been cut away, I checked H's body from head to toe, and from front to back. It was very clear that he only had injuries consistent with the impact and passage of a single bullet. It did however take me a little time to work it all out.

The entry wound was about 8mm in diameter, and just behind his right collarbone, but there was a much larger exit wound down the left side of his lower abdomen. There were other features making this a classic example of a high-energy bullet's track. The only explanation that fitted properly was that H was crouching, perhaps as he ran forward up a slope, and that

---

* Retired as Surgeon Captain Jolly OBE, and after the conflict, uniquely, was decorated by both sides.

he was hit from higher ground, at close range, from his front and right.

The bullet, having penetrated the apex of his right lung, passed behind his heart, bounced off the lower end of the thoracic spine and crossed the midline. It exited halfway between the navel and crest of H's left hip, still possessing considerable kinetic energy. The impact undoubtedly stopped H in his tracks and probably knocked him on to his back.[12]

Jolly explained that subsequently H would have lost a lot of blood, the effect of which could easily have misled Sergeants Norman and Blackburn. Commenting on the suggestion contained in Fitz-Gibbon's book that H had been hit in the buttocks and the back of the head, he said: 'I can confirm that this is completely untrue.'

Speculating that if H had arrived at the Field Hospital earlier, it might have been possible to operate and perhaps do something to stop his internal bleeding, Jolly continued:

In my heart of hearts, I do not think that H would have survived in the end. I base this judgement on the fact that he did not speak after he was hit, although he continued to breathe and have a pulse . . . I think that the ascending shock wave up the spinal cord, generated by that bullet as it changed direction . . . probably extinguished all his higher reflexes – like conscious thought, or any perception of pain. In a sense it turned the lights out . . .*

The day after Goose Green surrendered, Major-General Jeremy Moore, who had landed that morning, led the mourners at a field burial in a large temporary grave dug just above Ajax Bay. David Cooper, 2 Para's Padre and H's friend and confidant, conducted a simple and dignified service. Major Chris Keeble and his subordinate commanders carried H's body-bag down first into the

---

* Jolly says that on returning home he saw Sara Jones and at her request explained the truth to her in these words.

grave he was to share with sixteen others. Over three-quarters of them were officers or non-commissioned officers. This in itself was a remarkable illustration of the commitment and example that had been set by the leaders.

Action was still in progress elsewhere, so there were neither bugles nor a firing party; when the service ended, those present merely saluted as the RSM scattered a handful of earth over the bodies. The scene, under the dome of a perfect blue sky, with a frigate swinging at anchor in the bay below, its guns trained skyward against possible air attack, was filmed and relayed back to the UK and around the world. The row of silver plastic body bags, each identified by surname, hand-written with a black marker-pen, brought home vividly the human cost of war.

The Falklands was the first British active service campaign in which the next-of-kin were given a choice of whether or not to repatriate bodies. Sections of the media agitated for a change in the regulations, which, until then, had been insistent on the burial of servicemen where they fell. Perhaps the feminine instincts of Margaret Thatcher led her to direct that the wishes of the next-of-kin should be accommodated. When asked, however, Sara firmly chose the traditional soldier's resting-place – on the field of battle alongside his comrades. It was not a straightforward decision, and was made more difficult by other widows looking to her for a lead.

When the hostilities ended, the Commonwealth War Graves Commission was invited by the Ministry of Defence to design and build a military cemetery so that the bodies in temporary graves could be transferred and laid to rest in perpetuity. In fulfilling the Commission's remit, its architectural adviser, Professor Sir Peter Shepheard, based his concept on a North Wales sheepfold: oval in shape, built in rough-hewn stone.* Two of the Commission's stonemasons† carefully constructed the site and the result is a small,

---

* A decision was taken subsequently to 'dress' the stones.
† Jim Hallahan and Rory O'Connor.

beautiful cemetery overlooking San Carlos Water, with only the wind and the cries of gulls wheeling overhead to disturb the peace. Here H's grave and those of thirteen others are lovingly tended.

Inscribed on H's headstone of Portland limestone is a quotation from Sir Francis Drake's prayer:

> It is not the beginning but the continuing of the same
> unto the end.

On the wall immediately to the east of where he lies is a memorial in slate on which are engraved the names of the 174 sailors, soldiers and airmen lost in the conflict who have no known grave but the sea.

Commander Tim Jones, H's younger brother, who was serving in the South Atlantic at the time, represented the family at the re-burial. Other services were held in the United Kingdom. Among them was a memorial service in Aldershot conducted for all those in the Parachute Regiment who died. In Exeter Cathedral hundreds of members of the Devon and Dorsets, their families and Regimental well-wishers attended a service of thanksgiving for H's life. In both Brockenhurst and Kingswear, services were held for close family, friends and the local community.

Various permanent memorials were established too. A stone cairn commemorates the spot where H fell on the battlefield; and a memorial cross (made on the *Norland*), visible on the skyline from both Darwin and Goose Green, was erected by the islanders. In the grounds of Pangbourne College in Berkshire, famous for its nautical tradition, 'The Falkland Islands Memorial Chapel' was built by public subscription to commemorate all those who lost their lives in Operation Corporate at sea, on land or in the air.

For months after the war ended, speculation continued over the possibility, then probability, of H being awarded the Victoria Cross, Britain's highest award for gallantry. The VC was instituted by Royal Warrant, signed by Queen Victoria, on 29 January 1856, and has been in existence throughout the most ferocious and costly period in British history in terms of lives lost in battle, embracing both world wars, the Boer War and the Indian Mutiny. Yet it has been awarded to only 1,351 men, three of whom won it twice. (Another was awarded to the American Unknown Warrior resting in Arlington National Cemetery, Washington DC.)

Over those one and a half centuries, various alterations and amendments to the Warrant have been made. Importantly, in 1902 King Edward VII made provision for a posthumous award. The key clause in Queen Elizabeth II's extant Royal Warrant, dated 30 September 1961, reads: 'Thirdly: It is ordained that the Cross shall only be awarded for most conspicuous bravery, or some daring or pre-eminent act of valour or self-sacrifice or extreme devotion to duty in the presence of the enemy.'

The method by which all honours and awards for Britain's Armed Forces are submitted, processed and bestowed is complex and fraught, often generating considerable heat and emotion. One senior officer declared that after the war, 'medals' posed more problems than anything the Argentinians had done during it. The age-old problem is that the allocation – the so-called 'medal quota' – never is, or ever has been, sufficient to recognise all deserving cases. Thus, the process is inherently competitive, and very selective. Indeed, it is often argued that Britain is too parsimonious in this matter compared with other nations. Whilst probably true, the corollary is that the resultant recognition has greater value and commands more respect.

After Operation Corporate, the formal recognition, or otherwise, of members of all three Services, as well as those involved in other capacities, such as merchant seamen and civilians, followed the normal pattern. The scars of commission and omission are still evident. Many deserving cases were left off the list, and some contributions were under-valued. A very few should not have been recognised at all, according to some on the spot.

In the case of the Victoria Cross, 'bravery' is quantified as a ninety per cent possibility of being killed in performing the deed under consideration. Furthermore, signed statements of three independent witnesses should accompany a recommendation.[13] Like other things relating to H, even in death matters were not straightforward, and controversy dogged his award.

First, the citation does not bear all the requisite signatures. Second, some considered that H's action was more foolhardy and impetuous than brave. But even if true, that is irrelevant and should be discounted on the basis of the above quoted third clause of the Warrant. Last, there was suspicion that his nomination was directed from above rather than originated from below.

Those who quibble with H's VC now appear more concerned with process than substance – but that was not the case at the time. Although, undeniably, H displayed gallantry of the highest order in ignoring or overcoming the mortal danger he faced as he charged directly at the enemy; and notwithstanding that his action met the 'possibility of death' criterion in every last respect, or that his was an example of extreme devotion to duty, his name was not initially submitted for formal recognition. It seems that it was blocked somewhere up the chain of command.

At Northwood, Lieutenant-General Sir Richard Trant had been Land Deputy to the Commander-in-Chief for Operation Corporate since the initial landings. After the conflict was over – the Argentinians surrendered in Stanley on 14 June – and a tricky period of disengagement, readjustment and Argentine repatriation was complete, the demands of administration reasserted themselves. On the matter of honours and awards, General Trant recalls: 'When the citations started to arrive they were extremely sketchy. After extracting the details from Jeremy Moore's headquarters in Port Stanley they were rewritten at Northwood. No citation arrived for H.'[14]

Any senior headquarters worth its salt keeps a finger on the pulse of its command. HQs are meant to have a good feel for developments – both official and unofficial – from their various feeder links and channels. It was no surprise, therefore, that Northwood's collective antennae picked up rumblings. As Dick Trant put it: 'From what we had heard, the CO 2 Para's action had been one of extreme gallantry, and potentially worthy of the highest recognition. In the end, after a direct request for a citation for H, one arrived.'[15]

There was nothing amiss here. This was part and parcel of command, as it has always been – it was Trant's duty to monitor the matter for his Commander-in-Chief – and he is clear that no one leant on him from above. The supporting witness statements* from the field, from Major Rice, Sergeant Norman and Lieutenant Thurman RM,† are now in the Public Record Office. However, a copy of Thurman's contemporary five-page hand-written state-ment‡ concludes unequivocally:

> It is my present opinion that Colonel Jones's action led directly to *[the words 'led directly to' have been struck through and substituted with:]* precipitated the surrender of the enemy. It came at a critical phase in our advance. Further delay would have resulted in heavier casualties bearing in mind the enemy artillery fire.
>
> I was therefore of the firm belief that the success of the Darwin/Goose [Green] attack was a direct result of Colonel Jones's action coming, as it did, at a critical phase in the battle.

The citation, having been edited and finalised at Northwood, was submitted to the Ministry of Defence. Although the Victoria Cross is always a personal rather than a corporate decoration, the Commander-in-Chief would have been mindful of the inseparable linkage of the VC with the gallantry of 2 Para at Goose Green, for which they now carry the battle honour 'Darwin and Goose Green' on their Colours. The final recommendation was the Joint Com-mander's: 'Colonel Jones acted with conspicuous bravery and daring, totally disregarding his own safety in order to maintain the

---

* Major Rice recognises passages from his signed statement in the final citation. Sergeant Norman remembers making a statement to 'a senior officer', but not signing a citation.
† Thurman was one of the RM liaison officers attached to 2 Para.
‡ Seen by the author.

momentum of the attack. Colonel Jones is recommended for the posthumous award of the Victoria Cross.'

In London, a series of top-level Honours and Awards committees in the MOD and Cabinet Office considered the submission. When the deliberations were complete, the Defence Secretary sent a formal recommendation to The Queen: to bestow the Victoria Cross posthumously on H, and on Sergeant Ian McKay, who had displayed conspicuous gallantry on Mount Longdon with 3 Para. Longdon was one of the fiercest concluding battles of the campaign.

Their citations* were promulgated in a Supplement to the *London Gazette* of 8 October 1982. Her Majesty approved at the same time 680 other awards for gallantry and distinguished service to members of the Armed Services, and to civilians.

The Queen's Investitures are awesome occasions, known to have given the most distinguished subjects sleepless nights – even nightmares – about doing or saying the wrong thing. In fact, Her Majesty speaks to each recipient with a remarkable mixture of informality and warmth, seeming genuinely delighted at the opportunity to talk after recognising formally each achievement.

Many are so overwhelmed by the splendour and yet intimacy of the occasion that afterwards they cannot remember precisely what their Sovereign said, although they do recall she seemed uncannily well informed.

In this case, because the award was posthumous, Sara, accompanied by David and Rupert, had a private Audience with The Queen in the State Dining Room, adjoining the Ball Room where the main Investitures take place. Sara remembers The Queen putting them at their ease by talking about the Russian guns captured at Sevastopol in the Crimea, from which all VCs are struck, and remarking, 'I've got a bit of that metal somewhere and I was looking for it before you arrived.' Perhaps she added that there was enough left for another eighty-one medals, which according to the logisticians is so. But Sara does not remember.

---

*See Appendix for H's.

This was only the seventh occasion in her reign that Her Majesty had made such an award – H's being just the fifth Victoria Cross to a Briton since the Second World War.* She duly presented Sara with H's VC – a crimson-ribboned bronze medal in the shape of a Maltese Cross, inscribed simply 'For Valour'. It is now on permanent display in the National Army Museum, to which Sara has loaned it.†

After the Investiture, recipients are photographed and well-known personalities interviewed in the Quadrangle of Buckingham Palace. After the emotion of the ceremony, this was another ordeal for Sara, but she handled it deftly. She was widely reported next day as saying:

> I am collecting this award for the whole Battalion. I know H would have been the first to say it belonged to them. He would have been so pleased, not for himself – he didn't like a fuss – but for 2 Para, who really deserve this award.

Some reports continued:

> Later Mrs Jones said: 'The Queen knew all about the action at Goose Green. She had clearly studied the citation. I have been asked – rather insensitively – if I feel H acted recklessly in doing what he did. I was delighted with what The Queen had to say about it. She put it so much better than I could have done.
>
> 'H did what had to be done. The whole thing had come to a grinding halt, half an hour earlier. Something had to be done to get things moving again. H knew what was needed and he went

---

* The previous four were awarded between September 1950 and November 1951, during the Korean War. They were to Major Kenneth Muir of The Argyll and Sunderland Highlanders, a posthumous VC; Lieutenant Colonel James Carne VC DSO DL, CO of the Glosters; and, attached to the Glosters: Lieutenant Philip Curtis VC of the Duke of Cornwall's Light Infantry; and Private Bill Speakman VC, of the Black Watch. Four Australians and one Gurkha have also been honoured.

† The photograph on the back cover is of H's actual medal.

ahead and did it. He was that sort of man. I believe he acted in the only way possible at the time and I am very, very proud of him.'

The question of how far H would have progressed up the Army ladder had he survived has generated abiding interest. In 3 Commando Brigade, all five of the surviving commanding officers became at least major-generals. Hew Pike subsequently rose even higher, to lieutenant-general. As Brigadier Julian Thompson rated H one of his best commanding officers, the assumption must be that he too would have achieved general rank.

Had H survived both Goose Green and 2 Para's second battle, on Wireless Ridge – the final battle preceding the fall of Stanley, where the Battalion again distinguished itself – he would have been awarded at least a DSO,* had he not already earned the VC. Completing another year in command of 2 Para – command tours are never less than two years – he would then, aged forty-three, almost certainly have been selected for command of a front-line brigade, either in Germany or in Northern Ireland. These posts are invariably escalators to the top.

Whether he would have achieved the highest rank and become a member of the Army Board of the Defence Council is more uncertain. This is not because he lacked the ambition or ability – far from it – but because at that level timing, luck and balance play an important part, especially when an officer is controversial, as H could only have continued to be.

At some stage, a highly ranked H would probably have had blazing rows with more senior officers, government ministers or influential MOD civil servants. Admittedly, he had matured at each promotion and was learning slowly to bide his time and compromise where necessary. Even so, he was high-principled and the kind of officer to contemplate resignation – aloud. Being

* Distinguished Service Order, the highest decoration, other than the VC, for gallantry in action.

essentially progressive and broad-minded, he would probably not have opposed the main social issues of the 1990s, such as equal opportunities and tolerance of minority lifestyles, which caused much concern within the Services in that decade. Nevertheless, such an outspoken officer would have been vexed by the march of 'political correctness', which he would probably have loudly derided. But of greatest potential conflict would undoubtedly have been the chronic under-funding of defence by successive governments. H would have been at his most intransigent and outraged as each cut bit deeper, and a critical equipment project he favoured was cancelled, or the barrack improvement programme – already twenty years behind schedule – postponed yet again.

His tendency would be to interpret such decisions as posing unacceptable risks to, or attacks upon, his soldiers and his command, and would have taken his opposition right to the wire. At that stage, possibly, balance and a sense of perspective might have deserted him. Civil servants are adept at advising ministers on how to cope with recalcitrant senior officers who loudly proclaim their principled opposition too often. Whitehall first suggests that such officers are politically naïve, or even unsound, and they become marginalised. Should the trouble persist, their next tendered resignation is banked.

The resignation of General Sir Herbert Jones, of Falklands fame, would have made a big splash, but only for a day or two. It would be 'spun' that funding for other government projects was more pressing, and the essential point that often such over-simplifications tend to be superficial non sequiturs would have been obscured. H would have departed, lamented within the ranks as a colourful and principled character, to be a well-off landowner, or whatever else might appeal.

Describing the family's progress since H's death is more straightforward. The day after Sara was widowed, she agreed to be interviewed by the press in the garden of her married quarter, Leipzig House. Her brother John, who worked in public relations, organised matters and was at her side.

The media already had a hero; now they discovered a heroic wife. Sara showed herself to be brave, proud and devoid of any bitterness or self-pity. Yet her vulnerability was clear and at one stage she wept. She remembered those bereaved with her, and paid tribute to the achievements of H's Battalion, then explained to the scores of reporters and photographers present: 'He died as he lived, a soldier. He would not have wanted it any other way.' Next day that was on every front page.

In the weeks that followed Sara received hundreds of kind letters, including a long hand-written one from Prince Charles, as Colonel-in-Chief of The Parachute Regiment. Replying to them all was a daunting task. As Sara's life as a widow stabilised, she immersed herself in her family and took on a variety of outside commitments. When controversies arose, her judgement proved excellent. Her chairmanship of the Falklands Families' Association, for example, brought her into conflict with the Trustees of the South Atlantic Fund, whose trust deeds were so tightly drawn that the relief and benefit intended by the donors was often thwarted by absurd bureaucracy. Sara fought tenaciously when reimbursement of the high cost of travel to the Falklands for widows, who wanted privately to visit the graves of their loved ones, was deemed inadmissible without first a doctor certifying a psychiatric need.

Never a self-publicist, Sara has preserved her private life and yet kept up with events. She has given the occasional interview when one of her charities, like the Poppy Day Appeal, could benefit, or where Service widows' issues have been at stake. These invariably strike the right chord, and it was no surprise when she was elected Woman of the Year in 1983. Several years later she was appointed a Justice of the Peace. Sara is now a figure of national standing in her own right – no longer is she solely the widow of H Jones VC. Sylvia Shortis, the wife of one of H's former Devon and Dorset commanding officers, put it well: 'Had H survived, we would never have known Sara's true capabilities.'

When Mrs Thatcher left office, Sara's name was submitted for a life peerage, but the recommendation was lost in the turmoil of that cataclysmic event. When her name was later resubmitted, it was made clear that she would be expected to take the Whip and align herself with a political party as a working peeress. This she was reluctant to do in view of the conflicting calls on her time, and her name was withdrawn. She was appointed a Commander of the Order of the British Empire (CBE) in 1995.

Since H's death the only external event to hurt her deeply has been the Channel Four television programme *Secret History*, shown in July 1996. It drew on Spencer Fitz-Gibbon's critical *Not Mentioned in Despatches*, although the programme was not his. Acting in good faith, a number of H's former officers and men – and others such as Admiral Lewin and Major-General Thompson – took part. However, after many of the interviews had been edited down to seconds of screen-time, a mostly negative picture of 2 Para's former Commanding Officer and his action on Darwin Ridge emerged. The overall perception created was that the Battalion had been engaged in an unnecessary battle during which their Commanding Officer had unprofessionally got himself killed.

Years later, Thompson recalled his own unhappy experience with this programme:

> I was talked into it against my better judgement, having initially refused to take part. I bitterly regret doing so. It seems [to me] the programme was . . . cut to denigrate H. I made a point of saying to camera that H lacked support, and that if he was under pressure, it was my fault. This was left out by the programme makers, presumably because it was not part of the 'plot'.[16]

The programme generated much protest in advance – which served to boost viewing figures – and even more critical comment afterwards. Reporters Fox and David Norris, both present on the battlefield, wrote effective rebuttals.[17] There was a flurry of critical letters in *The Times* and *Daily Telegraph*. However, one from General Sir Anthony Farrar-Hockley, an adviser to the programme, judged that the producer had 'made a valuable contribution to the history of the Falklands War'.[18] Notwithstanding, Sara was distressed that viewers were left with the impression that her husband might have died pointlessly and carelessly. It was the manner in which the programme had been produced that hurt her most. She felt that H had somehow been betrayed and his memory diminished by some of those involved in the programme's making.

Of the many consoling letters Sara received, one was especially comforting and reassuring. Field Marshal Lord Bramall, who had been CGS at the time, wrote:

> You must not let any of that film on Goose Green bother you . . . [those interviewed] who are all honourable chaps now bitterly regret taking part because they were used.
>
> H's action and heroism, although indeed somewhat unusual for a commanding officer, definitely turned the course of the whole battle and inspired and led Dair F-H's Company who were, up to that time, completely stuck to surge forward. This is what won the battle and made it possible for the surrender negotiations to be so successful. Without H the whole battle would probably have bogged down with an appalling effect on the whole campaign.
>
> So nothing in the film, despite all the awful cutting and snide commentary, can take away from the fact that Goose Green, in which one weak battalion of no more than 300 bayonets took on and defeated 1,400 Argentines, was one of the British Army's finest feats of arms and virtually decided the whole campaign. Without H to inspire and lead the Battalion as he did, that most important victory would *not* have been won.[19]

This helped to restore Sara's equilibrium at a difficult time. Fortunately, most other events involving her and her family since H's death have been wholly positive.

Both her sons won competitive Army scholarships, and attended Reading University before being commissioned from Sandhurst into their father's original Regiment. David served in the Devon and

Dorsets for ten years, being decorated with a Queen's Commendation for Valuable Service for his work in Northern Ireland. In 1997 he joined the American electronics multinational, Motorola, where he is now a director.

Rupert is a major, in mid-career. He was awarded the MBE in 2001 for his work whilst serving in the Ministry of Defence which, in equivalent terms, was several years ahead of his father's appointment to that Order.

Probably of most satisfaction to Sara has been the marriages of her sons and the arrival of her four grandchildren – all boys: two each to David and Claire (nee Blackstone)* and to Rupert and Lucinda (nee Brasher)†. All of them carry Herbert as a Christian name. H, usually more at ease with children than adults – and with a probable preference for grandsons – would have been overjoyed.

Sara, David and Rupert have between them been down to the Falklands several times since the war – first in 1983 for the opening of San Carlos Military Cemetery. They received a genuinely warm welcome from the essentially undemonstrative Islanders, and some lasting friendships were formed. On a more recent visit Sara would have noticed the substantial investment, part self-funded, poured into the islands. The major airfield at Mount Pleasant, constructed in 1985 at a cost of £310 million, provides a base for RAF reinforcement with a continuous all-weather air defence capability. A garrison of soldiers fulfils the equivalent ground defence task. Royal Navy ships visit regularly, and an international fishing industry prospers. Offshore prospecting for oil and minerals continues, although extraction from such distant, hostile waters is problematic.

Argentina has not relinquished her claim to the 'Malvinas', and probably never will. But she has pledged not to pursue it by force. Hostilities having been suspended, harmonious inter-governmental relations have been restored gradually at official level. Nevertheless,

---

* Toby Geoffrey Herbert born 24 September 2001 and Jamie Christopher Herbert on 22 January 2003.
† Henry Thomas Herbert born 10 November 1999 and Edward Amdsen Herbert on 12 January 2002.

strong residual suspicions of their neighbour still exist among the Islanders.

H would not have entertained the question of whether or not it was all worth it. Having accepted the Queen's Shilling and taken the Oath of Allegiance, sworn by all Service personnel, he had a duty to carry out the properly constituted orders of Her Majesty's Government. Servicemen and women are unique in this respect. Members of no other body have this sacred duty to lay down their life, if necessary, on their Sovereign's behalf, and H accepted that responsibility without demur.

Three days after H's death, *The Times* published an obituary attributed to 'A Friend'.[20] Part of it ran:

> H Jones has been portrayed as an extrovert ... but this was only part of him. It was always fun and stimulating to be with H; there was laughter, style and complete sincerity. There was discussion and argument and bravado, but never cant or shallowness, and not once in 22 years do I remember H acting or saying anything mean or cheap.
>
> His friends knew him to be a sensitive and essentially shy man. These were among his most endearing characteristics.
>
> Undeniably H Jones was one of the brightest stars of his generation in the Army and one who seemed destined to go to the top. His loss to the Service will be keenly felt. To his family and his many friends, the loss is acutely painful.

One of those friends, Lieutenant Colonel Dan Severson, H's American buddy at Warminster, was on leave in Kentucky when he heard the news. Dropping everything, he flew over to be with Sara and the boys. This spontaneous gesture – in the best American tradition – was much appreciated. Severson, who probably had a better understanding of H than most, and certainly a wider perspective, believed that 'H was the kind of hero who could be produced only by a great Army and a great Nation'.

Citation – The Victoria Cross

On 28 May 1982 Lieutenant Colonel Jones was commanding 2nd Battalion, The Parachute Regiment on operations on the Falkland Islands. The Battalion was ordered to attack enemy positions in and around the settlements of Darwin and Goose Green. During the attack against an enemy, who was well dug in with mutually supporting positions sited in depth, the Battalion was held up just south of Darwin by a particularly well-prepared and resilient enemy position of at least 11 trenches on an important ridge. A number of casualties was received. In order to read the battle fully and to ensure that the momentum of his attack was not lost, Colonel Jones took forward his reconnaissance party to the foot of a re-entrant which a section of his Battalion had just secured. Despite persistent, heavy and accurate fire the reconnaissance party gained the top of the re-entrant, at approximately the same height as the enemy positions. From here Colonel Jones encouraged the direction of his Battalion mortar fire, in an effort to neutralise the enemy positions. However, these had been well prepared and continued to pour effective fire onto the Battalion advance, which, by now held up for over an hour and under increasingly heavy artillery fire, was in danger of faltering.

In his effort to gain a good viewpoint, Colonel Jones was now at the very front of his Battalion. It was clear to him that desperate measures were needed in order to overcome the enemy position and rekindle the attack, and that unless these measures were taken promptly the Battalion would sustain increasing casualties and the attack perhaps even fail. It was time for personal leadership and action. Colonel Jones immediately seized a sub-machine gun, and, calling on those around him and with total disregard for his own safety, charged the nearest enemy position. This action exposed him to fire from a number of trenches.

As he charged up a short slope at the enemy position he was seen to fall and roll backward downhill. He immediately picked himself up, and again charged the enemy trench, firing his sub-machine gun and seemingly oblivious to the intense fire directed at him. He was hit by fire from another trench which he outflanked, and fell dying only a few feet from the enemy he had assaulted. A short time later a company of the Battalion attacked the enemy, who quickly surrendered. The devastating display of courage by Colonel Jones had completely undermined their will to fight further.

Thereafter the momentum of the attack was rapidly regained, Darwin and Goose Green were liberated, and the Battalion released the local inhabitants unharmed and forced the surrender of some 1,200 of the enemy.

The achievements of 2nd Battalion, The Parachute Regiment at Darwin and Goose Green set the tone for the subsequent land victory on the Falklands. They achieved such a moral superiority over the enemy in this first battle that, despite the advantages of numbers and selection of battle-ground, they never thereafter doubted either the superior fighting qualities of the British troops, or their own inevitable defeat. This was an action of the utmost gallantry by a commanding officer whose dashing leadership and courage throughout the battle were an inspiration to all about him.

Bibliography

Lisa Appignanesi and John Forrester *Freud's Women* (Weidenfeld & Nicolson, 1992)

Mark Adkin *Goose Green, A Battle Fought to be Won* (Leo Cooper, 1992)

Mark Adkin *The Last Eleven?* (Pen and Sword, 1991)

Michael Bilton and Peter Kosminsky *Speaking Out: untold stories of the Falklands War* (Deutsch, 1989)

Tim Card *Eton Renewed* (John Murray, 1994)

Channel Four Team *Untold Story*

Michael Clapp and Ewen Southby-Tailyour *Amphibious Assault Falklands* (Leo Cooper, 1996)

Mike Curtis *Close Quarter Battle* (Corgi, 1998)

Lieutenant R J Dickinson *Officers' Messes, Life and Customs in the Regiments,* (Midas Books, 1973)

Martin Dillon *The Dirty War* (Arrow, 1991)

Christopher Dunphie and Gary Johnson *Gold Beach* (Leo Cooper, 1999)

Spencer Fitz-Gibbon *Not Mentioned in Despatches* (Lutterworth Press, 1995)

Robert Fox *Eye Witness Falklands* (Methuen, 1982)

John Frost *2 Para Falklands, Battalion at War* (Buchan & Enright, 1983)

Linda Goodman *Sun Signs* (Pan, 1988)

H JONES VC

Max Hastings and Simon Jenkins *The Battle for the Falklands* (Michael Joseph, 1983)

Max Hastings *Going to the Wars* (Macmillan, 2000)

Toby Harnden *Bandit Country* (Hodder & Stoughton, 1999)

Tim Heald *Networks* (Hodder & Stoughton, 1983)

Rick Jolly *The Red and Green Life Machine* (Century, 1983)

Ernest Jones *The Life and Work of Sigmund Freud* (3 vols.) (Hogarth Press, 1957/8)

Herbert Jones *The Well of Being; The Blue Ship; Romanel; Finlay; The Dwellers in Dusk* (John Lane, The Bodley Head Ltd, 1920–7)

John Keegan *The Mask of Command* (Jonathan Cape, 1987; Pimlico, 1999)

Henry Leach *Endure No Makeshift* (Leo Cooper, 1993)

Ken Lukowiak *A Soldier's Song* (Orion, 1993)

Martin Middlebrook *Operation Corporate* (Viking, 1985)

Martin Middlebrook *The Fight for the 'Malvinas'* (Viking, 1989)

James Morris *Pax Britannica: Climax of an Empire* (Penguin, 1979)

Ewen Southby-Tailyour *Reasons in Writing* (Leo Cooper, 1993)

Margaret Thatcher *The Downing Street Years* (Harper Collins, 1993)

Julian Thompson *No Picnic* (Leo Cooper, 1985)

Sandy Woodward *One Hundred Days* (Fontana, 1992)

Notes

Chapter 1: American Influences

1 *The Life and Work of Sigmund Freud* by Professor Ernest Jones (3 vols.).
2 *Freud's Women* by Lisa Appignanesi and John Forrester, p. 228.
3 Appignanesi and Forrester, op. cit., p. 192.
4 From *The Well of Being*, poems by Herbert Jones.
5 Professor Jones, op. cit., Vol. 2, pp. 121–2.
6 Woodrow Wilson letter to David Benton Jones dated 27 July 1910.
7 David Benton Jones letter of 28 July 1910.
8 Woodrow Wilson to David Benton Jones, 26 September 1914.
9 Letter to President Wilson addressed to the White House, dated 2 March 1914.
10 Letter to Thomas D. Jones (and others) from Woodrow Wilson dated 20 January 1924.
11 Ted Bennett to Tim Jones.
12 *The Well of Being, The Blue Ship, Romanel, Finlay* and *The Dwellers in Dusk*, all published between 1920 and 1927.
13 First verse of Sonnet XVII in *The Well of Being*.
14 The Oaks and the Snuggery.
15 Will of Herbert Jones, dated 5 November, 1974.
16 Conversation with author, 21 February 2000.

Chapter 2: Early Life

1   Deeds dated 28 May 1940.
2   Interview with author, October 1999.
3   Interview with author, April 2000.
4   Interview with author, June 2000.
5   Interview with author, June 2000.

Chapter 3: 'Floreat Etona'

1   *Eton Renewed*, Tim Card, p. 242.
2   *Eton Chronicle*, 25 September 1982.
3   Autobiography of Winston Churchill, grandson of the famous statesman.
4   Letter to author.
5   *Eton Chronicle*, 25 September 1982.

Chapter 4: 'Serve to Lead'

1   Letter to author, September 1994.
2   Letter to author, March 1996.
3   Ibid.
4   Survey taken for *Networks* by the writer and broadcaster Tim Heald.

Chapter 5: 'Primus in Indis'

1   Letter to author, December 2000.
2   Letter to author, April 2001.

Chapter 6: Wider Horizons

1   Conversation with author, June 2000, and letters.
2   Interview with author, November 2000.

NOTES

Chapter 7: Increasing Responsibility

1   Letter to author, December 2000.
2   Interview with author, May 1998.
3   Interview with author, November 2000.
4   Conversation with Lt. Col. Mike Martin, late Royal Hampshire
      Regiment, March 2000.
5   Conversation with author, November 2000.
6   *Pax Britannica*, James Morris, p. 236.
7   *Northern Ireland Directory 1968–1993*, W D Flackes and Sydney
      Elliott, 1980.
8   Interview with author, January 1996.
9   Letter to author, July 1994.
10 Interview with author, January 2001.
11 Report dated 13 December 1973 and letter of 21 February 1996.

Chapter 8: The Watershed

1   Conversations with and letters to author, January 2001.
2   Interview with author, June 2000.
3   Conversations with author, June 2000.
4   Interview with author, January 2001.
5   Various interviews conducted by the author.
6   *The Dirty War*, Martin Dillon, p. 174.
7   Conversation with the author, November 2000.
8   Letter to author, 13 January 2002.
9   Interviews with author, August 1994 and August 2000.
10 Letter dated 13 January 2002.
11 Conversations with author, December 2001.
12 Conversation with author, January 2001.
13 Conversation with author, August 2001.
14 E-mail to author, 11 March 2001.

Chapter 9: Command

1   Letter to author, dated 3 April 2001.
2   Ibid.
3   Interview with author, February 2001.
4   Interview with author, 24 July 2000.
5   Conversation with author, June 2000.
6   Letter to author, 3 January 2001.
7   Conversation with author, 6 August 2000.
8   Interview with author, 24 July 2000.
9   Conversation with author, March 2001.
10 Interview with author, 29 November 2000.
11 Ibid.
12 Conversation with and letter to author, December 1993 and
    January 1994.

Chapter 10: Going to War

1   *The Voyage of the Beagle*, Charles Darwin.
2   *Endure No Makeshifts – Some Naval Recollections*, Henry Leach
3   *The Battle for the Falklands*, Max Hastings and Simon Jenkins,
    p 78.
4   Extract from Hew Pike's journal.
5   Ibid.
6   *Eye witness Falklands*, Robert Fox, pp. 34 & 84.
7   *Amphibious Assault Falklands*, Michael Clapp and Ewen
    Southby-Tailyour, pp. 4–5.
8   Ibid., p. 143.
9   Ibid., p. 97.
10 Ibid., p. 135.

Chapter 11: Action

1   Conversation with author, 31 July 2000.
2   Conversation with author, 29 March 2001.

3   Interview with author, 8 May 2001.
4   Ibid.
5   Conversations with author, 31 July 2001 and December 2001.
6   *The Fight for the 'Malvinas'*, Martin Middlebrook, p. 180.
7   *Eye witness Falklands*, Robert Fox, p. 53.
8   Correspondence with author, 31 September 2001
9   *Not Mentioned in Despatches*, Spencer Fitz-Gibbon p. 60.
10 Ibid., p. 62.
11 Ibid., p. 63.
12 Ibid., p. 63.
123 Ibid., p. 63.
14 Ibid., p. 75.
15 *The Mask of Command*, John Keegan, p. 329.
16 Ibid., p. 328.
17 Fitz-Gibbon, op. cit., p. 79.
18 Ibid., p. 83.
19 Conversation with author, 6 December 2000.
20 *Army Field Manual – The Infantry Battalion in Battle* (1964):
        Chapters XIX and XX (updated 1979/80 by Code 70740).
21 Fitz-Gibbon, op. cit., p. 109.
22 Correspondence with author, September 2001.
23 Interview and conversations with author between 1995 and
        2001.
24 Interview with author, 6 December 2000.
25 Fitz-Gibbon, op. cit., p. 109.
26 Ibid., p. 109.
27 Interview with author, 6 December 2000.
28 Conversation with author, 6 August 2000.
29 Ibid.
30 Conversation with author, 8 June 1995.
31 Middlebrook, op. cit., p. 186.
32 Fitz-Gibbon, op. cit., p. 125.
33 Conversation with author, 6 August 2000.
34 Conversation with author, 8 June 1995.

35 Letter to Sara Jones from Michael Farebrother, Headmaster, St Peter's, 1982.
36 Interview with author, 4 May 2001.

Chapter 12: The Aftermath

1   Account by David J Kenney, an American historian, author and intelligence analyst, covering the Falklands conflict.
2   *Goose Green*, Mark Adkin, p. 176.
3   E-mail to author, 16 September 2001.
4   *The Fight for the 'Malvinas'*, Martin Middlebrook, p 193.
5   E-mail to author, 7 October 2001.
6   Conversations with author, November 1996 and September 2001.
7   Conversation with author, 25 April 2001.
8   Interview with author, 25 May 2000.
9   Leader in *Daily Mirror*, 2 June 1982.
10 *Not Mentioned in Despatches*, Spencer Fitz-Gibbon, p. 121, note 39.
11 Ibid., p. 121, note 39.
12 Interview with author 24 January 2001 and subsequent conversations.
13 Military Honours and Awards Pamphlet, 1960.
14 Conversation with author, 3 September 2001.
15 Ibid.
16 Letter to author, 18 October 2001.
17 *Daily Telegraph*, 15 June 1996, and *Daily Mail*, 11 July 1996, respectively.
18 *The Times*, 15 June 1996.
19 Letter to Sara Jones dated 15 July 1996.
20 Author of this biography.

Index